The River aI Environment Us

An Environmental Guide for Recreational Users of Rivers and Inland Waterways

by Tim Stott

Published by

BRITISH CANOE UNION

Endorsed by:

| Amateur Rowing Association | Inland Waterways Association | Royal Yachting Association |

Preface

The recreationalist who paddles, rows or sails small craft without engines has an unrivalled opportunity to explore, discover and observe the environment of rivers and inland waterways. These craft offer great advantages to the recreationalist wishing to explore the water environment as, when handled correctly they cause no erosion, noise or pollution and they leave no trace of their passing. Such craft are used throughout the world for exploring wilderness areas and observing wildlife without disturbance.

You can enjoy the environment and wildlife of many inland waters if you purchase a licence from the appropriate navigation authority; for canoeists some of these licenses are included with British Canoe Union membership. Many other inland waterways are private and permission to use them must be given by the owners of the banks; the British Canoe Union has secured agreements to use some of them on a restricted basis.

As an environmental scientist with research interests in rivers, and also as a kayaker and open canoeist, I enjoy both studying and spending leisure time on rivers and canals. I have, for a number of years, felt a growing need to integrate these disciplines into a book which is intended to interpret, explain and illustrate the basic features, operation and management of the river and waterways environment for the recreational small boat user. Such recreationalists may include canoeists, sailors, rowers or indeed any user of small craft on rivers and inland waterways.

There are a number of excellent guide books now available to those wishing to navigate rivers and inland waterways. There is also a range of textbooks available, and a growing body of research, which deal both generally and specifically with aspects of the river environment. They examine how river systems work, how external factors such as pollution or human interference may be changing how they work, and how we may wish to manage and conserve rivers and inland waterways in the future. For the sake of simplicity, from here on the general terms 'river' or 'river environment' will be used to include all inland waterways navigable by small craft - be these canals, lowland rivers and broads and some upland rivers.

As the recreational use of our rivers and inland waterways becomes more popular, the need for a better understanding of 'how rivers work' has never been greater. This book collates recent and current research and information on aspects of recreation, river hydrology and fluvial geomorphology, wildlife and conservation, and river management. It looks at how river systems seem to be responding to issues such as land use conversion and polluting discharges. Part 1 is intended to be an introduction for those with little or no prior knowledge and develops ideas up to and including Key Stage 4 of the National Curriculum. Part 2 is intended for those who wish to find out more about any of the introductory themes covered in Part 1 and explores some other aspects of rivers at a more advanced level. It is intended that the material in Part 2 will, to some extent, bridge the gap between the academic researcher and the recreationalist wishing to find out a little more. Part 2 may well be of interest to aspirant or even experienced coaches who wish to improve their environmental knowledge and awareness. Both Part 1 and Part 2 have suggestions for further reading should the reader wish to follow up any of the subject areas in more detail. There is a list of useful addresses and the book has its own Internet Web Site accessed from the author's home page at:

http://www.staff.livjm.ac.uk/ecststot

There are links in to a range of other sites and organisations concerned with rivers, inland waterways and recreation. This book is not intended to be used as an identification guide to the plants and animals you might find on rivers and inland waterways in Britain - there are plenty of excellent identification guides recommended in the Further Reading sections for this purpose. Rather, Chapter 2.3 describes and illustrates only those plants and animals considered to be the most likely you will encounter.

With a more environmentally aware and knowledgeable population of river users in Britain, we will be better informed to understand the future changes which our rivers are likely to undergo. These changes may be they the results of human impacts, past river or catchment management or mis-management, recreational impacts or even global climate change. More knowledgeable recreationalists will be better placed to be involved in making the important decisions which will face Britain's rivers in future. I hope you enjoy reading and using this book, or even just parts of it.

Dr Tim Stott
Cheshire, 1999.

Acknowledgements

During the two years it has taken to write this book I am greatly appreciative of the continued support and guidance given by the members of British Canoe Union's (BCU) Access Committee and Environment Panel: Colin Kempson and Carel Quaife have managed the project on behalf of the BCU and Darren Male of the BCU Environment Panel has given advice and made helpful comments on earlier drafts of the text and tested Part 1 on 14 year old canoe club members. Simon Dawson, the BCU Water Quality Adviser, made constructive comments on Section 2.4, and Martin Varey allowed me to use extracts from his undergraduate dissertation in Section 2.1. Alan Meegan of the Amateur Rowing Association provided the information and statistics on ARA and supplied Plate 2.3 and the rowing picture on the back cover.

I would also like to thank all those who have read and commented on earlier drafts of the book and particularly: Dr Hugh Mantle OBE and Geoff Griffiths (retired) Senior Lecturers at Liverpool John Moores University, for helpful comments on the second draft; Professor Dave Huddart of Liverpool John Moores University for his thorough proof-reading of the final draft and for useful suggestions; staff of the Environment Agency (EA) organised by Andrew Graham (EA Recreation and Navigation Officer), who read and made comments and in particular, Dr Nigel Holmes for his thorough proof reading and many helpful comments at the second draft stage; Neil Edwards, Executive Director of the Inland Waterways Association (IWA) and Tony Harrison of IWA for helpful comments; Alan Meegan of the Amateur Rowing Association for providing information and commenting on the rowing section in Chapter 2.1 and for Plate 2.3; Jerry Eardley and Tony Ellis of the Royal Yachting Association have been supportive and have made helpful comments at the various draft stages. Carl Mitchell of the Wildfowl and Wetlands Trust made useful comments on the section on birds.

Finally, I owe a great debt to my wife Kath for her tolerance in putting up with my long hours at the computer.

Illustrations

Many of the illustrations in this book are not original. Where they are reproduced exactly as they were first published, permission has been obtained, and payment made where required, to the copyright holder, and this is indicated in the figure caption by the words *source* or *after* followed by the author's name. Every effort has been made to obtain permission from the relevant copyright holders, but where no reply was received I have assumed that there was no objection to me using the material.

I am grateful to:

Philippa Mitchell for drawing Figures 2.3.1, 2.3.2, 2.3.3, 2.3.4, 2.3.5, 2.3.6, 2.3.7, 2.3.8, 2.3.10, 2.3.11, 2.3.13, 2.3.14, 2.3.15, 2.3.16, 2.3.17, 2.3.18, 2.3.19, 2.3.20, 2.3.21, 2.3.22, 2.3.25, 2.3.27, 2.3.28, 2.3.29, 2.3.30, 2.3.31, 2.3.32, 2.3.33, 2.3.34.

Meike Stephenson for drawing Figures 2.3.9, 2.3.12, 2.3.23, 2.3.24, 2.3.26.

Thomas Nelson and Sons Ltd for permission to use Figures 2.2.2, 2.2.3, 2.2.4, 2.2.8, 2.2.9, 2.2.10, 2.2.12, 2.2.13, 2.2.14, 2.2.16, 2.2.17, 2.2.18, 2.2.20, 2.2.21, 2.2.22, 2.2.24 from David Waugh's book *"Geography: An Integrated Approach (1990)"*.

R. B. Bunnett for permission to use Figure 2.2.19 and Plate 1.9 from *"Physical Geography in Diagrams, 4th Edition (1988)"*.

The Reader's Digest Association Limited for permission to use Figure 2.4.2 from *"The Living Countryside – Along the Riverbank © 1985"*.

Foreword

The growing number of initiatives throughout this decade, at local, national and international scale, which have been aimed at protecting the environment and ensuring that people learn to live more harmoniously with it, has prompted the BCU into supporting this publication. The publication of an environmental guide for river and waterway users has been an aim of the BCU for some years. As we enter the 21st Century I feel this is an appropriate time for us all, and river and waterway users should be no exception, to reflect back and to look forward to the new millennium with optimism to meet the challenges which lie ahead.

As river and waterway users we are afforded access to some of the most beautiful habitats in our environment and we must all aim to do our bit, however small, to protect and enhance the environment in which we live and work. I firmly believe that the deeper knowledge and understanding that this book will help to foster among river and waterway users will help us to achieve this aim. I do hope you enjoy reading and learning from this book as much as I have.

David Gent, BCU Chairman,
Nottingham, 1999.

The River and Waterway Environment
for Small Boat Users

Contents

Part 1: An Introduction

List of Figures

Part 1

Section 1.1

Section 1.2

Section 1.3

Section 1.4

Part 2

Section 2.1

Section 2.2

Figure 2.2.1: Mechanisms of rainfall generation (after Dobson & Virgo, 1964).

Figure 2.2.2: The drainage basin system for a region such as the British Isles (after Waugh, 1990).

Figure 2.2.3: A model showing the water balance (after Waugh, 1990).

Figure 2.2.4: The storm hydrograph (after Waugh, 1990).

Figure 2.2.5: The impact of building Harlow New Town on the mean unit hydrograph of Canon's Brook, Essex (after Collard, 1988).

Figure 2.2.6: The impact of ditch excavation on a forested catchment at Coalburn in the North Pennines (after Collard, 1988).

Figure 2.2.7: The impact of ditch excavation on a forested catchment at Coalburn in the North Pennines (after Collard, 1988).

Figure 2.2.8: Rainfall and runoff figures for the river Don (after Waugh, 1990).

Figure 2.2.9: Types of flow in a river (a) laminar flow, (b) turbulent flow (after Waugh, 1990).

Figure 2.2.10: The wetted perimeter, hydraulic radius and efficiency of two differently shaped channels with the same cross-sectional area (after Waugh, 1990).

Figure 2.2.11: (a) Velocities in a straight symmetrical channel, (b) an asymmetrical channel showing velocities through the cross-section of a typically meandering river.

Figure 2.2.12: Why a river increases in velocity towards its mouth, (a) mountainous or upper course of a river, (b) lowland or lower course river (after Waugh, 1990).

Figure 2.2.13: A typical long profile of a river (after Waugh, 1990).

Figure 2.2.14: Transport processes in a river or stream (Source: Waugh, 1990).

Figure 2.2.15: The relationship between velocity and particle movement (after Hjülstrom, 1935) (Source: Clowes & Comfort, 1982).

Figure 2.2.16: Cross-section of a flood plain showing levees and bluffs (after Waugh, 1990).

Figure 2.2.17: The structure of a delta (after Waugh, 1990).

Section 2.3

Figure 2.3.28: Chub (*Leuciscus cephalus*) (illustration by Philippa Mitchell).

Figure 2.3.29: Eel (*Anguilla anguilla*) (illustration by Philippa Mitchell).

Figure 2.3.30: Perch (*Perca fluviatilis*) (illustration by Philippa Mitchell).

Figure 2.3.31: Pike (*Esox lucius*) (illustration by Philippa Mitchell).

Figure 2.3.32: Brown Trout (*Salmo trutta*) (illustration by Philippa Mitchell).

Figure 2.3.33: Salmon (*Salmo salar*) (illustration by Philippa Mitchell).

Figure 2.3.34: Common Frog (*Rana temporaria*) (illustration by Philippa Mitchell).

Figure 2.3.35: (a) *Aeshna juncea*, one of the commonest of the larger dragonflies with a wingspan of about 95 mm; (b) *Ischnura elegans*, the Common ischnura damselfly (about 30 mm long); and (c) dragonfly and damselfly larvae compared.

Figure 2.3.36: Life in fast flowing streams.

Section 2.4

Figure 2.4.1: Maps to show: (a) water abstraction, and (b) average rainfall in the UK.

Figure 2.4.2: The effect of pollution control measures on fish diversity in the River Thames, 1957-87 (source: The Reader's Digest, The Living Countryside – Along the Riverbank © 1985).

Figure 2.4.3: The chemical quality of rivers and canals, 1988-96 (source: Environment Agency, SEPA, Environment and Heritage Service).

Figure 2.4.4: Biological water quality of rivers and canals, 1990-96 (source: Environment Agency, SEPA, Environment and Heritage Service).

List of Tables

Part 1

Part 2

List of Plates

Part 1

Plate 1.1: The Nant Ffrancon valley in Snowdonia is a good example of a U-shaped valley enlarged by glaciers and now occupied by the River Ogwen (taken by the author).

Plate 1.2: Using an orange to estimate the speed a river is flowing (taken by the author).

Plate 1.3: V-notch weir structure used to measure stream discharge (taken by the author).

Plate 1.4: Crump weir structure measuring discharge of a small river (taken by the author).

Plate 1.5: Baseflow flume for accurate measurement of low flows in a small river (taken by the author).

Plate 1.6: Spore containing capsules of moss (taken by the author).

Plate 1.7: (a) Students using nets and white trays to sample and examine invertebrates (taken by the author).

Plate 1.7: (b) The white tray with the contents of net emptied (taken by the author).

Plate 1.8: (a) The River Severn at Newtown in mid-Wales before construction of the flood alleviation scheme in 1970.

Plate 1.8: (b) The River Severn at Newtown in mid-Wales after construction of the flood alleviation scheme in 1970.

Plate 1.8: (c) The River Severn at Newtown looking upstream from the Long Bridge in 1900 before the flood alleviation scheme was constructed in 1970.

Plate 1.8: (d) The same view as in Plate 1.8 (c) taken in 1999.

Plate 1.8: (e) View of Long Bridge at Newtown on R. Severn in 1960s (prior to construction of flood alleviation scheme in 1970).

Plate 1.8: (f) Same view of Long bridge during severe floods in 1964.

Plate 1.8: (g) Broad Street, the main street in Newtown, in December 1964 as the flooding recedes.

Plate 1.9: The River Brent in London heavily polluted with rubbish (source: Bunnett, 1988)

Plate 1.10: An algal bloom can turn water into a 'green pea soup' (taken by the author).

Plate 1.11: Afforestation of an upland catchment is preceded by ploughing and ditching to help the young trees to get established (taken by the author).

Plate 1.12: Sailing on lowland rivers: the Norfolk Broads (taken by the author).

Plate 1.13: Whitewater kayaking on the upper reaches of the river Dee at Llangollen, Wales (taken by the author).

Part 2

Plate 2.1: The Tees Barrage artificial whitewater course was opened near Middlesborough in 1993 (taken by the author).

Plate 2.2: Canolfan Tryweryn Whitewater slalom course where reservoir releases from Llyn Celyn Dam provide reliable water suitable for World Championship Canoeing Events (taken by the author).

Plate 2.3: Recreational rowing craft in the River Avon (photograph by Alan Meegan, ARA).

Plate 2.4: A typical V-shaped valley on a tributary of the River Severn in mid-Wales (taken by the author).

Plate 2.5: High Force waterfall on the River Tees in Co. Durham.

Plate 2.6: Thornton Force in Kingsdale near Ingleton, North Yorkshire (taken by the author).

Plate 2.7: The Allt Mhor in the Cairngorms, a typical Scottish river in its upper course (taken by the author).

Plate 2.8: Rapids at Grand Tully on the River Tay in central Scotland are used as a canoe slalom training venue. (taken by the author).

Plate 2.9: A meander on the River Forth near Stirling in central Scotland (taken by the author).

Plate 2.10: Cuckoo Flower (*Cardamine pratensis*) (taken by the author).

Plate 2.11: Marsh Marigold (*Caltha palustris*) (taken by the author).

Plate 2.12: Common Reed (*Phragmites australis*) on the Norfolk Broads (taken by the author).

Plate 2.13: White Water Lily (*Nymphaea alba*) (taken by the author).

Plate 2.14: Ragged Robin (*Lychnis flos-cuculi*) in water meadow (taken by the author).

Plate 2.15: Mute Swan (*Cygnus olor*) (taken by the author).

Plate 2.16: Sand Martin (*Riparia tipaiia*) nest tunnels in the bank of the River Beauly, NE Scotland (taken by the author).

Part 1:

A Basic Introduction to the River and Waterway Environment

1.1   Introduction

During the past 20-30 years there has been a rapid increase in the search for recreation of all types. More wealth and leisure time has been accompanied by increased popularity in individual and group activities, especially those requiring relatively costly equipment: many water sports fall into this category. Similarly, more people now own cars than ever before, and this has allowed people to get out to rivers and canals more easily and to transport small boats and other bulky and/or heavy equipment with them.

This increase in car ownership, the increase in free-finance and an increasingly leisure orientated and flexible population has increased pressures on the environment. As more and more people want to escape from urban pressures, there is an increasing need for provision of car parks, toilets, picnic areas, nature trails and information to cater for those who want to be on, or beside, rivers and canals.

Water in general provides a major attraction not only to those who wish to take part in active water sports but also for those who seek a day out in the country and quiet enjoyment of the countryside. Britain has a wide variety of inland waterways, i.e. navigable rivers, canals and drainage channels which have been recognised for over 30 years as having an important recreational role. In 1996 it was estimated that there were about 8640km (5370 miles) of waterway (IWAAC, 1996) which were navigable by craft of at least 2.13 m (7 ft) beam. The 2790 (1734 miles) system of navigable waterways managed by British Waterways (BW) - mainly canals but including a few rivers - is now primarily seen as a recreational resource (although the system still carries some commercial craft and has drainage and water supply functions). A further 860km (535 miles) of navigable rivers managed by the Environment Agency (EA) in England and Wales and 160km (100 miles) by the Broads Authority are also used for leisure purposes. Thus Britain is well endowed with attractive rivers and canals (Inland Waterways) and land associated with them (canal tow paths and river banks). This environment not only supports a great diversity of plants and animals, it is also popular with people seeking recreation other than that provided by traditional and often overcrowded resorts.

1.1.1   History of Rivers and Inland Waterways

As well as providing an unique resource for sport and recreation, Britain's rivers and canals are vital to the economy of the country, providing water for domestic, industrial and agricultural use. They form the **habitat** of countless forms of plant and animal life, and they provide some of the most beautiful scenery we have. Rivers and canals criss-cross the countryside in such a way that it is difficult to avoid them. They both have plants and animals that make them unique, but at the same time there are slight variations which make a river different from a canal, and often one section of a river very different from another.

Around 12 000 years ago, the melting of huge ice sheets at the end of the last ice age left a network of rivers that has moulded the landscape since that time. Many of these rivers now flow in 'U'-shaped valleys enlarged by valley glaciers during the ice ages (see Plate 1.1).

Glaciers have deposited rock material called **boulder clay** or **till,** all over the landscape. On top of these ice age deposits, soils and vegetation have slowly developed but at the same time the river network has re-worked these sediments in valley bottoms. As the climate warmed, plant and animal life began to colonise the landscape, and for thousands of years rivers might have had a large influence on our first settlers who had moved north from mainland Europe. The earliest Palaeolithic (old stone age) settlers would have been able to cross the English channel on foot when sea level was much lower than today. The Mesolithic (middle stone age) hunters and gatherers gradually gave way to the Neolithic (New Stone Age) farmers. All would have encountered rivers as natural obstacles. Later rivers became important routes into the centre of the country, and as the human population expanded they became navigation ways and the focus for settlement and trade.

Navigable rivers provided a network through lowland Britain, and as trade flourished in the eighteenth and nineteenth centuries, artificial waterways were built to link the main systems (Figure 1.1.1).

These canals had their heyday during the **industrial revolution** in the eighteenth and nineteenth centuries, feeding factories with raw materials such as coal, wool and iron ore, and filtering manufactured goods such as cloth or steel, through to estuaries and ports. Rivers and canals shared this important role in history for a relatively short time: once the railways had captured most of the transport market, canals began a century of decline.

River wildlife arrived soon after the ice age ended. As the huge ice sheets and glaciers melted, a wide drainage system was established across Northern Europe. Animals and plants could spread uninterrupted along these new waterways, which were both fertile and free from competition. The initially rapid **colonisation** of Britain slowed down when the sea finally channelled out the Straits of Dover around 7 500 years ago during a period of rapid climate improvement known as the 'Boreal'. During the '**climatic optimum**' (the warmest climate we have had since the last ice age), mean temperatures in Britain were higher than today. We then moved into the warm wet 'Atlantic' climatic period. By this time most of the important elements of river life were already here. The climate has worsened since then, passing from the warm and wet 'Atlantic' period through the warm sunny 'Sub-Boreal' to the cooler wet climate of the 'Sub-Atlantic' which we know today.

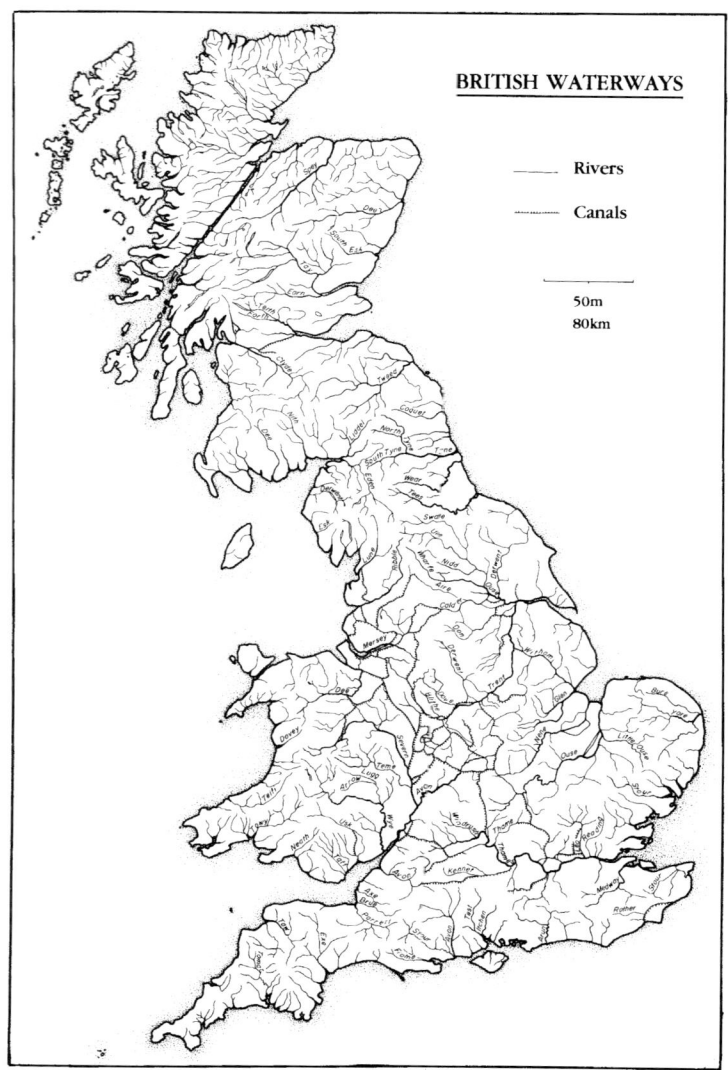

Figure 1.1.1: British Waterways (after Hopkins and Brassley, 1982)

The impact of humans on the landscape has seen massive increases. Almost all of the **primary forest** that blanketed Britain 6,000 years ago was initially cleared by successive Neolithic, **Bronze** and **Iron Age** cultures. Forest was cleared to make way for agriculture among other things, and this has continued right up until this century when at last we are beginning to see that we cannot go on clearing forests and that we now need to re-plant them.

Today, many rivers serve as wildlife 'corridors' with trees on the banks which provide cover in which wildlife can live and breed and use to migrate along.

In the recent past many species, the beaver for example, have become extinct. To counter-balance this there have been new arrivals, either expanding naturally or through accidental introductions by humans. When the first true canals were built towards the end of the eighteenth century they provided a potential wildlife habitat which was probably taken over by wildlife more as the use of canals has declined since their heyday in the **industrial revolution**. The contrast between rivers and canals is, on the one hand very marked: natural rivers can change overnight into torrents of floodwater. This is contrasted by the relative constancy of canal levels. However, some inland waterways have been specifically built as drainage channels, and these can, at times, flood. Rivers generally flow quickly, even in navigable lowland areas, while canal water makes slow progress, held up by lock gates and the need to keep levels constant. In spite of these contrasts, rivers and canals have a great deal in common and it is the differences, both between them and within them, which have given rise to the diverse uses of rivers and waterways for recreation purposes which we see emerging today.

1.1.2   Human Uses of Rivers and Canals

1.1.2.1   Early Use of Rivers and Canals

To the early settlers rivers were the way of reaching into the heart of the country. They could also be boundaries, a flood hazard, they created barriers to travel and may have been sources of disease. The benefits, which included a water supply for stock and people, a source of fish (an important protein source in winter) and the means of disposing of rubbish and sewage, must have outweighed the problems. Gradually, settlements grew up by rivers, often at important fording, or bridging points, or where they could be used for transport or power. This potential for power was harnessed at first for corn mills and later in the eighteenth and nineteenth centuries the huge mills of the Pennine valleys in Yorkshire and Lancashire capitalised on the power of water for 'fulling' (cleansing and thickening) cloth. River water was also controlled to supply water meadows to produce grass for stock early in the year. Fords, bridges and the deepening of pools were probably the first artificial interruptions to river flow. Later weirs, flood banks and mill leats were built which allowed the flow to be diverted into channels for traffic, or to prevent flooding.

It is thought that the Romans improved on the existing river pattern by building cuts such as Car Dyke, from Lincoln to Peterborough, and Foss Dyke from the River Trent to the River Witham at Lincoln. Following the Roman effort it seems likely that little happened over the next thousand years and the dykes probably fell into disrepair. However, the fifteenth and sixteenth centuries saw a great increase in works to improve river navigation. The major river systems were the Thames, Severn, Great Ouse and Trent. The Severn was thought to have been navigable to Welshpool in the sixteenth century and by the seventeenth century it was a prosperous thoroughfare for coal and other manufactured goods such as woollen cloth. In 1643 the Soar was made navigable and others such as the Hampshire Avon, Wey Navigation and Great Ouse, were canalised. This often just involved widening and deepening the waterway, while in others it required the construction of flash or pound locks or reservoirs to maintain water levels. The perfection of the **flash lock** (actually a movable weir, or barrage, across a river or drainage cut) made it possible to dam and then suddenly release a mass of water, thus allowing a shallow-draft barge to float over a minor obstruction. Pound locks, the early versions of the locks we see in canals today, invented near Utrecht towards the end of the fourteenth century, allowed commercial canal transport by barge to develop on a major scale. The use of waterways increased from an estimated 1 102km of navigable waterways before 1660 to 1 866km by 1724. River transport was much cheaper and more efficient than the use of roads. One horse could draw two tonnes on the road, but could pull 50 - 100 tonnes on water, and the roads were rough, sometimes impassable in winter and robberies were frequent.   However, some of the problems associated with inland waterways included water shortages (during dry spells some sections of river became impassable), rights of passage, delays while bargaining for water and the necessity to get goods and fuel to and from the nearest rivers. When cargo was transferred to seagoing vessels near river mouths, the dumping of ballast formed mounds and this, together with the constant need to dredge channels in the lower courses of rivers, as well as the coming of trains, eventually led to a decline in inland water-borne trade.

Some of the first canals used for navigation were constructed to bypass hazards on otherwise navigable river courses; they linked different water levels above and below falls or rapids. The complex engineering involved in canal construction and operation rose steadily. Bigger locks were built, and large differences in water level were overcome by constructing great **lock staircases** such as those at Bingley on the Leeds and Liverpool Canal. Sometimes sudden changes in level were overcome by the canal lift. In this procedure, canal barges were floated onto a metal box filled with water. The box was then raised or lowered vertically within a lift framework, the load being counterbalanced by a weight of water held in an adjoining container, or lifted and lowered by the direct application of electrical power. The Anderton lift in Cheshire is one such example.   The first long distance canal was the Newry (30km long) in Ulster, opened in 1742. Later, the St Helens canal on the north bank of the Mersey, was completed in 1761.

By the time of the 1968 Transport Act, the network of waterways looked after through the British Waterways Board (BWB), were classified into three groups:

(a) **Commercial waterways** 555km (347 miles): to be maintained by the BWB in navigable condition for use by commercial freight-carrying vessels, (b) **Cruising Waterways** 1 738km (1 086 miles): to be maintained by the BWB in navigable condition for use by powered pleasure craft, eg. the Llangollen Canal is a statutory cruising waterway,

(c) **Remainder Waterways** 835km (522 miles): to be dealt with by the BWB in the most economical manner possible, whether by retaining, developing, eliminating or disposing of them.

1.1.2.2 Current Trends

We saw in Section 1.1 how the increased availability of the private motor car may be an important factor in allowing recreationalists to visit rivers and waterways more easily, and to transport their small boats with them.

Research was carried out for British Waterways (BW) to measure the number of visitors and visits to canals in 1984, 1986 and 1989. The figures for 1989 are given below together with figures for the Kennet and Avon Canal based largely on 1989 data:

Table 1.1.1: Visits to BW navigable waterways (source: Inland Waterways Association, 1994)

Activity	All canals			Kennet & Avon Canal
	Visitors (millions)	Visits (millions)	Visits/km/yr	Visits (millions)
Hire boating	0.37	0.4	160	0.005
Private powered boating	0.57	2.1	820	0.06
Restaurant/trip boats	0.62	1.1	430	0.08
Canoeing	0.24	1.4	540	
Other unpowered boating	0.53	2.8	1090	0.12
Fishing	0.98	17.3	6700	0.17
Informal visits	7.28	132.5	52000	10.92
TOTAL	10.59	157.6		11.36

The figures above are dominated by the informal visitors who make up 84% of all visits to inland waterways (mainly canals, but some rivers too). Informal visitors, however, tend to spend much less time, their visits typically last 1 - 2 hours, whereas other activities last much longer. Informal visitors tend to be concentrated at "**honey pot**" sites whereas other users tend to be more evenly spread. The visit rate to a particular inland waterway will, of course, depend on how attractive it is and on how many people live nearby. For example, the visit rate for the Kennet and Avon canal (139km in length) is 79 000 visits per kilometre per year compared with the average for all canals (2570km) of 50 000 visits per km per year.

1.1.2.3 How Far Do Visitors Travel ?

Some evidence for how far visitors travel to get to canals was obtained in the Kennet and Avon study and in an earlier study at nine sites distributed across the waterways system. The Kennet and Avon study gave an average distance travelled by visitors of 18.4 miles (29.6km), with 9% travelling 7 miles (11.3km) or less. The earlier study gave an average of 4.7 miles (7.6km), with 1% travelling more than 50 miles (80.5km) and 61% travelling 1 mile (1.6km) or less. Visitors to the Kennet and Avon canal are clearly prepared to travel greater distances: this may be due to the large number of attractive features on the canal and the fact that by the second survey, ten years later, people had more money available to spend on recreational visits. Both survey results show that waterways are largely local recreational resources for informal visitors.

1.1.2.4 Numbers of Boats on Waterways

No comparable surveys have been carried out for recreational use of rivers, but there is evidence to support the general impression that navigable rivers are more intensively used than canals. The National Rivers Authority (NRA) (Thames) (the NRA is no longer in existence and is now replaced by the Environment Agency, EA) quoted a figure of 7 million informal visits to locks per year; this gives a rate of 34 700 visits per kilometre per year on the 202km of non-tidal Thames. Allowing for visits to other lengths of the riverbank, the total visit rate is clearly much greater than that for canals. Furthermore, there are 4 000 powered and unpowered craft registered on the 470km of BW rivers and 40 000 on the 800km of EA's navigable rivers, an average of 35 boats per km. In comparison there are 18 000 boats licensed on BW's 2400km of canals, an average of 7.5 boats per km. This may be sub-divided: powered craft 6.6 per km; hire craft 0.6 per km with business and unpowered craft both 0.1 per km. The NRA figures include short-term licences (which make up perhaps 20% of the total) but BW figures do not.

1.1.2.5 Rate of Growth in Recreational Use of Waterways.

A measure of the rate of growth can be obtained by comparing the 1984 and 1989 figures, although the estimate is only approximate because of the dominant effect of weather on outdoor activities. These give an annual growth rate of 2.5%, but it should be remembered that this was a period of strong economic growth when personal incomes were rising relatively rapidly. Considering other related activities, those walking a distance of

3.2km (2 miles) or more at least once per month increased by 1.2% per year between 1977 and 1987; and the number of rambling clubs affiliated to the Rambler's Association increased by 2.3% per year between 1975 and 1987. It may be concluded that informal visits to waterways are probably increasing at 1.5 - 2% per year, which is probably slightly higher than the growth rate for visits to urban and country parks. Thus, though there may continue to be a small increase in boat numbers on canals and inland waterways over the next 5-10 years, this is unlikely to be significant.

Figure 1.1.2 illustrates some of the many uses to which rivers, canals and inland waterways can be put.

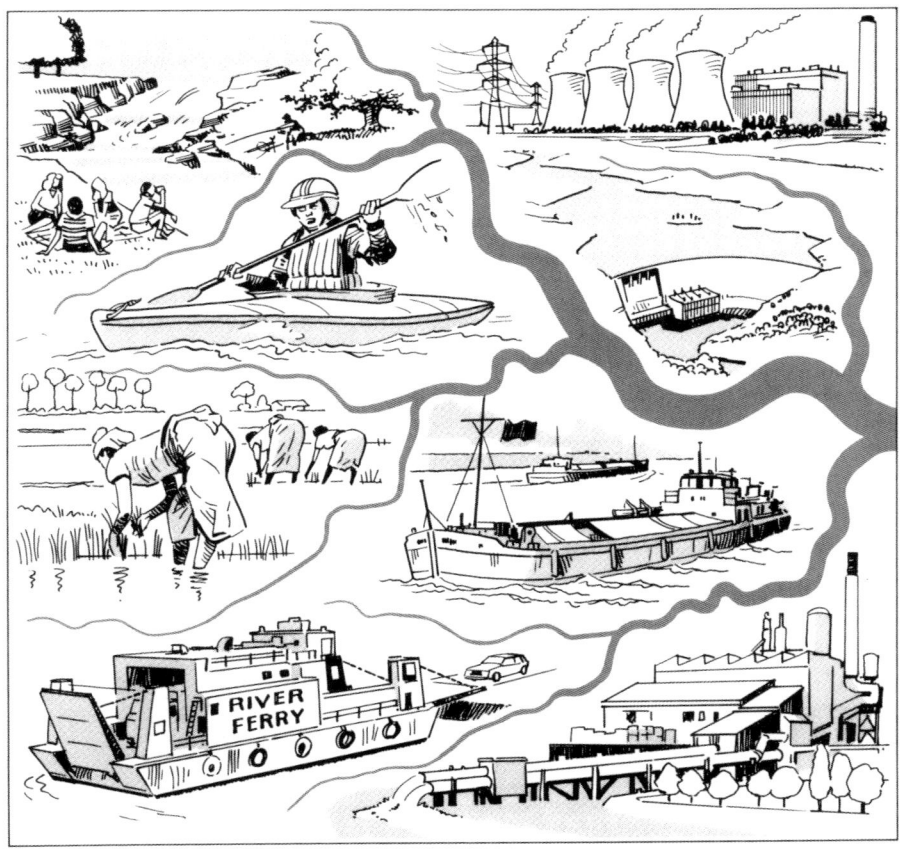

Figure 1.1.2: Some of the many uses to which rivers, canals and inland waterways can be put (source: Richards, 1990)

1.1.2.6 The Range of Recreational Uses of Rivers and Inland Waterways

This section outlines the main recreational uses to which our rivers and inland waterways and associated land are put. Table 1.1.2 summarises these uses.

Table 1.1.2: Main Recreational Uses of Rivers and Inland Waterways.

Boat Uses	Non-boat Uses
Canoeing Inland Touring Marathon Racing Slalom Racing Wild Water Racing Rodeo/Freestyle Sprint Racing White Water Recreation Canoe Sailing Canoe Polo Bell Boating	Angling Art / Photography Camping Caravans Dog Walking Gorge Walking Gun And Field Sports Historic Conservation Horse Riding Jogging Mountain Biking Nature Study and Wildlife Conservation
Rowing Competitive Rowing Recreational Rowing Touring	Orienteering Rambling Sightseeing & Picnicking Sub-Aqua Diving
Sailing Dinghy Sailing (Wet) Windsurfing Yacht Sailing (Dry)	
White Water Rafting	
Pleasure Cruising Trail Boats Narrow Boats Broad River Cruisers	
Other Pleasure Craft: Rowing Boats Pedal Boats Gondolas Dragon Boats Skiffs & Punts	
Commercial Freight	

Since the 1950s there has been a national growth in almost all water based activities, particularly in angling, canoeing and sailing, and although rowing has experienced a gradual overall increase, current Amateur Rowing Association (ARA) pilot participation projects, which include the National Rowing Programme and its core programme, Project Oarsome, aim to attract more young people into the sport (see section 2.1). Angling is estimated to be growing at a rate of 7% annually. The Sports Council consider that sailing is entering an area where the quality and appropriate location of facilities will be more important than an increase in provision. The British Canoe Union (BCU) has experienced an increase of 60% in its individual membership over the period 1980-1997. However, it is estimated that only 25% of canoeists belong to the BCU; nevertheless it would not be unreasonable to state that the number of people participating in canoeing has doubled over the past 20 years or so.

1.1.2.7 Towards Sustainable Recreational Use of Our Waterways

Waterways have always been an integral part of the way many people spend their leisure time. Rowing, cruising, sailing and fishing have been popular water sports for many years, but it is also for the aesthetic value that millions of people visit a waterside environment while at leisure. Public houses, parks and footpaths located along rivers, canals and on the seafront are honeypots for visitors who just enjoy being by water.

The demand for countryside recreation, and in particular opportunities for water based recreation, is on the increase. Those who have responsibility for managing the countryside now have to ask: 'How do we satisfy recreational demands, while at the same time conserve the countryside as a flourishing natural habitat, so that the recreational visitors do not destroy the very things they come to enjoy ?'

This issue of **'sustainability'** is one of the most important which the leisure and tourism industries are having to consider at present. Achieving a level of recreational activity that can be sustained by the natural environment requires planning, management and monitoring. The first step in this process is to prepare strategies which co-ordinate and guide the numerous, often conflicting interests, and to advise on the most appropriate course of action.

A sustainable strategy has been compiled for the River Thames. This valuable natural resource is one of the busiest waterways in Europe. In a joint effort between the National Rivers Authority (NRA, now the Environment Agency) and the Sports Council undertook an in depth survey, the report of which is entitled 'Space to Live, Space to Play: A Recreation Strategy for the River Thames', (NRA, 1995). With a vast diversity of users who have different expectations, achieving a sustainable level of recreational use on the River Thames, and many other waterways in Britain, is a priority for all those involved in their management.

1.2   How and Why Rivers Flow: An Introduction to River Hydrology

Some recreational uses of rivers, particularly white water kayaking, rafting, rodeo and play boating and recreational touring, require moderate to high river levels to enjoy the sport.   Some of the best upland rivers don't reach such moderate to high levels very often, and when they do it may only be for relatively short periods of time. Large dams have been built on some rivers to store water in reservoirs. This water can be released at times of low flow to maintain river levels or, by arrangement it can be released at certain times for recreational users. Examples of these will be examined in more detail Parts 2.1 and 2.2. An understanding of how and why it rains, where most rain falls and how rainfall affects how rivers flood is therefore useful to the small boat user for these reasons:

*   being able to access and understand weather forecasts at the right time will allow the recreational user to understand when, where and how much rain will fall,

*   an understanding of the relationship between rainfall and **runoff** will allow the recreational user to plan and time river journeys appropriately and to be in the right place at the right time to enjoy their recreation and minimise damage to the environment.

1.2.1   Distribution of Water on Earth

All life on Earth depends on the presence of water which we can find naturally in three states: solid (frozen as ice, snowflakes or hailstones), liquid (water, fog, cloud droplets, rain) and gaseous (invisible as water vapour). Water on planet Earth is contained in the **hydrosphere**, the Earth-atmosphere system that extends some 8-16 km above the Earth's surface and to about 0.5 km below it.

Water is readily available for life in the oceans where around 97.5% of all water on planet Earth is found. The remaining 2.5% circulates over the land.

As Figure 1.2.1 shows, the amount of the world's water available as freshwater for drinking, or in our rivers available for recreational use, is very small indeed. But life on land can only exist because water easily changes its state when heated or cooled, through the processes of **evaporation, condensation,** freezing and melting. What this all means is that water circulates around the planet, between the oceans, the atmosphere and the land in what is called the water cycle. Without circulation of this water, driven by the sun's energy, rivers would simply not flow. Rivers are natural watercourses that form the land based part of the global water cycle (Figure 1.2.2).

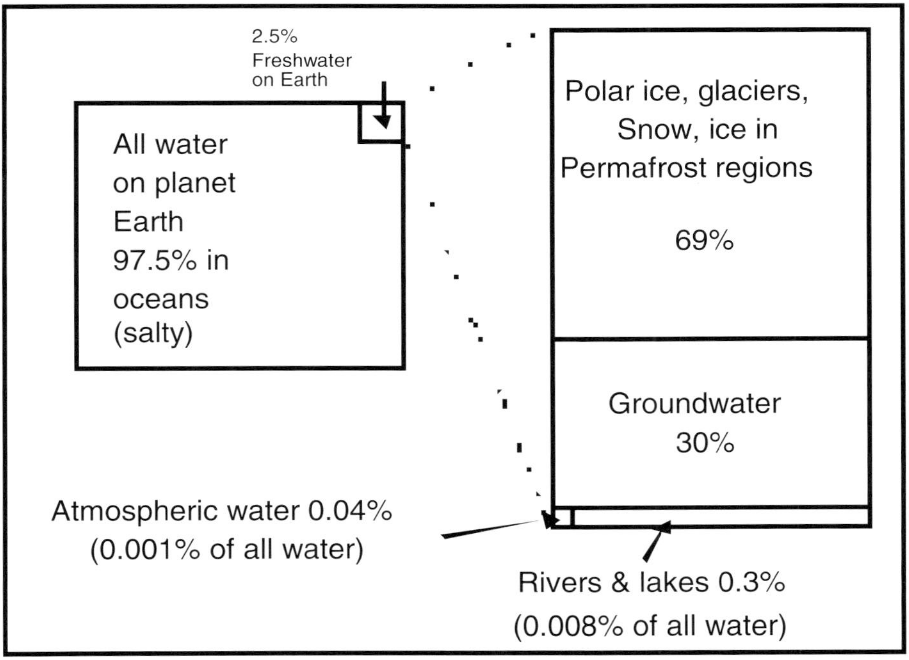

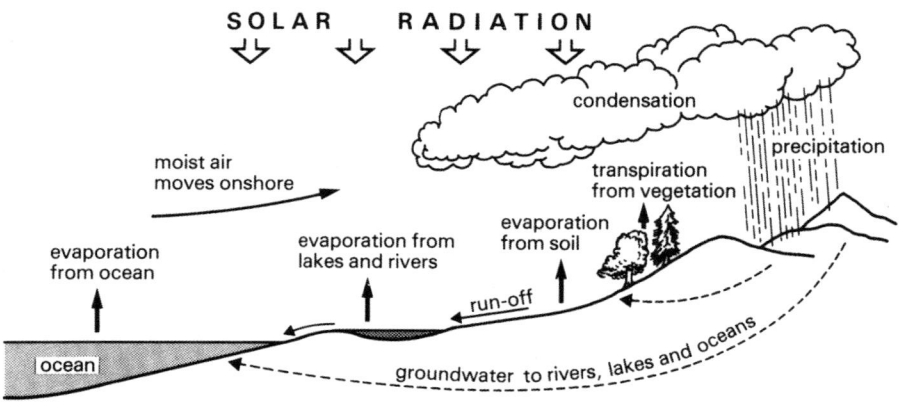

2.5% Freshwater on Earth		Polar ice, glaciers, Snow, ice in Permafrost regions 69%
All water on planet Earth 97.5% in oceans (salty)		Groundwater 30%

Atmospheric water 0.04%
(0.001% of all water)

Rivers & lakes 0.3%
(0.008% of all water)

Figure 1.2.1: The world's freshwater resources as a proportion of planetary water.

SOLAR   RADIATION

condensation

precipitation

moist air
moves onshore

transpiration
from vegetation

evaporation
from soil

evaporation from
lakes and rivers

evaporation
from ocean

run-off

ocean

groundwater to rivers, lakes and oceans

Figure 1.2.2: The Water Cycle (after Clowes and Comfort, 1982)

Rivers are one of the most important ways by which water finds its way from the land, where it falls as precipitation, back to the sea. It is this 'rainfall-runoff' part of the water cycle that most concerns the recreational user and we shall now examine this in more detail.

The development of a river depends on there being a gradient on the land surface and an adequate supply of water from rain, snowmelt, an overflowing lake or a groundwater spring. Clouds form when moisture is evaporated from the Earth's surface. The vapour condenses on tiny invisible particles of dust or sea salt to form small droplets that we see as clouds. Usually hills and mountains cause rain bearing clouds to shed their rain by the rise in altitude (see Section 2.2.1 for a more detailed explanation). The rain falls to the ground, moves downhill and wherever hard or **impermeable** rock forms the surface, water may flow as a sheet, picking up loose material (dust, soil or rock particles) as it goes. Once the water reaches a more **permeable** surface the flow may join up into more distinct **rivulets**. The force of the water combined with the debris being carried, will help to gouge out less resistant rock and gradually a course or channel will develop. This channel is usually called a stream when small (up to 4 m wide) and a river when one or more streams have joined to make it larger, though there is not really a generally accepted point at which a stream suddenly becomes a river.

Canals on the other hand, are defined as being artificially cut. However, many canals have developed from rivers. Usually rivers or streams supply the water to canals. The Llangollen branch of the Shropshire Union canal, for example, is fed by water from the river Dee at the Horseshoe falls upstream of the town of Llangollen. Some canals, such as the Soar in Leicestershire, use rivers as part of the canal system.

1.2.2   Drainage Basins and Rivers: How Rivers Work

1.2.2.1 What's a drainage basin ?

A **drainage basin** or **catchment area**, as it is sometimes known, is an area of land drained by a river and its **tributaries**. Its boundary is marked by a ridge of high land beyond which any precipitation will drain into the next adjoining drainage basin. This boundary is called a **watershed**. A drainage basin can be described as an open system which forms part of the water cycle (Figure 1.2.1). When viewed as a system, the drainage basin has inputs, outputs and storage points within it like this:

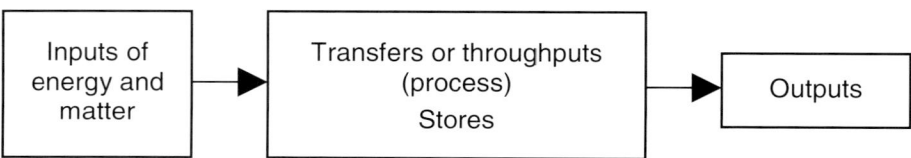

So, in terms of a river system:

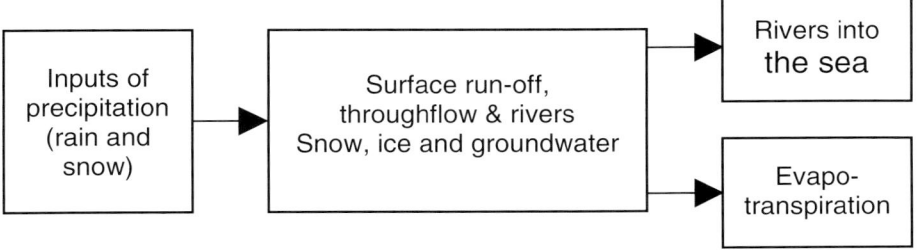

Section 2.2 gives greater detail of the transfers or throughputs (processes) and storage points within a drainage basin.

Figure 1.2.3 illustrates a drainage basin with the inputs, transfers, storage points and outputs indicated.

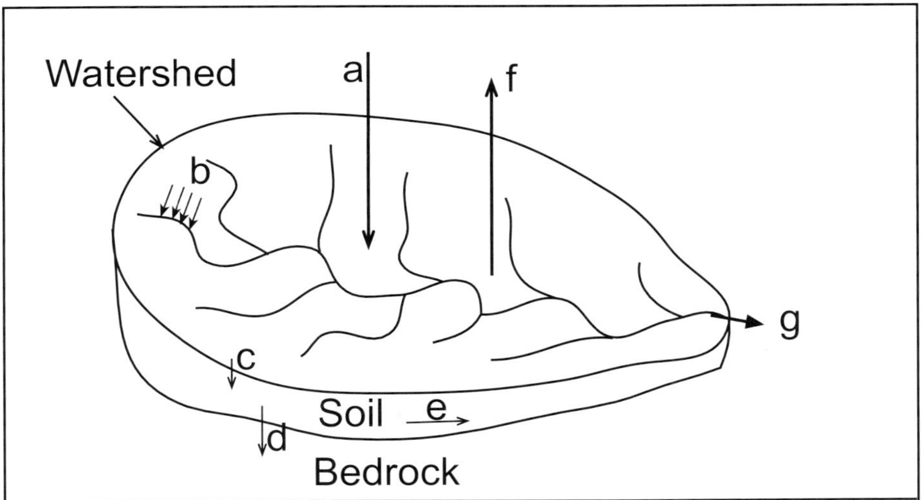

Watershed

a = precipitation (input) e = throughflow
b = surface runoff   f = evapotranspiration
c = infiltration   (output)
d = percolation   g = channel flow (output)

Figure 1.2.3: Diagram to show the drainage basin with the inputs, transfers, storage points and outputs indicated.

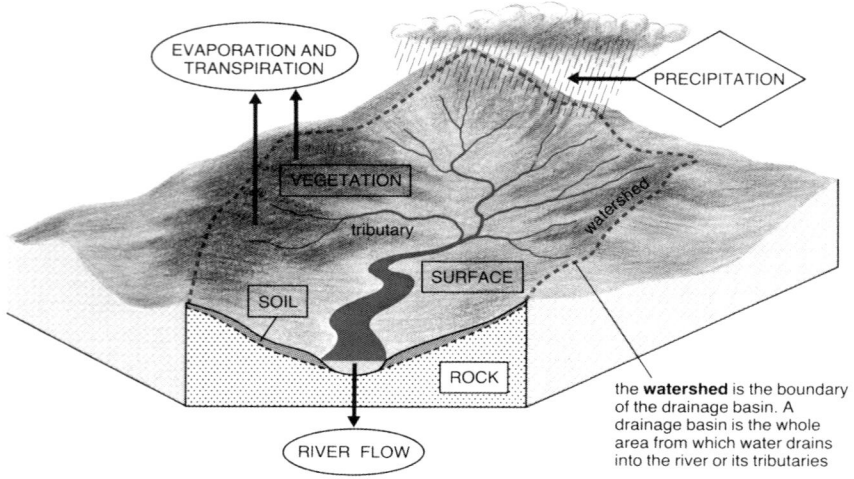

Figure 1.2.4: Simplified view of a drainage basin water cycle (after Richards, 1990)

1.2.2.2   Where Does the Rain Go ?

When it rains, droplets of water reaching the ground surface will pass into the soil by **infiltration** providing there are air spaces for it to pass into. When these air spaces have been completely filled by water, the droplets will no longer be able to pass into the soil. Providing the ground is sloping, water will flow over the surface as **overland flow** until either it is able to pass into the soil further downslope or it reaches a stream channel. Water which gets into the soil on a slope may move downhill through the soil, either by moving from one pore space to the next, or by entering natural soil pipes. This movement of soil water downslope is called **throughflow**.   If the underlying rock is porous or permeable, soil water may pass into the rock by **percolation**. It may flow out at some late⸴ date through a spring.   The precise pathway which water follows affects the time it takes to get from being rainfall back into the sea. Table 1.2.1 shows some possible pathways

Table 1.2.1: Water pathways through a drainage basin.

A FAST ROUTE	B MEDIUM ROUTE	C SLOW ROUTE
rain	rain	rain
overland flow	infiltrates soil	infiltrates soil
stream channel	throughflow in soil	percolates rock
flows into sea	stream channel	flows out of spring
	flows into sea	into stream channel
		flows into sea

1.2.2.3 How Much Flow ?

The channel flow or output (j on Figure 1.2.3) of the drainage basin can be measured at a specific point in the river. The amount of water flowing in the channel at a particular point in time is known as the river's **discharge**. This is simply the cross-sectional area (shaded below) of the water flow in the channel multiplied by it speed:

Discharge)   =   Speed x Cross-sectional area (shaded)
(m^3 / s)   (m/s)   (m^2)

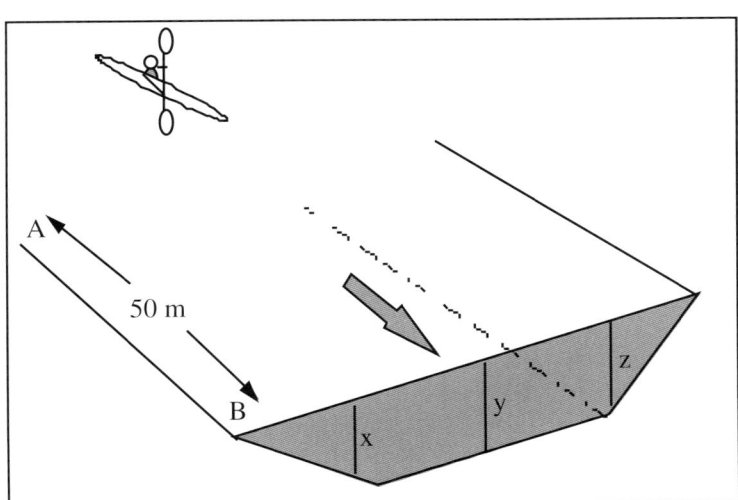

Figure 1.2.5: Diagram to show measurements needed to estimate river discharge.

Let's work out the speed first. A reasonable idea of how fast a river is flowing can be gained by timing how long something floating takes to travel between two fixed points along the bank - say from A to B on the diagram. Measure the distance between A and B in metres (though this could be done quite accurately by counting how many 1 m paces), then time (in seconds) how long it takes a small drifting object, (like the kayak in the picture) to travel the distance between A and B. Plate 1.2 shows some students using an orange for this exercise.

You can then calculate the speed like this:

Speed (in metres per second) = $\dfrac{\textbf{distance (metres)}}{\textbf{time (seconds)}}$

Let's say, using the example in the picture, that it took the kayak 2 minutes (120 seconds) to drift the 50 m from point A to point B. Then we can work out the speed for the river:

Speed = $\dfrac{\textbf{50 (m)}}{\textbf{120 (s)}}$ = **0.42 metres per second**

We can change this to km per hour. There are 1000 m in one km so to change 50 m to km divide it by 1000 = 0.05 km. There are 60 x 60 = 3600 seconds in one hour, so divide 120 seconds by 3600 to convert it to hours = 0.033 hours. Now do the calculation again:

$\dfrac{\textbf{0.05}}{\textbf{0.033}}$ = **1.5 km per hour**

In this example the river is flowing quite slowly and you could quite easily walk faster than this, say at 4 km per hour.

Now let's work out the cross-sectional area. This can be done as follows:

Cross-sectional area (m^2) = **width (m) x average depth (m)**

If you have a small boat the width can easily be measured with a tape measure or even just a long piece of string as shown in Figure 1.2.6.

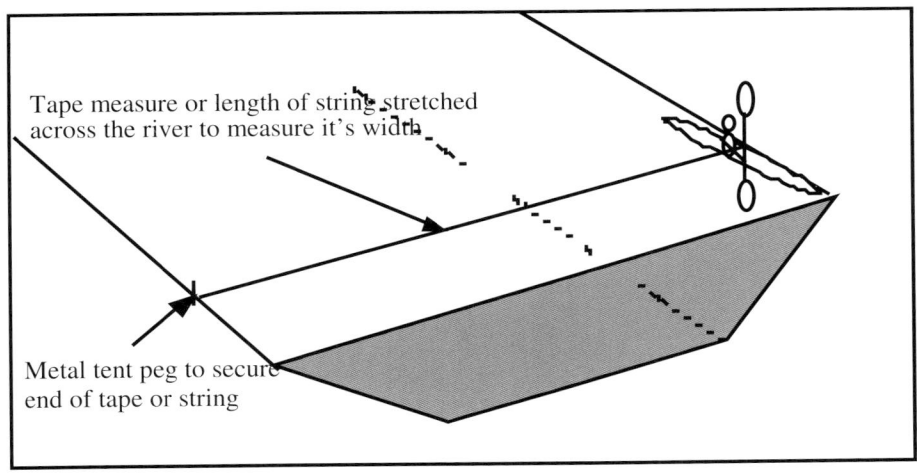

Tape measure or length of string stretched across the river to measure it's width

Metal tent peg to secure end of tape or string

Figure 1.2.6: Measuring river width.

Let's say the width of this river is 20 m exactly.

To measure depth, tie a weight onto the end of your piece of string so that it can be lowered into the river until it touches the bed. Once the weight is on the bed, pull the string tight and pinch the point where it breaks the water surface. You can then draw it out and measure off the length of string that was submerged against a metre rule or tape measure. You can make the job a little easier by marking your string every 10 cm with a waterproof marker and stick a piece of tape every metre. In Figure 1.2.7 the kayaker is measuring the depth at 6 evenly spaced points across the river as s/he moves from point A to F.

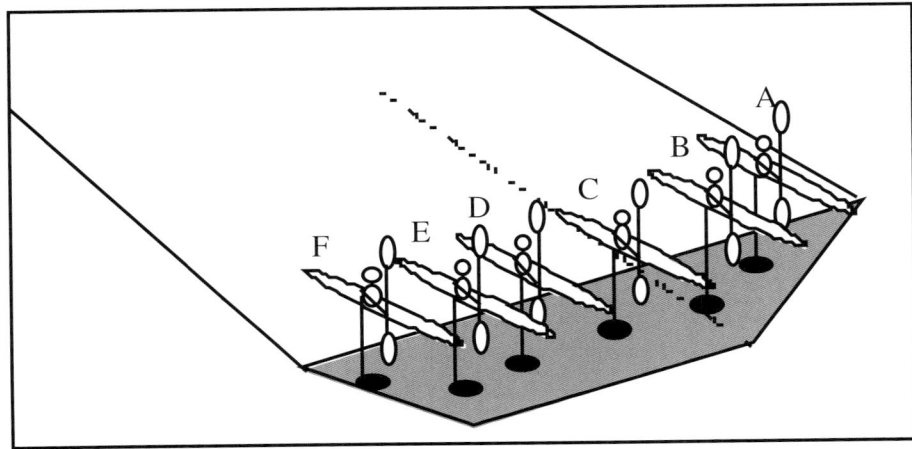

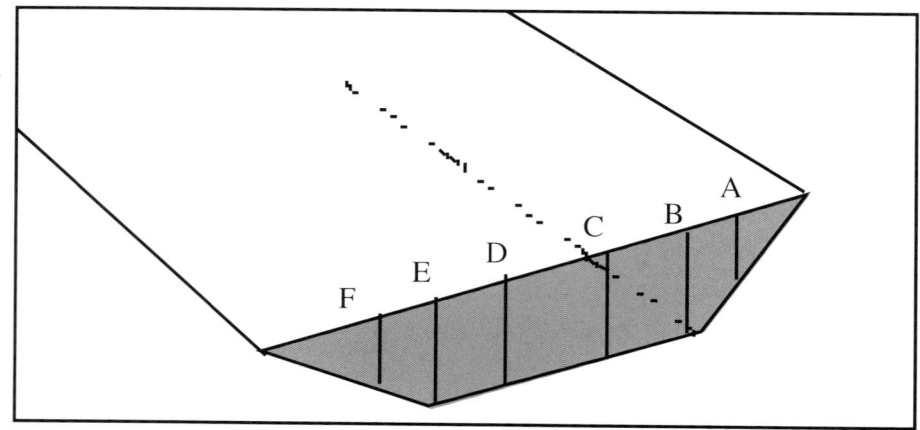

Figure 1.2.7: Measuring river depth.

We now have six evenly spaced depths across the river. In this example the depths in m are:

A = 0.8; B = 1.5; C = 1.5; D = 1.5; E = 1.5; F = 0.7

So, we work out the average depth by adding up these depths and dividing by the number of depths, like this:

$$\text{Average Depth} = \frac{0.8 + 1.5 + 1.5 + 1.5 + 1.5 + 0.7}{6} = \frac{7.5}{6}$$

$$= \underline{1.25 \text{ m}}$$

You will remember that the width of the river was 20 m. So we can now work out the cross-sectional area of the river at this point:

Cross-sectional area (m²)   =   **width (m) x average depth (m)**
    =   20 x 1.25
    =   <u>25 m²</u>

Now we know the cross-sectional area and the speed, we can go ahead and calculate the discharge:

Speed (m/s)	**x**	**Cross-sectional area (m²)**	**=**	**Discharge (m³ / s)**
0.42 m/s	x	25 m²	=	<u>10.5 m³ / s</u>

So, it is possible to estimate the discharge of a river using simple equipment and a small boat, which is fairly manoeuvrable like a kayak, open canoe or rowing boat. If you don't have a boat available, and the river is deep, then try to find a bridge. You can then measure the width of the river along the bridge and the depth could be measured from the bridge also by lowering your weighted piece of string from the bridge. Then it will be more difficult to mark the point where the string breaks the water surface - so fixing different coloured pieces of tape at known distances along the string may help here.

At various points in rivers you may see **stage boards** installed by river engineers to help them to assess the river level easily. You could perhaps get permission to install your own (usually from the Area Environment Agency Office). Later, we shall see how the discharge of rivers can be continuously recorded.

Once you have mastered this technique you can then begin to conduct a range of investigations to find answers to some of these questions:

Does the width of the river always increase on going downstream ?

Does the depth of the river always increase on going downstream ? Is the depth across the river always even ?

How do depth and speed vary on river bends ?

By how much does the discharge increase on going downstream ?

By how much do the speed, depth, width and discharge vary over time ? What is the highest the stage reached ? What is the lowest ?

By finding out the answers to some of these questions you will be beginning to understand how a river flows, how it responds to rainfall and what are its extremes. In Part 2.2 we will investigate these matters further and look at how records of river flow are kept, and how they may be used for river management purposes.

The changing cross-sectional area of a river may be monitored by a river gauging station. Plates 1.3 – 1.5 show photographs of structures used to measure river discharge.

River users will almost certainly have come across such structures. Though some have been specifically built for the purpose of gauging flow, others date back to times when rivers were used much more than today for transporting goods. Weirs were built in order to hold the flow back and make the river deep enough for transport boats. Chester weir is one such example from Norman times. Such stone, concrete or metal structures in the channel usually present a hazard to the small boat user and in most cases a **portage** will be necessary in order to pass by safely.

The cross-sectional area of the river at the flow structure is measured, and the change in cross-sectional area as the river level (or stage) rises and falls is monitored almost continuously. Today, a variety of instruments are used to do this. Some, such as a pressure transducer, work on pressure changes near the river bed. As the river stage rises, the pressure near the bed increases and this change is logged in a **data logger**, typically every 15 minutes. However, as rivers rise, not only does their cross-sectional area increase, but their average speed may also change. Thus, gauging station operators also need a good knowledge of how speed and cross-section area are related. This is normally a simple linear relationship obtained by measuring the speed of flow at many different river levels and plotting them on a graph known as a 'rating curve' shown in Figure 1.2.8.

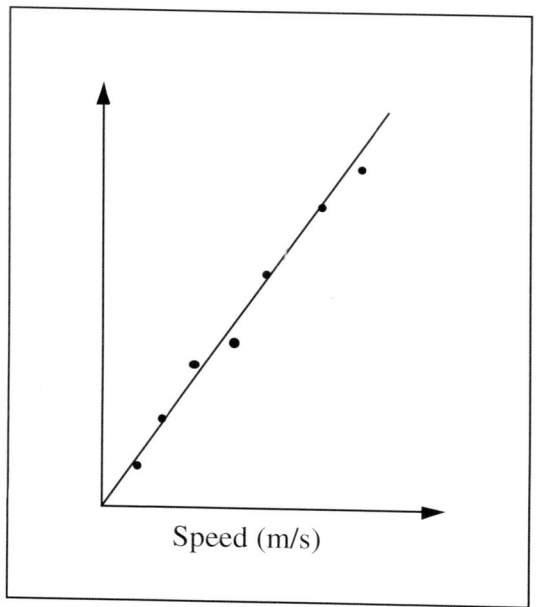

Speed (m/s)

Figure 1.2.8: The relationship between river stage and speed. A rating curve.

Using this relationship, river hydrologists are then able to estimate the cross-sectional area of the river and its speed continuously. They can therefore work out the continuous discharge which tells us how much water is flowing in the river at any time over the whole period over which records have been kept.

1.2.2.4 Rainfall-runoff response

If water takes the fast route (see Table 1.2.1) where the rain does not infiltrate the soil, and provided the rainfall is heavy and continuous, flooding of the river may well result. For a canoeist wanting to paddle in the white water upper reaches of a river, then these are usually the ideal rainfall-runoff conditions.

A river that rises rapidly has what is known as a 'flashy' regime - it rises and falls relatively quickly. The rainfall-runoff response is rapid as shown in what is called the storm **hydrograph** (see Part 2.2.4). Figure 1.2.9 (a) shows a hydrograph where water takes the fast route. Water taking the medium route may produce a storm hydrograph as in Figure 1.2.9 (b) and water taking the slow route may cause a very slow rise in the hydrograph as in Figure 1.2.9 (c). In fact, the portion of the streamflow below the dashed line, known as **baseflow**, is maintained by soil throughflow and groundwater when it doesn't rain.

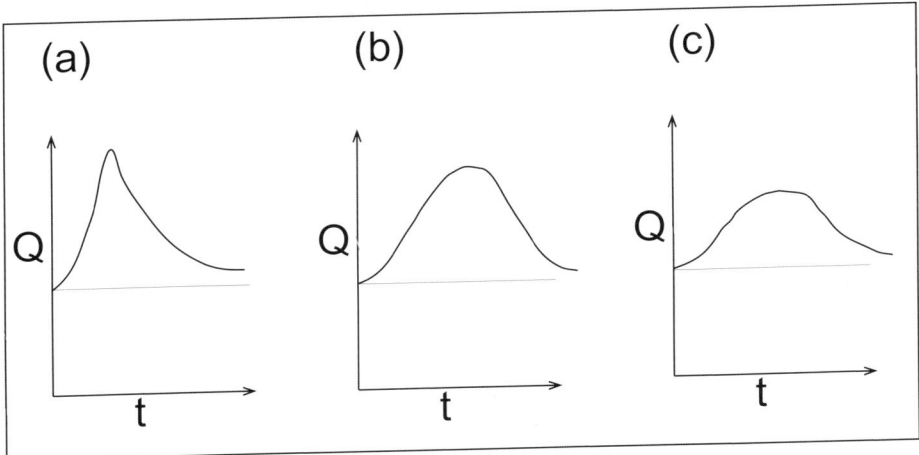

Figure 1.2.9: Storm hydrographs for (a) fast, (b) medium, and (c) slow runoff pathways in a drainage basin. Q = discharge, t = time.

It may be obvious by now that the pathway that the water takes will depend firstly on whether or not it can infiltrate the soil surface, and secondly whether or not it can percolate into the bedrock.

The rate at which rainfall can infiltrate into the ground surface is known as the ground's **infiltration capacity** (IC). Different land uses and ground surfaces have different infiltration capacities. For example, a well dug dry flower bed will have a high IC, an agricultural pasture may have a moderate IC whereas a tarmac road will have a low IC, probably near to zero. Part 2 gives more details on this and Table 2.2.1 shows some typical ICs. Thus, the land use in the catchment area surrounding a river will have quite an influence on infiltration rates and in turn how rapidly a river rises following rain. Other things which can affect this relationship include:

type of precipitation: prolonged rainfall will eventually cause the ground to become saturated and infiltration is replaced by surface runoff. Storms may produce rainfall that is so heavy that the rate at which water is reaching the ground surface may be greater than the rate at which the ground can absorb

23

it. In this case the excess water will rapidly become surface runoff and this will produce rapid rises in river levels. Heavy snowfall means that water is held in storage and river levels drop. However, as temperature rises then the meltwater soon reaches the main river. It is possible that the ground may remain frozen for some time and so melting snow enters the ground. Some of the most severe flooding in Britain has been caused by snowmelt.

basin size and shape; if a basin is small it is likely that it will reach the main channel more rapidly than in a larger basin where the water has much further to travel. **Lag time**, the time between the peak rainfall and the peak discharge in the river, will therefore be shorter in a small basin. A more circular basin will have a shorter lag time because all points in the basin will be roughly equidistant from the gauging station, whereas in an elongated basin it takes longer for water from the extremities of the basin to reach the outlet (see Figure 1.2.10).

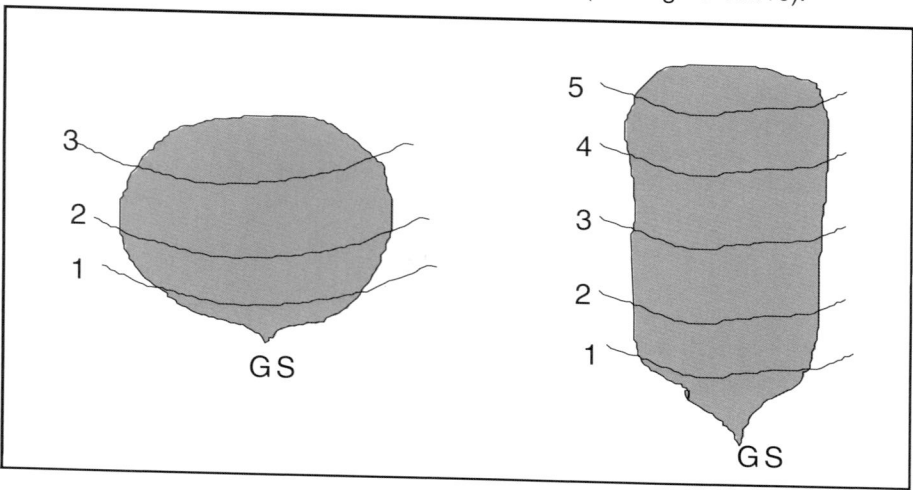

Figure 1.2.10: Travel times for water falling on different shaped drainage basins. GS = gauging station where river flow is measured. Lines show time (in hours) for rain falling in the basin to reach the gauging station.

steepness of slopes: in mountainous catchments where slopes are steep water is likely to reach the river more quickly.

temperature: extremes of temperature can restrict infiltration (frozen ground in winter, hard dry ground in summer) and thus increase surface runoff.

land use: vegetation intercepts rainfall and stores moisture on its leaves and branches before it evaporates back into the atmosphere. This may help to prevent flooding as less water will reach the streams and rivers. Dense forests can intercept up to 80 per cent of rainfall (30 per cent of which may later evaporate), whereas arable farmland may only intercept 10 per cent. Such interception may be less in winter in Britain when deciduous trees lose their leaves and crops have been harvested leaving bare earth. Vegetation, especially trees, also takes up water from the soil through roots and so reduces throughflow. The effect of mature coniferous plantation forest on runoff in the headwaters of the river Severn compared with the moorland river Wye is discussed in Part 2 (Section 2.2.4).

**urbanisation,** the building of towns and cities, has increased the flood hazard since water cannot infiltrate through tarmac and concrete. Gutters, drains and **culverts** carry water as quickly as possible to the nearest river to reduce flood risk in urban areas. Small streams may be canalised so that friction is reduced and water flows away faster. However, this may, in some cases, only move the flooding problems further downstream !

**rock type (geology):** rocks which allow water to pass through them are said to be **permeable**. Some rocks such as chalk contain numerous pores which can fill with and store water. These are called porous rocks. Other rocks such as limestone allow water to flow down cracks called joints or along bedding planes. These rocks are said to be permeable. Both of these rock types allow water to percolate into them so there is less surface runoff and a limited number of streams. In contrast, **impermeable** rocks such as granite, do not allow water to pass through them and so they produce more surface runoff and many streams.

**soil type:** this controls the speed of infiltration, the amount of storage and the rate of throughflow. Sandy soils with large pore spaces allow rapid infiltration and do not encourage flooding. Clay soils, on the other hand, have much smaller pore spaces and the particles sometimes swell up when wetted. This reduces infiltration and throughflow but encourages surface runoff and increases the risk of flooding.

**drainage density:** this refers to the number of streams in a given area. The density is highest on impermeable rocks (like granite) and clay soils and lowest on permeable rocks (like sandstone, limestone and chalk) and sandy soils. The higher the drainage density, the greater the chance of flash floods - a sudden rise of water in the river. In some British rivers such as the Findhorn, in NE Scotland for example, the rise in the hydrograph has been so sudden that witnesses have observed a 'standing wave' of water advancing down the river !

1.2.2.5   River Energy and Work

The amount of water reaching the river, and flowing in it, is very important, as it affects the amount of energy the river has to do work (Figure 1.2.11):

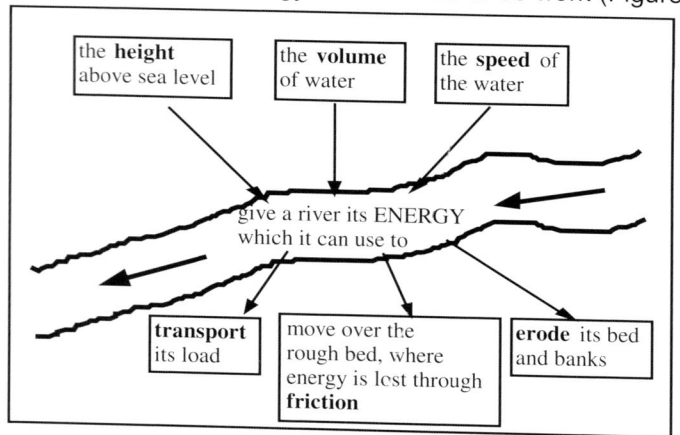

Figure 1.2.11: River energy: the sources of the energy and how it is used.

A river's energy depends on the volume of water, its speed and the height of the river above sea level. In simple terms we can say that this energy will mainly be used to overcome friction with the bed and the banks. In some rivers this may use 95% or more of the river's energy. Any energy left will be used to carry material and to erode the bed and banks. Figure 1.2.12 shows some of the processes of river erosion.

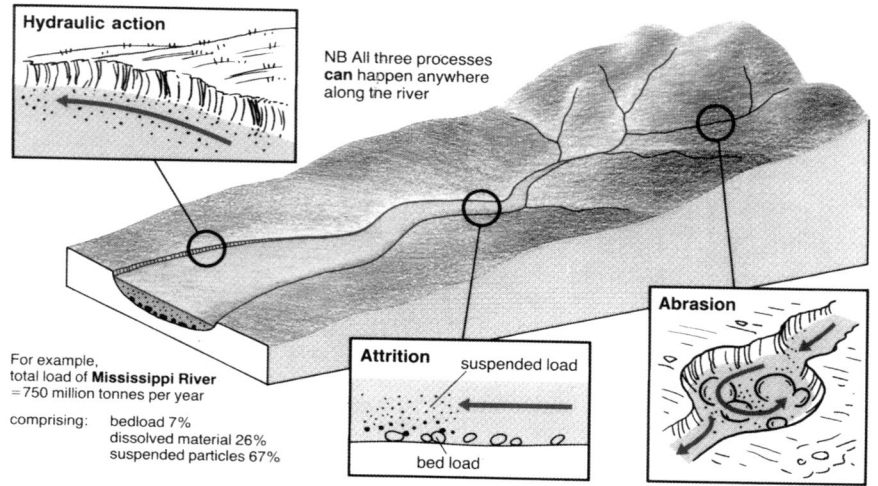

Figure 1.2.12: Some of the processes of river erosion (source: Richards, 1990). This is discussed in more detail in sections 2.2.6 and 2.2.7.

26

1.2.2.6   Landforms produced by rivers

Figure 1.2.13 shows some of the features produced by rivers.

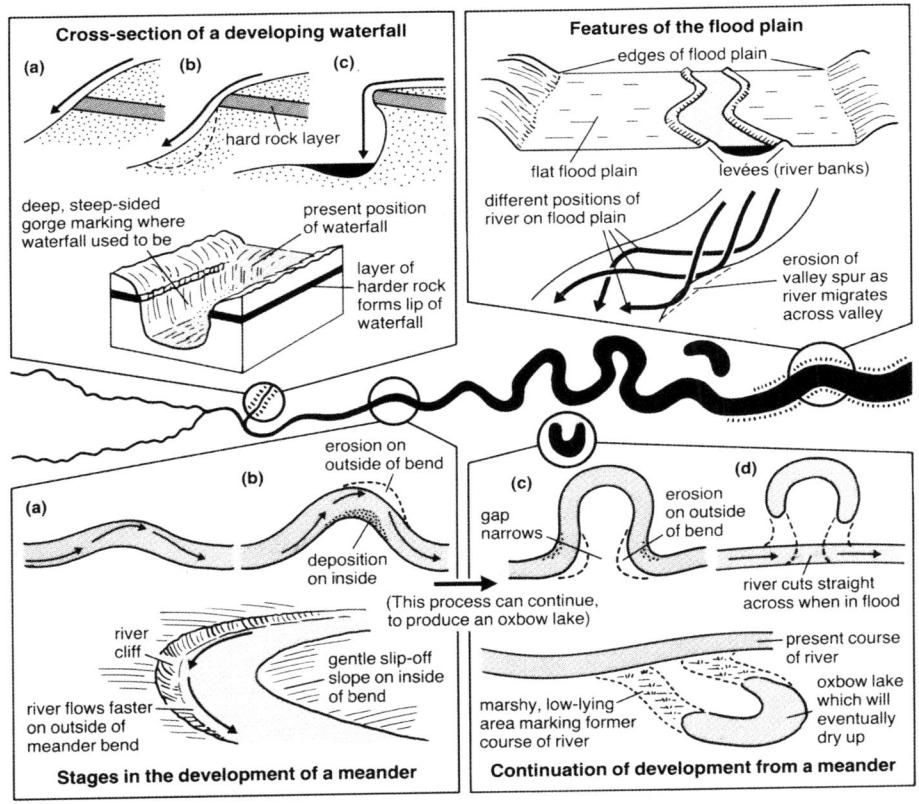

Figure 1.2.13: Some of the features you might expect to find along the course of a river (source: Richards, 1990)

The general location along the river course where these features may be seen is indicated. The movement of water along a river channel is a very complex subject and the various processes involved lead to a great variety of physical landforms that can be seen in river basins of all scales throughout the world. River courses may be conveniently divided in an idealised way into three main sections: the upper, middle and lower (see Figure 1.2.14).

Interlocking spurs

Waterfall

Rounded hills

Wide valley floor

Braiding

Ox-bow lake

Delta

Figure 1.2.14: Upper, middle and lower courses of a river (source: Doherty and McDonald, 1992)

Plate 2.7 shows the Allt Mor in the Cairngorms, a typical Scotish river in its upper course. Plate 2.8 shows the middle course of the River Tay at Grand Tully, and Plate 2.9 shows the lower course of the River Forth near Stirling in central Scotland. In the idealised upper course, the narrow V-shaped valley is characterised by the presence of **interlocking spurs**, rapids and small waterfalls.

In the idealised middle course, the river channel is much wider and the river flows between rounded hills. The river begins to **meander** as it hits flatter country. In a meandering stream the water flows in a corkscrew path as the water tends to be flung to the outside of the bends and to compensate for this a return flow develops over the stream bed towards the inside of the bends (see Section 2.2.6 for more details). The river profile in the middle course often consists of a series of steps as hard rock bands may inhibit the river's efforts to form a smoothly curving graded profile (as illustrated in section 2.2.1).

In the lower course the river channel reaches its maximum width and maximum sinuosity (the number and width of bends). Meanders can migrate a few metres downstream every year by continuous erosion from the outside of the bend with deposition on the inside of bends. In this way the floodplain alluvium is transported downstream. The lower course is characterised by **floodplains**, **ox-bow lakes**, and **levees**. Floodplain sediments may be cut through by the river and may form steps or platforms on the valley sides called **river terraces** (see section 2.2.10).

So, we have seen how a number of things can affect the rainfall-runoff response in any particular drainage basin. A basic knowledge and understanding of these is important to the river user because:

- we will be better placed to predict and understand when river levels will be up or down, and this can help when choosing a suitable river for a particular recreational pursuit since an understanding of the way a river flows and how it responds to rainfall and snow melt can be useful in planning your visits to the river in question,

- we can better understand the likely effects of different land and river management practices on the river hydrology and runoff response, so that as recreational river users we can make informed decisions about our rivers and inland waterways in future.

1.3   An Introduction to Living Things in Rivers and Inland Waterways

1.3.1   What's in River Water ?

Planet Earth differs from other planets in our solar system in that we have water. Oceans covers over 70% of the Earth's surface, but in terms of volume only about 2.5% of the planet's water resource is freshwater. Of this freshwater, almost all of it is held either as ice and snow in ice sheets, ice caps and high mountain glaciers, or as **groundwater** in **porous** or **permeable** rocks. This leaves only 0.3 % (or 0.008% of all water on Earth) as 'biological' freshwater (i.e. in rivers, canals and lakes on the surface). Nevertheless, there is a large annual turnover - addition and loss, inflow and outflow - from this 'pool'. On average these surface fresh waters are replaced in days or months compared with **residence times** of thousands of years for the oceans.

The other more obvious difference between the freshwater of rivers and canals and that of the oceans is the salt content of the water. Sea water has around 35 g of salts in every litre, whereas in freshwater this is normally less that 0.1 g per litre. This is because water flows into the oceans but leaves only by evaporation: whilst some salts are precipitated (solidify out), those dissolved in the in flowing water have been concentrated over time. As well as being made up of water molecules (hydrogen and oxygen), natural water contains a range of other chemicals which are picked up from the air (as rain falls), or from the surface of vegetation or dissolved from the soils and rocks of the Earth's surface. Table 1.3.1 gives concentrations of some of the most common **ions** in natural waters.

Table 1.3.1: Concentrations of some of the most common ions in natural waters (after Moss, 1988).

Ions	Fresh water (Barton Broad, K[1])	Average Sea water[2]
Sodium (Na^+)	2.1	475
Potassium (K^+)	0.23	10.1
Calcium (Ca^{++})	2.8	10.3
Magnesium (Mg^{++})	0.46	54.2
Chloride (Cl^-)	2.4	554
Sulphate (SO_4^{--})	-	28.6
Bicarbonate (HCO_3^-)	3.4	2.4

[1] data from Moss (1983); [2] data from Moss (1988)

Despite the major differences in residence times and salt content between surface freshwater and oceans, there are some remarkable similarities in terms of the variety of life. Water, as a medium in which to live, is so different from air that its properties and the problems organisms have to overcome in order to live in water will be emphasised in this Section.

1.3.2   How Life In Rivers Developed

There seems to be little doubt that life started in water, but no certain evidence that the water was initially fresh or salt. The earliest **fossils** are of **micro-organisms** - like bacteria and blue-green algae - which we know must have at least a covering film of liquid water to stop them drying out. Representatives of all the earliest organisms are found in both the sea and fresh waters. However, it does seem clear that the first animals which possessed more than one cell began life in the sea, whereas some plants started life in the sea, while others did so on the land.

The pattern of where plants and animals live along canals and rivers may sometimes seem haphazard, but there are various reasons why a particular species is present or absent. As a general principle, the basic need for animals, either directly or indirectly, is the presence of plants for food, shelter and breeding sites. The more diverse the habitats and vegetation the greater the variety of small animals there will be.

As was stated in Section 1.1.1 earlier, river wildlife arrived shortly after the ice melted and the melt-water established a wide drainage system across Northern Europe and animals and plants spread along these new waterways. When the sea finally flooded the Straits of Dover during the **climatic optimum** around 7, 500 years ago (when average temperatures were warmer than today) the rapid colonisation of British rivers ended and Britain became an island. Human impact on the landscape has steadily increased and certainly many species, such as the beaver for example, have become extinct in quite recent times. To counter-balance this, there have been new arrivals, either expanding naturally or through accidental introductions by humans (such as the mink described in section 2.3).

1.3.3   Things Which Affect Plant And Animal Life

The factors that affect plants and animals that live in streams, rivers and canals can be divided into two groups. One group covers those aspects of the physical and chemical environment around us and are called **abiotic** factors. The other group concerns the animals and plants themselves who compete with each other for space, food, light etc. and these are called **biotic** factors. These are dealt with in turn below.

Abiotic Factors

1.3.3.1 Flow

Sometimes also called the current, the speed and type of flow in a river can favour or eliminate certain plants or animals. For example, the upland sections of a river tend to be steeper and often rainfall is higher. Here the flow is fast in places and varies greatly over short distances. Further downstream, the construction of weirs creates a locally faster flow, and canal locks can do the same when in use. These fast flowing sections may contain plants and animals not found elsewhere, such as certain kinds of moss.

Fast flowing sections of rivers tend to have a high proportion of mosses and liverworts with few, if any, flowering plants. This is because mosses and liverworts are small and grow close to the bed of the stream which makes it more difficult for the current to dislodge them. The variety of flowering plants usually increases lower down rivers where the flow is slower. Section 2.2.6 shows how flow is usually fastest near the surface in the middle of the channel (where it is straight) and on the outside of bends.

1.3.3.2 Nature of the bed

The nature of the bed or **substrate** - whether it is rough or smooth, will affect the living creatures that can exist. One of the greatest differences between canals and rivers is the nature of their bed. Canals tend to have relatively smooth silt and clay linings whereas river beds may vary from smooth rock through cobbles and pebbles to sand, silt or clay as the river goes from source to sea. Both the rock type and nature of the flow will affect the bed material. Fast flow will tend to transport pebbles, knocking them together, breaking and rounding them as they move down the river. Some parts of rivers, such as the inside of meander bends, tend to favour deposition of bed material. Other areas, such as the outside of meander bends where flow is fastest, tend to favour erosion.

Mosses tend to grow on rocks, because if they grew on silt or mud they would be constantly buried. On the other hand, taller flowering plants favour silt or mud beds, because there are more nutrients available and in more mobile coarser sediments, plants with tall stems are more likely to get broken. Greater amounts of silt or **suspended sediment** carried by a river can reduce the number of snails, water lice and other tiny creatures that live on or in the river bed.

1.3.3.3 Channel width and depth

Width is not as important as depth in affecting the animals and plants that colonise an area. The shallower a stream or river, the more the light can penetrate the water (unless the suspended sediment content is high). On the other hand it may be more likely to dry out in summer. Some plants, like common reed, cannot grow under water, whereas sweet-grass can grow submerged or emergent. In some disused canals the depth can be reduced gradually by silting and build up of dead plants until it is more or less filled up completely with plants and no open water remains. This is less likely to happen in rivers though, because floods tend to erode and wash away silt regularly keeping the channel clear. Animals, less dependent on light than plants, can exist at much greater depths.

1.3.3.4 Light

Water reflects light at the surface and only absorbs the red part of the light spectrum that gets through causing everything below about 3 m to have a bluish tinge. Because red light is important for **photosynthesis**, the process by which plants make their food, plants tend to grow in shallow water, though in very clear water they can grow at depths of up to 10 m. Some plants, like water lilies, overcome this problem by having floating leaves. The amount of light is affected by the **turbidity** (suspended solids content), discolouration (caused by peat for example) or pollution (see Sections 1.4 and 2.4).

1.3.3.5 Temperature and Oxygen

The temperature of water and its oxygen content are linked, and best dealt with together. Because oxygen is relatively insoluble in water and the solubility decreases as the water gets warmer (within limits), higher temperatures will generally speed up plant growth although the oxygen supply may decrease. **Invertebrates** cannot regulate their body temperature so it varies with that of the water. Therefore, they occur in greater numbers in summer and some pass the winter as inactive stages such as eggs or pupae. The upper reaches of rivers tend to have colder water, but a lot of turbulence, which increases oxygen absorption. Lower down the river the temperature tends to be higher, the water is smoother, and there is a breakdown of **organic matter** and a higher plant and animal population, all combining to lower the oxygen level. Canals are slower moving and generally have even less oxygen. Where pollution is high, particularly where sewage or **farm effluent** gets into rivers, a lot of oxygen is used up in the breakdown of organic matter. Once oxygen levels drop to very low levels, only blood worms can survive in large numbers and gradually other organisms such as plants and fish die (see Section 1.4).

1.3.3.6 Nutrients

In the freshwater environment nutrients are chemical compounds such as nitrates and phosphates which are necessary for healthy plant growth. More chemical compounds will dissolve in water than in any other natural liquid. Section 1.3.1 outlined some of the chemicals which natural water contains. Generally there is a natural process of enrichment called **eutrophication,** from the source of a river to the sea. These nutrients come from a variety of sources: some are washed in on soil and silt from the land surrounding the river; some fall in as leaves and dead plant matter; some are dissolved out of the rock over which the river flows. The upper reaches generally tend to be nutrient-poor (oligotrophic) but as more are added to the river from runoff, dissolving of the bed rock, deposition of silt, and the breakdown of dead plants and animals, the water becomes richer in nutrients. Many plants which live in rivers absorb nutrients from the water through their leaves and stems as well as through roots. It seems likely that nutrient levels in rivers are rarely limiting for plants and although they may stop growing, they do not die. The various physical and chemical qualities of rivers and canals combine and interact to provide **habitats** for plants and animals.

Biotic Factors

1.3.3.7 Competition

The distribution of plants and animals in rivers is not only determined by their tolerance to the above abiotic factors. Biotic factors are also involved. For example, the presence of the right type of food, the space and the presence or absence of other competitive species. Clearly, consumption by one species will reduce the amount of resource available for others. The species which is less efficient at turning the resource (e.g. food) into more of its own species (by reproduction) will eventually die out and become extinct if there is competition with other species.

1.3.3.8 Human interference

Finally, management interference and in some cases mis-management by humans can overcome all of the above factors to a greater or lesser extent. For example, construction of reservoirs and weirs will change the river's flow, width and depth and sediment load, which in turn may alter the distribution and types of animals and plants. Planting or felling trees on a riverbank may alter the amount of light reaching the water. The shading effect of overhanging trees can alter the river's temperature, in turn affecting oxygen levels. Dredging of silt and sediment from the bottom of rivers and canals can totally alter the nature of the bed allowing new species to colonise rapidly. The addition of sewage or farm effluent to a river can add so much organic matter that the extra oxygen used up in its breakdown can lead to the death of fish and other animals. Section 1.4 deals with management of rivers and canals in more detail.

1.3.4 Introducing Freshwater Plants and Animals

This book does not aim to describe all the plants and animals you are likely to see on, around, or in the rivers and inland waterways of Britain. There are plenty of keys and guides that are specifically dedicated to helping you to find and identify such plants and animals. These are given in the further reading sections at the end of Part 1 and Part 2. Part 1 explains how plants and animals may be classified, how they are named and introduces the various stream and river habitats where you are likely to find them. Part 2 describes the common plants and animals you may find and explains how some of them are adapted to life in or around rivers. This book will deal mainly with the plants and animals that you are likely to see with the unaided eye - though a simple magnifying glass will be useful for a closer look at some of them. Sometimes reference will be made to smaller organisms if they are thought to be of interest.

1.3.4.1 Plant Groups

Plants make their food by photosynthesis. The green colouring in plants is called **chlorophyll** and this enables plants to absorb energy from sunlight and use it to combine carbon dioxide (from the air) and water (from their environment) to make sugar and all the other substances they need for food.

Sub-divisions of the plant kingdom are:

1.   Spore producing plants (non-flowering plants)
          (a) Algae
          (b) Liverworts and Mosses
          (c) Ferns

2.   Seed-bearing plants:
          (a) Conifers
          (b) Flowering Plants:
                    (i) Monocotyledons (parallel veins in leaves)
                    (ii) Dicotyledons (branching veins in leaves)

We shall now consider the basic characteristics of each group in turn.

1. (a)   Algae

Seaweeds are the largest algae but they are quite simple structures with no proper roots, stems or leaves. In the freshwater environment, however, some of the simplest algae are single-celled and cannot be seen without a microscope. They can turn water 'pea-soup' or bright green in colour. Larger ones are filamentous and form slimy growths or tough mats in ponds, ditches, rivers and canals.

1. (b)   Liverworts and Mosses

Liverworts are small, flat, green plants, usually growing close together in very moist, shady places such as in the mouths of caves or on a stream bank near the water-line. Some can look like small, overlapping, strips of dark green cabbage leaf stuck to the rock or the bank. Liverworts have no stem and their 'roots' are only single cells like root hairs.

Mosses are familiar as green, cushion-like growths seen on walls, roofs and at the base of tree-trunks in woodland. Each 'cushion' is made up of hundreds of separate plants. Each moss plant has a slender stem with simple, tiny, overlapping leaves.

Mosses and liverworts produce microscopic reproductive spores and the capsules which contain these spores can often be seen sticking out of the tops of the plants (see Plate 1.6). The capsules will break open, releasing the spores.

1. (c)   Ferns

Bracken is probably the most widespread and familiar type of fern. Ferns are usually found in shady damp woods, gardens or on shady banks. Many ferns have underground stems as well as roots and large well-developed leaves. These contain water-conducting tissues that are connected to the roots and stem. The spores are produced in special structures under the leaves.

2. Seed bearing plants

All the plants described so far reproduce by single-celled spores. The most familiar plants, however, reproduce by seeds, which are made up of many cells and contain a tiny **embryo** plant as well as a store of food for the early growth of the seedling.

2. (a)   Conifers. These are seed bearing trees but the seeds are produced in cones. The leaves are usually small and often needle-like. Examples are pine, larch, spruce and cypress.

2. (b) Flowering plants. These produce their seeds from flowers. There are two main groups:

(i) those with parallel veins in leaves are called 'monocotyledons', which means that the seeds of these plants contain only one **cotyledon** (or food storage organ). All the grasses, including the cultivated grasses, such as wheat, barley and maize are in this group. So are some of the plants that have bulbs or other underground storage organs; for example, daffodils, bluebells, tulips, crocuses, irises, lilies, onions and leeks. The leaves can usually be recognized because the veins run parallel to each other down the length of the leaf and in many cases the leaves are narrow and long,

(ii) those in which the leaf veins form a network branching from a midrib are called 'dicotyledons'. The seed contains two cotyledons. This group includes all the flowering plants not mentioned so far; the garden flowers and wild flowers (herbaceous), shrubs and trees (woody). Their leaves are broad and net-veined, that is, there is usually a large middle vein with other veins branching from it to make a visible network.

1.3.4.2   Animal Groups

All animals get their food by eating plants and/or other animals. Most animals are able to move freely. The animal kingdom is divided into several main groups, called 'phyla' (pronounced 'fila'; singular = phylum), six of which are listed next:

Cnidarians
Platyhelminthes
Annelids
Molluscs
Arthropods
$\left\{\begin{array}{l}\end{array}\right.$
Crustaceans
Insects
Arachnids
Myriapods

Vertebrates
$\left\{\begin{array}{l}\end{array}\right.$
Fish
Amphibia
Reptiles
Birds
Mammals

The vertebrates are animals that have a skull and a backbone (vertebral column). All the other groups are sometimes referred to as 'invertebrates', that is, animals without backbones. Although this is a convenient description, it is not really a proper subdivision of the animal kingdom. We shall now look at each phylum in turn:

Cnidarians

Cnidarians (pronounced 'nid-air-ians') are sea anemones, corals and jellyfish. They nearly all live in the sea, but some, called Hydra, do live in freshwater, and they live by attaching themselves to an object and catching food with their stinging tentacles. They are difficult to see in rivers with the naked eye.

Platyhelminthes

The flatworms that live in ponds and streams are usually about a centimetre long or less. They are found under stones or under the floating leaves of pond plants and they glide about by means of the movements of the **cilia** that cover their bodies. Some members of the flatworm phylum are parasitic. Tapeworms live in the intestines of vertebrates and absorb the digested food there. Flukes are parasitic flatworms; some of them cause tropical diseases in humans and others, such as the liver flukes, cause diseases in animals. They are found in ponds and streams and some are fairly tolerant of pollution.

Annelids

Annelids are worms with tubular bodies that are divided up into segments (rings). They also have fine bristles that help them grip the soil or sand, or help them to swim. Earthworms are annelids; other examples include lugworms and bristle-worms living on the sandy coasts between tide marks. In the freshwater environment true worms such as the red Tubifex worms (which have haemoglobin in their blood similar to humans) are found in silt and mud and are good indicators of organically polluted water.

Molluscs

Snails and freshwater limpets have only one shell but swan mussels and pea cockles have a shell in two hinged sections and are called bivalves. Slugs have an internal shell. All have a foot. This is the structure on which they creep along or which holds them on to a rock. About 15 kinds of snail live in the wetlands of the British Isles. Some are adapted land dwellers, some are aquatic and several are truly **amphibious.**

Arthropods

These animals have a hard, jointed, skeleton like a suit of armour outside their bodies. They also have jointed legs and antennae ('feelers'). Their bodies are made up of segments and are usually clearly divided into three regions called head, thorax and abdomen.

(a) Crustaceans include shrimps, crabs, prawns and woodlice. They all have more than six legs (e.g. crabs have ten).

(b) Insects have six legs, a body in three segments, and, in most cases, one or two pairs of wings. Most of the animals you come across will probably belong to this huge group. Many of them will be the nymphs or larvae of flying adults. Insects can be divided into two sub-classes based on their life cycles. Flies, beetles, butterflies, wasps and earwigs are examples of insects. Insects such as fleas and lice are thought to have 'lost' their wings in the course of evolution.

(c) Arachnids are water spiders, water mites and land spiders. They have eight legs and a body in two segments.

(d) Myriapods. The name means 'many feet' and the group consists of centipedes and millipedes.

Vertebrates

These animals all have a vertebral column ('backbone') and a skull. There are five classes:

(a) Fish live in water and have streamlined bodies covered with scales. They have fins and breathe by means of gills. The common fish include barbel, bream, bullhead, chub, dace, eel, grayling, gudgeon, lamprey, loach, minnow, perch, pike, roach, rudd, salmon, sticklebacks and trout.

(b) Amphibia are frogs, toads and newts. They have four limbs and smooth moist skins without scales. They spend much of their time on land but they can live in water and most of them have to return to water to lay their eggs. On land they breathe with lungs. In water they can breathe through their skin. Examples which you could see on shallow, sheltered and well-vegetated parts of rivers and canals include great crested newt (warty newt), smooth newt (common newt), palmate newt, common toad, natterjack toad and common frog.

(c) Reptiles also live on land but their skins are dry and covered with scales. They lay eggs with leathery skins and they do not have to breed in water, like the amphibians. Most lizards have four limbs, but some, like the slow worm and snakes, have no limbs. You are most likely to see reptiles when they are basking in the sun in spring (mid-March to May) when they have emerged from their hibernation. Those you could see include sand lizard, viviparous lizard (common lizard), slow worm, grass snake, smooth snake and adder (viper).

(d) Birds are 'warm-blooded' vertebrates. They have feathers, wings and beaks and they reproduce by laying eggs. The most common examples you will see on or around rivers include: coot, dipper, grey heron, grey wagtail, mallard, moorhen and mute swan. Others such as little grebe, great crested grebe, garganey, goosander, kingfisher, red breasted merganser, sand martin and teal may be a little more difficult to see.

(e) Mammals are vertebrates that are also 'warm-blooded' but their bodies are covered with hair. Their young are born 'alive', rather than hatched from eggs, and are suckled on milk. The water dwelling mammals you may see on rivers include otters, mink, water voles and water shrew. Other mammals that may visit the river environment include Daubenton bat, fox, mole, polecat, rat and weasel.

1.3.4.3 Naming Plants and Animals

'Common' names have been used when they exist but not all organisms have one. A plant or animal may also be known by several different common names. Scientific names, which are always given following the common names if they exist, are understood universally. Do not be put off because they are in a form of Latin - gardeners use them all the time, often without realising it (*Primula*, *Iris* and so on)! They consist of two words printed in *italics,* the first always has a capital letter and is the genus (plural genera) and is a group of closely linked species. The *genus* name corresponds to our surname in the human community; the second (no capital) is the *species*, (the plant or animal itself) and, like our Christian names, many are used over and over again. Sometimes a third name is added to show a small, usually geographical, variation. For instance, the duck genus *Anas* contains several species, such as *Anas penelope* (Wigeon) and *Anas crecca* (Teal). When only the initial letter of the genus is given this means it is the same as the last genus mentioned. In some cases organisms are so alike that only the *genus* will be given.

A group of related genera form a *family* - the duck genus *Anas* (together with *Aythya* and others) belonging to the Duck family, *Anatidae.* Families are used here when appropriate to make the book easier to use but are not always included.

1.3.4.4 Freshwater Habitats

As described in section 1.2 the source of all our streams, rivers and inland waterways is rain. Most of our streams and rivers are of natural origin, even though their courses may have been altered by humans. Although their sources may be diverse, rivers can be divided into three, or even four, regions. Near the source of an upland river the current will be fast flowing. A more significant factor for freshwater life, is the bottom substrate which moves continually. The upper part of the river's course is sometimes also called the **headstream** and may be susceptible to fluctuations in temperature and volume. It therefore supports relatively little, but often very specialised, life.

Below this is the middle course sometimes also called the troutbeck region. The current here is still fast flowing but its volume is more constant. The river will now be larger and the substrate more stable, consisting of boulders with areas of exposed gravel on bends, sometimes forming islands in mid-channel. The troutbeck is so-called because it is a haven for trout which feed on the mayfly and stonefly nymphs which live there. Although there may only be a few species of insects living in the troutbeck, their populations can be large.

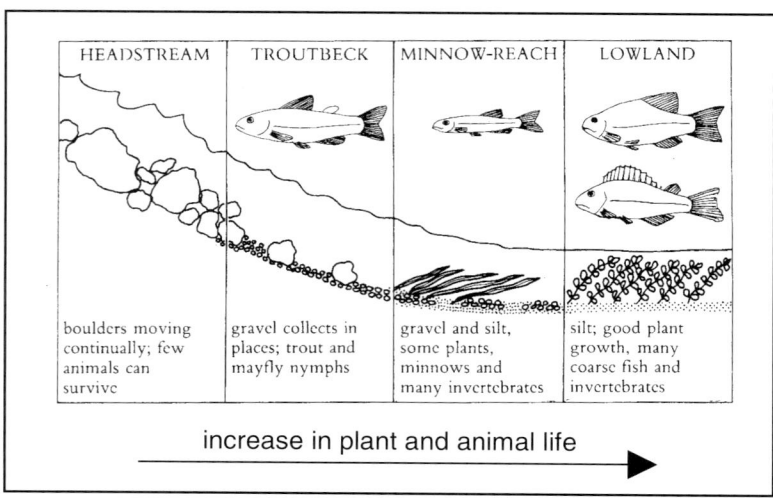

Figure 1.3.1: The four major regions of a river: headstream, troutbeck, minnow-reach and lowland. As the turbulence of the current decreases and the bed material becomes more stable, a greater abundance of animal and plant life can flourish (after Sterry, 1982)

As the river moves to flatter gradients, the turbulence of the flow generally decreases as it enters lowland regions. The volume of water carried by this region is greater because subsidiary streams have now joined the main flow. The river will have acquired more nutrients by this stage and the bottom is even more stable. In some parts, pools may be created and silt may gather in the slower moving areas. This allows for a greater diversity of species and this is the first region where plants can successfully colonise the water and the water's edge in any number. Where the river approaches the coast, and the volume of the river has increased even more, is usually the most productive part of the river and large fish populations will be present. These would not survive were it not for the extensive range of **invertebrates** also found here, together with healthy plant communities.

Canals

Canals have been with us for hundreds of years; indeed some date back to Roman times. Although many are redundant today, they were formerly the main transport highways. To allow canals to operate over gradients, lock gates were built and there were often a series if the gradient was steep. During the operation of a lock gate water is lost from the higher reach of the canal, and to replace the necessary volume of water, large areas were excavated adjoining the canal. These 'flashes' also served as turning points for barges. Today they often provide refuges for wildlife especially if the canal is well used.

A canal is, in effect, a long, continuous pond. In general, there is only a slow flow of water and the environment is quite stable. In former years, canals were colonised by animals and plants from the then numerous village and agricultural ponds. Nowadays, as ponds disappear rapidly, canals are becoming increasingly important as wildlife havens. One problem that ponds and canals have in common is that they eventually fill in. Decaying plant material ultimately forms a stable enough layer for emergent vegetation to grow across the width of the canal. The final stage is for trees such as alder and willow to colonise it, and this effectively destroys the freshwater habitat and the life it supports. If a canal is to continue to be navigable by boats and provide a habitat, it must be periodically cleaned. British Waterways and other navigation authorities maintain waterways and canals in their control, whereas the Waterway Recovery Group and Restoration Committee promote the restoration of canals. The Restoration Committee does the political lobbying and advising while the Waterway Recovery Group does the physical work of restoring canals.

Figure 1.3.2 shows how the presence of vegetation in ponds is very important to animals, particularly to invertebrates. This, to some extent applies to slow moving sections of rivers and canals. A great many species use under water plants for shelter, as a source of food and for anchorage.

Generally, there are a greater number of species of animals found amongst the weed of a pond, river or canal than in the bottom mud or open water.

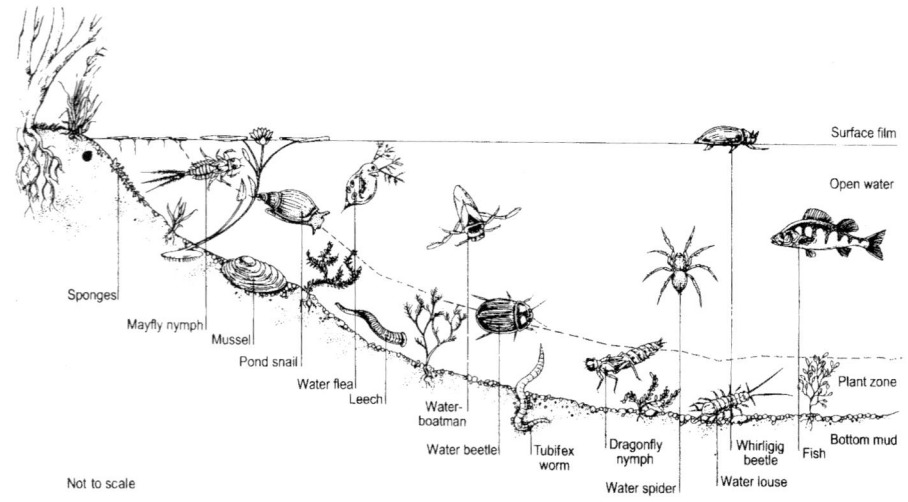

Figure 1.3.2: Pond zones and typical animals (after Clegg, 1974)

As can be seen from section 1.3.3, life in streams, rivers and canals is affected by a range of factors to which the plants and animals which live in them must adapt. The difficulties of coping with flowing water, of obtaining nutrients, and reproducing have been overcome in a variety of ways by colonising plants.

Algae, mosses, liverworts, lichens, herbs, grasses, sedges, trees - an infinite variety of plants live in, and alongside, rivers. For hundreds of plants, running fresh water is the only habitat in which they can survive. For others, it is one of a range of habitats in which they can be found. For the river community as a whole, plants are the producers of **organic matter.** They are able to do this by fixing energy from the sun through **photosynthesis**. Though the river channel itself provides a variety of physical habitats (pools, riffles, side bars, mid-channel bars and islands), plants offer numerous more intricate variations: the surfaces of stems above and below the water, the undersides of leaves, crevices in bark, holes in tree trunks, inside flowers, amongst root mats etc. Physical characteristics of the site (e.g. flow **velocity**, temperature and oxygen, silt accumulation and light availability) may all be modified by the presence of large plants or **macrophytes**. Most algae in silty rivers, for example, are attached to the stems and leaves of water plants. From the recreationalist's point of view, plants in and beside the water can make or mar the beauty of a river or canal scene.

There is a huge variety in the river plants which have evolved to take advantage of the range of habitats from a river's source to mouth. In any natural cross-section the variation of water depth, flow velocity, substrate size, bank height, slope, aspect, period of inundation and soil type, all combine to form an intricate pattern of zones which different types of plants may inhabit. In addition, the type of plants that grow on a bare area change through time. This is the process of **succession**.

As an aid to understanding the very complex river ecosystem, it is useful to subdivide the river into:

- mid-channel
- channel edges
- bank sides
- bank tops

Figure 1.3.3 is a cross-section of a 'typical' small lowland river which illustrates these divisions. Reference will be made to these parts of the river ecosystem in section 2.3 later.

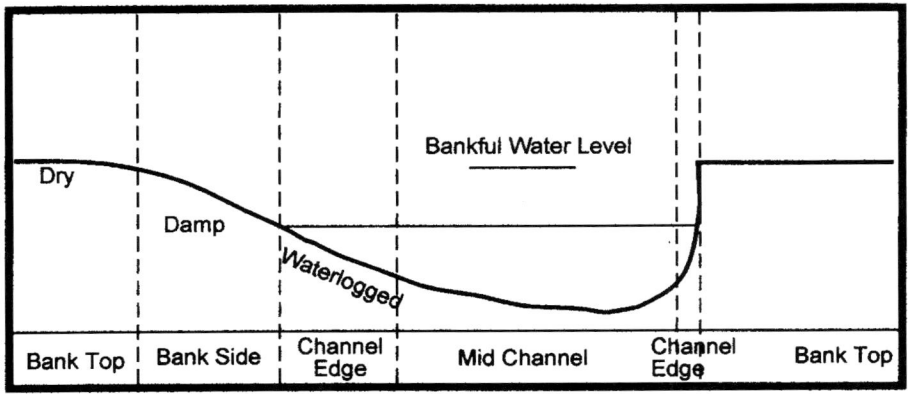

Figure 1.3.3: Cross-section of a typical lowland river divided by habitat types.

1.3.5   Observing Animals

If you do approach river wildlife carefully, you will be rewarded with some excellent observations. You may wish to write up some form of log, why not record what you see ? The best way to record your observations is to compile a good collection of photographs using a SLR camera and telephoto lens. A pair of binoculars (8 x 30 or 8 x 40 magnification) will allow you to observe birds more closely. A good pair of eyes is the most valuable aid to observing wildlife, along with a good nature guide to help with identification. A small hand lens is also useful with a magnification of x 8 to observe the more lowly forms of life.

Reading a guide before going onto the water, and aiming to observe one type of wildlife will be much more successful than trying to identify everything which grows, flies, crawls or swims. Always remember it is important to bring the book to the wildlife and not the other way around. The Further Reading list at the end of Part 1 gives some good guide books you could use. Most bookshops with a natural history section will be able to provide a selection of nature guides for you to choose from. Part 2.3 gives descriptions of the most common animals and plants you are likely to see. Membership of your local natural history or conservation group will improve your ability to observe and identify wildlife further. The Royal Society for Nature Conservation (address in Appendix III) will have their address, otherwise try the local library.

1.3.6 Practical Tips On How To Collect And Observe Small Animals And Plants

A net is probably the most useful piece of equipment for studying water life. It can either be bought or you can make your own. The frame should be rigid and around 0.25 m x 0.25 m (square or triangular). The mesh could be made from nylon net curtain with a mesh size of 2-3 mm. If the mesh is too large, insect **larvae** and beetles will escape through the holes; if it is too fine, it may become easily clogged and will be difficult to handle in a current.

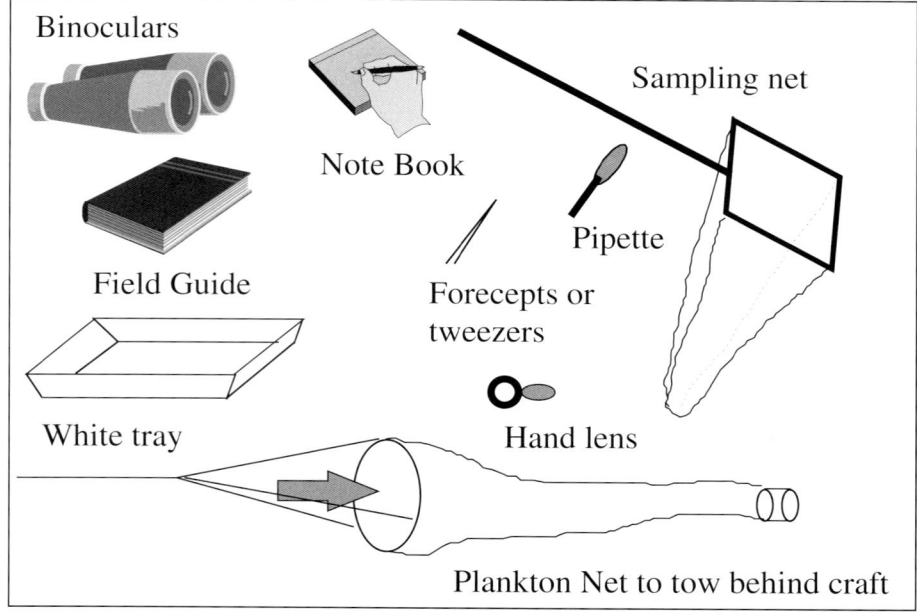

Binoculars

Note Book

Sampling net

Field Guide

Pipette

Forecepts or tweezers

White tray

Hand lens

Plankton Net to tow behind craft

Figure 1.3.4: Equipment used to examine aquatic plants and animals.

a

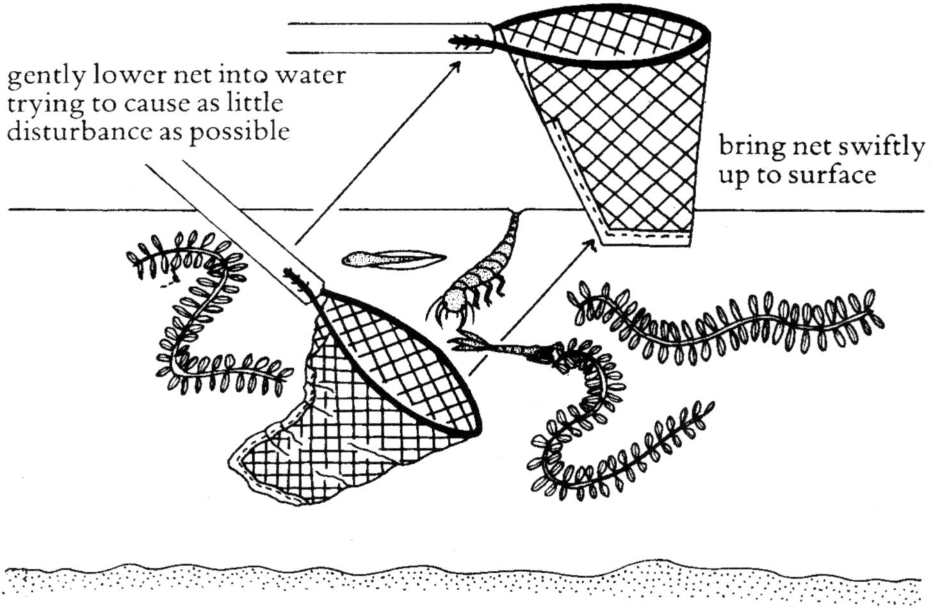

gently lower net into water
trying to cause as little
disturbance as possible

bring net swiftly
up to surface

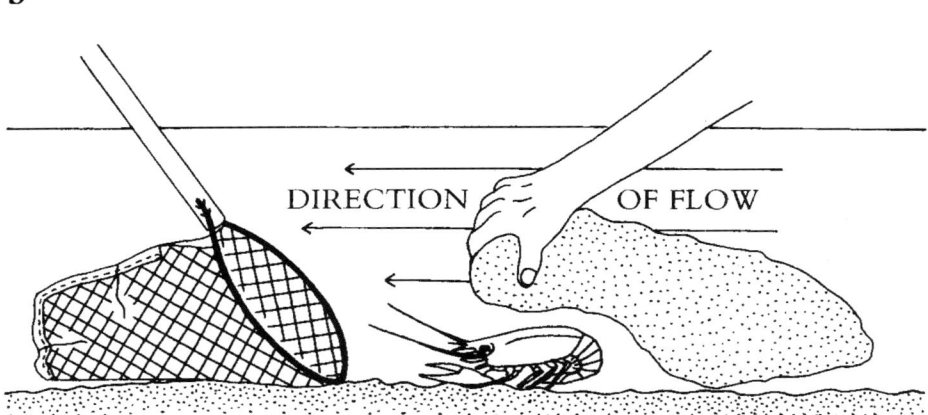

b

DIRECTION ← ← OF FLOW

lift boulders and stones while holding net
downstream; animals will be carried into net

Figure 1.3.5: Techniques for using a sampling net (after Sterry, 1982)

The animals and plants that drift around in the water and sometimes make it look like a 'green pea soup', are called **plankton**. If you want to catch the very smallest planktonic animals and plants, a much finer net will be needed. This can be make from one leg of a pair of tights. The plankton net in Figure 1.3.4 is a long net with such a fine mesh. The net ends in a plastic bottle in which the plankton accumulates as the net is drawn through the water. The ideal way to ensure that the net passes through a sufficient volume of water to collect a worthwhile sample of plankton is to tow it behind your boat. The distance you cover multiplied by the diameter of the aperture (which is kept under water during towing) will give you the volume of water from which you have collected plankton. However, the calculation of density of plankton population, which varies throughout the year, would require specialised equipment such as a microscope. The techniques for using a sampling net vary according to the strength of the current. When using it in still water, lower the net gently trying to cause as little disturbance as possible and then bring the net quickly to the surface (Figure 1.3.5 (a)); in flowing water hold the net downstream of some boulders with it facing upstream into the current. Then, as you disturb the bed either by gently moving it with your wellington boot or by lifting up the boulders and stones, any animals will be carried by the current downstream into the net (Figure 1.3.5 (b)).

Plate 1.7 (a) shows students using sampling nets and white tray, and Plate 1.7 (b) shows the white tray with the contents of the net emptied.

Do not take creatures that you collect home. Stream life will not stay alive for long unless you can keep it in a well aerated aquarium, and even then it is almost impossible to replicate the exact conditions of the river habitat where you collected your specimens. **Return everything you collect to the river** within a few hours, preferably to exactly the same spot from which you collected them.

1.3.7   The Interdependence Of Living Things In Rivers And Canals: Food Chains And Food Webs

Having become familiar with some of the types of plants and animals that live in rivers and canals, this section will illustrate how they depend on one another. One important way in which river organisms depend on each other is for their food. Many freshwater invertebrates such as water fleas feed on plants such as algae. These animals are called **herbivores.** Animals called **carnivores** eat other animals. A predator is a carnivore that kills and eats other animals. Scavengers or **detritivores** are animals that feed on detritus (dead and decaying plant and animal material). They eat the dead remains of animals killed by predators. These are not hard and fast definitions since predators sometimes scavenge for their food and scavengers may occasionally kill living animals.

Basically, all animals in rivers and canals ultimately depend on plants for their food. Even if a particular animal preys on other animals, it is likely that the animals they eat will have fed on plants. So a perch may eat a minnow, a minnow may eat a water flea, but the water flea has fed on microscopic plants. So, in fact, the minnow and the perch are ultimately dependent on the microscopic plants for their energy. This is called a **food chain**:

microscopic⟶ water fleas ⟶ minnows ⟶ perch
plants

The organisms at the beginning of the food chain are usually very numerous while the animals at the end are often large but fewer in number. The **food pyramid** in Figure 1.3.6 shows this:

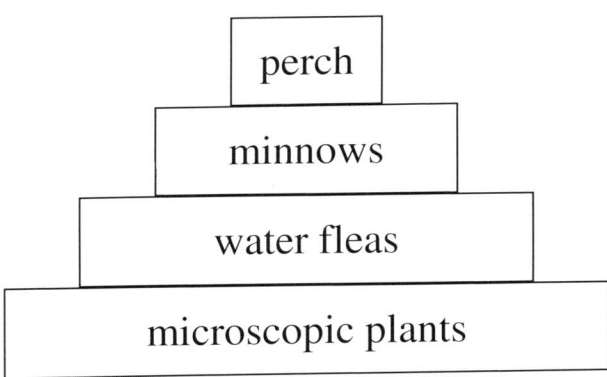

Figure 1.3.6: A food pyramid.

There will be millions of microscopic, single celled, green plants in a river. These will be eaten by the larger but less numerous water fleas, which in turn will become the food of small fish like minnows. The hundreds of small fish may only be able to provide enough food for four or five large carnivores, like perch.

Food chains are not really as simple as this, because most animals eat more than one type of food. A perch, for example, does not feed entirely on minnows, but takes fry of other fish, beetles and worms in its diet. To show these relationships more accurately, a **food web** can be drawn up as seen in Figure 1.3.7.

47

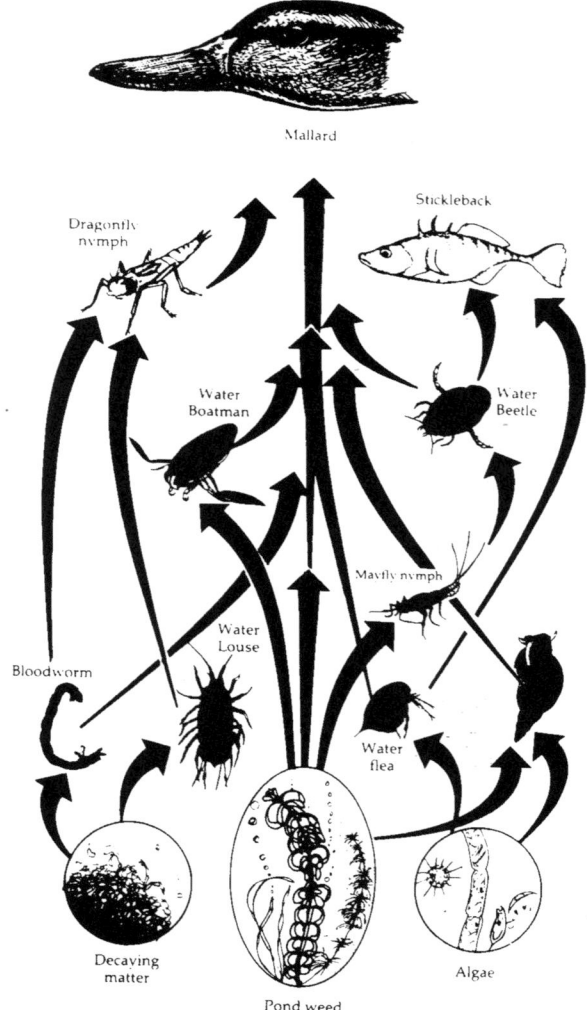

Mallard

Dragonfly nymph

Stickleback

Water Boatman

Water Beetle

Mayfly nymph

Water Louse

Bloodworm

Water flea

Decaying matter

Algae

Pond weed

Figure 1.3.7: A food web for a freshwater ecosystem (from Pondwatch Pack, Wildfowl and Wetlands Trust)

Food webs will change with the seasons and when the food supply changes. If some event interferes with the food web, all the organisms are affected in some way. We shall investigate this further in Section 1.4.

48

1.4 Managing Rivers and Inland Waterways: The Role of Conservation and Recreation

1.4.1 Why Rivers Are Managed

River management is about trying to look after rivers and keep them as we want them, but at the same time allowing them to be used for our benefit. We now need to think of ways of ensuring a **sustainable** future for our rivers and waterways. Sustainability is about improving the quality of peoples' lives whilst maintaining the capacity of the Earth to provide for future generations. The term 'sustainable' means ensuring that the needs of the present are met without compromising the ability of future generations to meet their own needs.

With respect to rivers and inland waterways we need to ensure that all forms of sport and recreation, development and transport are sustainable. In some cases the uses we wish to make of a river are conflicting. For example, birds breeding and rearing young may not be compatible with a recreational boating event in the breeding season on the same stretch of river. This section outlines some of the uses we make of rivers and how they can interact. Section 2.4 takes this further. It is quite likely that any section of river or canal that you know is already managed in one way or another. However, the type of management and the degree of control will vary widely according to the uses to which those particular rivers, or parts or rivers, are being put. The reasons why humans have an interest in managing rivers are discussed in this section.

1.4.2 Managing the Amount of Water

1.4.2.1 Water supply

'....Water is among the most essential requisites that nature provides to sustain life for plants, animals, and humans. The total quantity of fresh water on Earth could satisfy all the needs of the human population if it were evenly distributed and accessible...'

W. Stumm, 1986

If you examine the map of **water abstraction** (Figure 2.4.1 (a)) it shows that most water is abstracted in lowland Britain (south and east) where most of the population live. However, the rainfall map of the UK in Figure 2.4.1 (b) shows an uneven distribution. As a general rule, rainfall increases with altitude and in Britain most rain falls in the north and west where much of the land is mountainous and less populated. So, we have a basic problem in that most water is available in the north and west, yet the people who want it are in the south and the east. This is where rivers play an important role in transporting water from the relatively uninhabited uplands to the populated lowlands.

49

As rivers were used more and more for the abstraction of water to supply towns and industries situated along them, problems occurred during dry As rivers were used more and more for the abstraction of water to supply spells when river levels became too low. It became necessary to build dams and reservoirs on the upper courses of rivers where there were narrow valleys that could be dammed, so that a more constant water supply could be ensured. Today, anyone in England and Wales for example, wishing to abstract water from a river must obtain a licence from the Environment Agency. During times of low rainfall, when river levels naturally become low, water can be released from reservoirs to increase flow. This allows downstream abstraction for drinking water and industrial processes to continue even in dry weather. Reservoir releases can raise river levels especially for recreational purposes. The White Water canoeing and rafting facility on the Afon Tryweryn is one such example (see Plate 2.2). Others include the River Vyrnwy in North Wales, the North Tyne supplied by Kielder Water and the River Washburn in North Yorkshire.

1.4.2.2 Flood control

As settlements developed next to rivers flooding became a significant natural hazard on certain rivers. Some of the best land for farming, industry, commerce and private housing is on river floodplains. Since the discharge of most British rivers is at its highest during the winter months (November - March), suitably placed reservoirs can help to store some of the excess discharge, provided that the reservoirs are kept well below their full capacity at the start of the winter season in November. In this way, water produced by heavy rain storms in winter can be held back in the reservoirs and released slowly later so that the river does not burst its banks. This, along with the designation of 'flood storage areas' on lowland flood plains are ways in which the loss of human life, damage to property and animals can be reduced.

Another way which has been used for centuries has been to build earth flood banks called **levees** on top of the river bank to hold back flood water (see Figure 2.2.16). The removal of large boulders and coarse gravel from the bed of the river gives the bed a smoother profile and allows the velocity to increase. This helps to keep the channel free from obstructions such as whole trees or branches that become jammed in bridges. This is another aspect of reducing the risk of flooding.

A flood defence scheme, such as the one at Newtown on the River Severn (see Plate 1.8) can be very costly, but this one has helped considerably in reducing the flood hazard that was a regular occurrence in the town before its construction in the early 1970s. The scheme involved the removal of two weirs, straightening of the channel (in order to move water through the town as quickly as possible), and the building of high walls along that section of river in the town centre.

1.4.2.3 Hydro-electric Power

Hydro-electric power can often be generated where a dam has been constructed. Most hydro-electric schemes on rivers are specifically constructed for that purpose, but sometimes it has been possible to build reservoirs for the combined purposes of water supply, flood control and hydro-electric power generation. Such reservoirs then often serve an addition useful role for recreational purposes (e.g. sailing, windsurfing, etc).

1.4.3   Managing Water Quality

When harmful substances find their way into watercourses the term **pollution** is used. Pollution can be regarded as the introduction by human activities, directly or indirectly, of substances or energy into the environment which results in harmful effects that may endanger human health or harm living things and their ecosystems. Water pollution is a great threat to recreational activities on rivers and canals since 'clean' water is essential to the safe enjoyment of our activities (section 2.4.3 goes into more detail on this). Water carrying harmful **pathogens** can cause illnesses which can vary from an 'upset stomach' on the one hand, to certain diseases, which if left untreated can lead, in very rare cases, to death. This section outlines why pollution of our rivers occurs, the sources of pollutants and, most importantly, what you can do to help.

1.4.3.1 Why Pollution Occurs

As well as acting as a source of fresh water, rivers also serve as a convenient way to get rid of waste. Perhaps the greatest impact which human activities have had on the quality of water in the river systems of Britain has taken place since the beginning of the Industrial Revolution. In many rivers this impact has resulted in a poorer quality of water available for domestic use, agriculture, fisheries and recreation.

Before the Industrial Revolution, the rivers of Britain were less polluted and they contained far more fish and different plant life than they do today. Much of the industry which came with the Industrial Revolution grew up next to rivers because they used rivers as a source of power to drive waterwheels, and rivers also served as a means of transporting the raw materials and finished goods to and from the factories. The waste products of this early industry were usually dumped into the nearby river. As industry grew and the towns and cities expanded, both industrial and domestic waste (waste from peoples' houses) grew to alarming proportions - getting rid of it became an enormous problem. Rivers and waste land often seemed the best places to dump it.

By the end of the nineteenth century it was common practice to empty toilets directly into rivers. Other liquid waste, called **effluent**, from factories continued to enter rivers. This effluent often contained toxic waste that even kills bacteria. With some stretches of rivers becoming overloaded with nutrients, and no bacteria left to decompose the organic wastes (like human sewage) entering rivers, this gave rise in some locations to foul-smelling air and outbreaks of disease. Most of the fish died. (see Plate 1.9). This continued well into the 20th century, and only in the last 30-40 years have great efforts been made to clean up our rivers.

1.4.3.2 Sources and Control of Pollution

Figure 1.4.1 shows the increasing trend in the number of reported and substantiated water pollution incidents (1985-1996) in England and Wales.

In line with this trend the number of prosecutions has increased also. Membership of the European Economic Community has affected the United Kingdom's environmental policy, particularly in relation to water pollution law. Since 1973 the EC has agreed more than 300 measures relating to environmental protection. These measures generally take the form of a 'Directive' which lays downs objectives, standards and a timetable for their achievement. EC Directives which have been concerned with pollution of waters include: Dangerous Substances; Urban Waste Water Treatment; Nitrate; Detergent; Sludge to Land; Surface Water Abstraction; Bathing Water; Freshwater Fish and Shellfish.

Based on their origin, substances which cause pollution of rivers and inland waterways can be divided into two categories. These are: (a) point sources (those which originate from specific points along the watercourse, e.g. a sewage outflow or industrial waste) and, (b) diffuse sources (those which enter the watercourse from a wide area (e.g. agricultural land). This section looks at each in more detail.

(a) Point Sources

Point sources for pollution are those which originate from specific points along the watercourse.

(i) Industrial Wastes

Water companies regularly check consented discharges. In 1951, the Rivers (Prevention of Pollution) Act replaced the earlier 1876 legislation whereby prohibition of pollution was replaced by a system of discharge consents with new discharges being required to comply with minimum standards. These consented discharges carry an annual charge which is intended to be a financial deterrant on pollution. If tested water samples show an unexplained or unexpected level of pollution, detective work is immediately begun to find the source of the pollution while improvement or prohibition

Water pollution incidents: 1985-1996

England and Wales

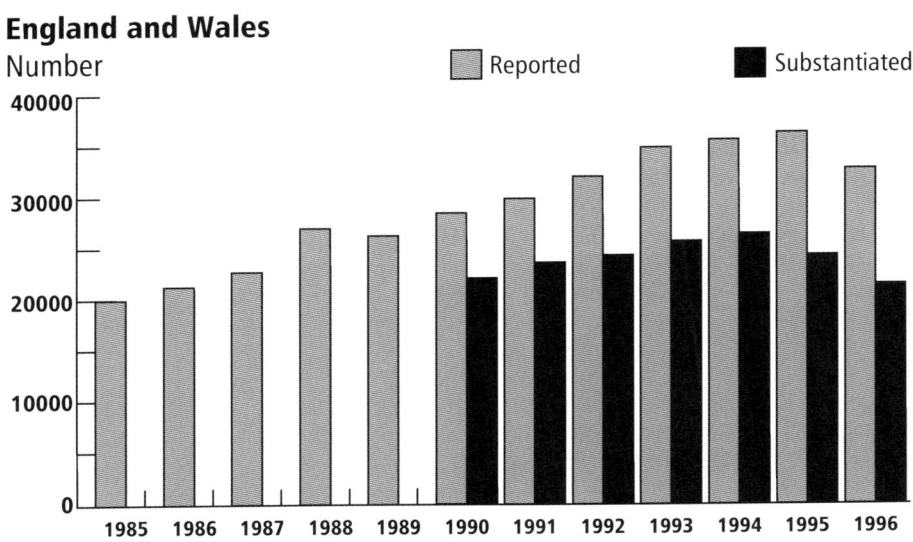

	Number				
England and Wales	1990	1993	1994	1995	1996
Reported incidents	28,143	34,296	35,291	35,890	32,409
Substantiated incidents	21,000	25,299	25,415	23,463	20,158
of which: major incidents		331	229	199	156
significant incidents		6,768	6,567	2,19	41,510
minor incidents		18,200	18,629	21,070	18,492
Prosecutions	282	286	237	151	139

Over 90 per cent of all substantiated incidents in 1996 were 'minor' incidents. The number of substantiated incidents was lower in 1996 than in any previous year in the 1990s. Between 1991 and 1996 the number of 'major' incidents fell by 60 per cent and the number of 'significant' incidents by 78 per cent. The number of prosecutions fell by 61 per cent between 1991 and 1996. Over half the substantiated incidents in 1996 were of pollution by fuels and oil and by sewage.

Source: *Environment Agency*

Figure 1.4.1: The number of reported and substantiated water pollution incidents (1985-1996) (source: Environment Agency).

53

notices are issued. Industry does not want to invest money in non-product related items, but this must be balanced against not only fines, which can be small (or 6 months imprisonment for a summary offence), but remediation costs and capital costs to prevent future occurrences can be huge. Additionally, the bad publicity can lead to loss of a company's share of the market. "Pollution Prevention Visits" by Environment Agency officers in England and Wales (or Scottish Environment Protection Agency (SEPA) in Scotland, and Department of the Environment in Northern Ireland), give free advice without obligation to industry on how to prevent pollution. This advice will not lead to criminal proceedings if the company commits to a practicably reasonable improvement plan. Prevention is better than Prosecution.

The Construction Industry is actually accused as the largest polluter, namely due to a lack of control on surface water runoff leading to suspended solids smothering the river bed and no control on oil tanks and barrels which can leak and wash out. These problems are usually due to the temporary and transient nature of the construction site.

Discharge of warm water from power stations raises river temperatures. This may in turn increase plant an animal growth but at the same time it decreases the solubility of oxygen. Less oxygen means that organisms that break down organic matter cannot work as well. So, although growth can increase in warm water in the short term, it is not sustainable in the long term.

(ii) Farmyard Waste

Farm slurry and silage (the winter feed made from compressed grass) effluent, yard washings, sheep dip and other toxic chemicals can find their way into nearby watercourses. Care must be taken by farm operators to dispose of these wastes carefully.

(iii) Sewage Treatment

The biggest source of possible pollution is sewage. This is water that has been used in our homes and in industry. It will have collected waste products that need to be removed at the sewage treatment plant. The standards to which sewage must be treated is set by the Environment Agency in England and Wales and regular checks are made to ensure that these standards are met. The constant aim is to ensure that there is the right amount of oxygen in the water. Pollution would cause the amount of oxygen to be reduced or, perhaps, even disappear. Animals and plants living in water need oxygen to survive.

One of the biggest problems in the UK results from unregulated Combined Sewer Overflows (CSOs), which overflow during storm conditions, resulting in foul sewage entering the river. Local Environment Agency Plans (LEAPs) are set up to manage this, and other related problems. Computer models of the drainage system, which are correlated against the actual catchment area, are built and these can be used to help plan possible ways of avoiding storm overflow from these CSOs occurring.

(iv)   Storm Drains

Storm drains, especially large culverts draining large urban areas, can be very important point sources after heavy rainfall. Rainwater can wash out many damaging chemicals (e.g. oil, diesel, petrol) and also many pathogens which are found in animal droppings (e.g. pets, rodents, vermin) and decomposing food (from streets, markets etc.). Also, defective foul water systems can inadvertently drain into urban culverts.

(b) Diffuse Sources

'Diffuse' means that the source of the pollution does not come from a single definable point but rather from a large area, or in fact anywhere from within the river's drainage basin.

(i) *Litter*

Litter is a diffuse source of pollution because it can enter a river or canal at any point. It can be dropped into the river by someone, or blown in from the banks or surrounding fields or towns. Litter can be broadly divided into two categories: that which is **biodegradable** (it will eventually gets broken down by micro-organisms) and non-biodegradable (things like plastics which persist in the environment for tens or hundreds of years). It is the non-biodegradable litter which is the worst offender simply because it persists as an eyesore for longer. Examples include:

Non-biodegradable	Biodegradable
Plastic & Glass Bottles	Builder's Wood
Aluminium Drinks Cans	Paper & Cardboard
Plastic Food Wrappers	Corks
Polythene Bags	Apple cores
Plastic String Or Netting	Orange peel
Fishing Line/weights	Banana skins

Most types of litter will, at some time or other, have an unwanted effect on wildlife. A clear plastic bag may be the answer to seeing what is for lunch, but underwater it is an invisible trap for aquatic animals that will kill them. Even the plastic retainers from a pack of beers can strangle birds and get caught behind the gills of fish. Small animals can become trapped in bottles, cans and polythene or become entangled in discarded netting, string or fishing line. Even biodegradable litter can persist in the environment for years (e.g. a banana skin can last for 2-5 years) and oxygen from the water is used as it slowly decomposes.

The best solution to the litter problem is prevention. **Always be certain that any potential litter you bring to a river or canal, you take away with you.** If you see anyone else dropping litter, if you are brave and tactful enough (!), a quiet word in their ear may be all that's needed to prevent it happening again. Otherwise, you might be able to pick it up in front of them so that they may see their offence. Every piece of litter you can collect and dispose of in a litter bin later will help to improve the river environment for yourself and others to enjoy.

(ii) _Fertiliser and Pesticides_

Inorganic fertilisers (chemicals in the form of small pellets) are spread on fields to provide essential nutrients like nitrates and phosphates to help maximise crop growth. Organic fertilisers like manure and slurry are also used to improve crop growth. However, if too much is applied the excess nutrients may be leached through the soil or will run off the surface to accumulate in watercourses. The usual method of slurry disposal is land spreading. However, choosing the right conditions, limiting the amount applied per hectare, and using slurry injection machines that introduce the slurry directly into the soil beneath the surface can all help to reduce the dangers from runoff.

The build up of these nutrients in waterways and lakes in particular can lead to a process called **eutrophication**. It can cause algae living in the water to grow excessively causing an **algal bloom** to occur in spring and summer. This excessive growth causes the water to turn bright green, like pea soup (see Plate 1.10), the algae use up the oxygen in the water and other organisms die.

Pesticides may reach fresh water by accidental direct spraying or drift, by runoff and seepage into groundwater, or by careless disposal of containers and unwanted chemicals. Sheep dip chemicals, particularly the new ones which are safer for farmers to use, can present very serious problems if they enter watercourses since invertebrates are extremely sensitive to them. Even though only low concentrations may get into the water, Figure 1.4.2 shows how the pesticide may be concentrated as it moves through a food chain.

A buffer zone several metres wide should be left unsprayed around the field, especially where there are streams or ditches. Likewise, spreading inorganic fertilisers next to ditches, streams, ponds or rivers should also be avoided because of the dangers of runoff causing eutrophication of the water. Again leaving a buffer strip can help reduce this problem.

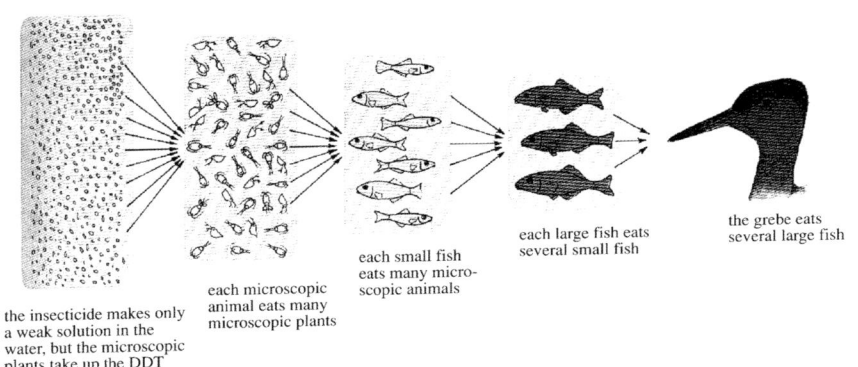

the insecticide makes only a weak solution in the water, but the microscopic plants take up the DDT

each microscopic animal eats many microscopic plants

each small fish eats many microscopic animals

each large fish eats several small fish

the grebe eats several large fish

Figure 1.4.2: How a pesticide becomes more concentrated as it moves along a food chain. The intensity of the shading represents the concentration of DDT (after Mackean, 1981)

(iii) *Acidification*

Table 1.4.1 shows the range of the pH scale:

Table 1.4.1: The pH scale

pH		Solution
1-2		H_2SO_4 (conc)
3		Lemon juice
4	acidic	Acid Water
7	neutral	Pure Water
10	alkaline	Hard Water
13		Calcium carbonate $CaCO_3$

Rain is naturally slightly acidic. It absorbs carbon dioxide from the air as it falls through the atmosphere. The carbon dioxide combines with water to form a weak carbonic acid giving the rain a pH of around 6.0 - 6.5. However, in industrial areas where atmospheric pollution is high and gases like sulphur dioxide and oxides of nitrogen are released from transport and industry, the rainwater can become more acid, sometimes as acid as pH 4.0. Figure 1.4.3 shows the effects this can have on the aquatic environment.

In extreme cases, some lakes in Scandinavia and Canada for example, have become more or less devoid of life due to this problem. The effects tend to be worst in upland areas in Britain where the geology is acidic and rainfall is high. One major solution lies in cutting our emissions of these gases, and everyday measures like using our cars less will help. In some upland drainage basins, crushed lime has been applied to the land from helicopters, to try to neutralise the soils and water.

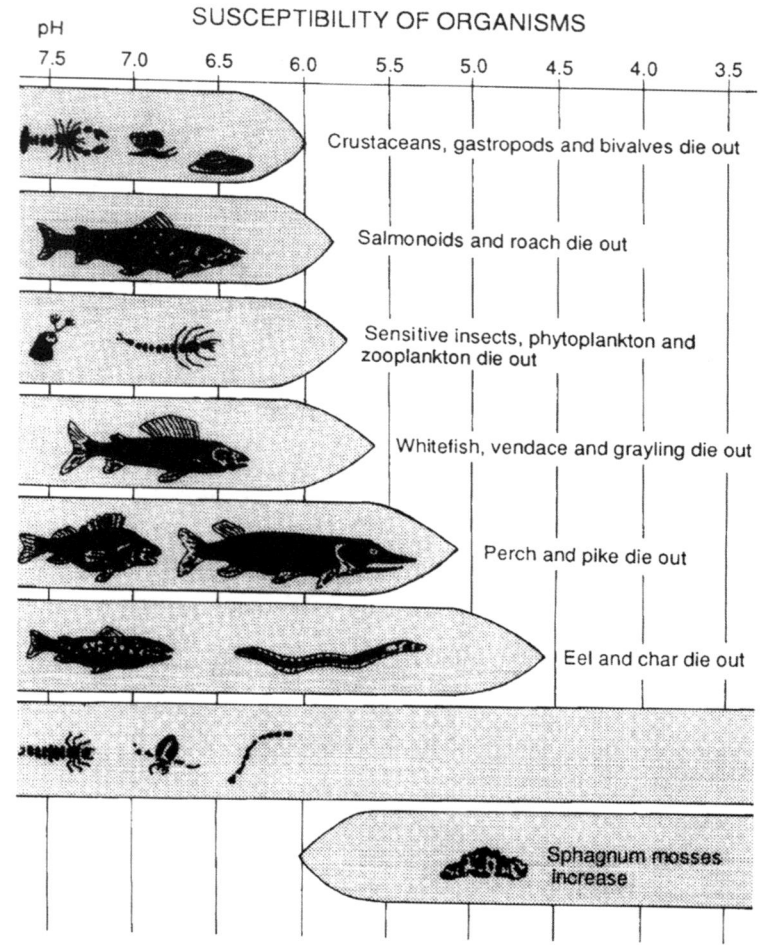

Figure 1.4.3: Effects of increasing acidity on life in water (after Lidstone, 1995)

This has been successful, but is expensive and only lasts 3-5 years. There is little in practical terms that a recreational river user can do about this problem, but everyone can campaign and support measures to cut air pollution, and aim to reduce your own personal effects as much as possible. Measures such as cycling more, sharing cars and using public transport as much as possible will all help.

(iv) Land use changes: afforestation, upland improvement for agriculture and urbanisation

Afforestation is the large scale planting of conifer plantations, usually takes place in upland areas of Britain where land is less expensive. However, evidence gathered over the past two decades suggests that intensive timber production can have adverse effects on the environment, and on the freshwater environment in particular. Due to the wetness of Britain's upland soils, it is usually necessary to precede planting of young trees by ploughing and ditching (see Plate 1.11).

Young trees are planted on upturned turves at the side of plough furrows so that their roots remain above the water table and competition from surrounding vegetation is reduced. However, this essential land preparation can release large quantities of sediment which results in a loss of nutrients from upland areas. This can have adverse effects on fish spawning, it can reduce the capacity of reservoirs and increase the cost of drinking water treatment, and it can lead to river channel instability and associated problems downstream. Forest authorities try to minimise these adverse impacts by insisting upon best practice in forest management as recommended in the 'Forests and Water Guidelines' (Forestry Authority, 1993).

Upland improvement for agriculture. Land in Britain's uplands is generally poor and can usually only support low intensity sheep grazing. Sometimes, farmers can improve wet upland areas by installing land drainage schemes or **moorland gripping**. Moorland gripping involves the digging of open drains to remove excess water from the soil, thus drying out the land and improving production. The adverse effects of this include the loss of valuable upland wetland habitats as well as the downstream effects on the freshwater environment, which are much the same as for afforestation.

Urbanisation usually takes place in lowland areas. The excavation required for the building of roads, houses and factories can temporarily release large quantities of sediment into streams and rivers, though the effect is usually short lived. However, one long term effect which urbanisation has been shown to have, is that it can contribute to increased flooding. Because urban areas tend to have lots of hard surfaces (e.g. roads and slate rooftops), there is little opportunity for rain water to infiltrate into the soil. Urban planners design drainage systems which will remove surface rainwater to a drain and into the nearest stream or river as fast as possible. The effect of this is to cause more rainwater to enter rivers more rapidly. The hydrograph will peak more rapidly, the flood peak will be greater and there is an increased risk of flooding.

1.4.3.3 Looking After The Water: Helping The River Bailiff

The Environment Agency (EA) in England and Wales, the Scottish Environment Protection Agency (SEPA) and Department of the Environment (DoE) in Northern Ireland are the government organisations which have responsibility for looking after our rivers and waterways. Small boat users are in the unique situation of being able to monitor the entire length of a river or inland waterway. The EA would like all river users (that's YOU) to help them by becoming a pollution detective.

If you see or hear of any pollution incidents or any of the following:

- poaching
- risks to wildlife
- fish in distress
- illegal dumping of hazardous waste

YOU are asked to report it by telephoning the Environment Agency's Emergency Hotline as seen in the Leaflet in Figure 1.4.4.

As a small boat user you may be in the best position to spot incidents of pollution. Report all incidents, however small, because they all add up to spoil the river environment. Most incidents will not be deliberate and the person (s) who are causing them may only be too pleased to find out and do something about it. For example, an oil leak from a motorised boat may go unnoticed by the boat owner for several months which not only causes river or canal pollution and a loss of fuel to the owner, but may also lead to the boat owner having costly mechanical problems to deal with later. The more people who are on the look out, the more incidents of pollution that can be reported and dealt with, the cleaner Britain's rivers and waterways will be.

ENVIRONMENT AGENCY

- Damage or danger to the natural environment
- Pollution
- Poaching
- Risks to wildlife

- Fish in Distress
- Illegal dumping of hazardous waste
- Flooding incidents (for reporting flooding only)

DON'T IGNORE IT, REPORT IT!

ENVIRONMENT AGENCY EMERGENCY HOTLINE

0800 80 70 60

CALL FREE, 24 HRS A DAY, 7 DAYS A WEEK

ENVIRONMENT AGENCY

Help us to protect the environment.

Your prompt action helps us protect the environment.

Please don't use this number for routine or general enquiries or you may prevent someone else getting through in an emergency.

For **GENERAL ENQUIRIES**, ring your local Environment Agency Office on:

0645 333 111

DURING OFFICE HOURS ONLY

To help us protect the environment, please keep this leaflet near your telephone and carry the card with you when you go out.

Figure 1.4.4: The Environment Agency's Pollution Hotline.

1.4.4   Managing Wildlife

Whether you paddle on wild upland rivers, row on calm lowland sections or tour peaceful canals, without Britain's varied wildlife much of the pleasure of boating would be lost. Throughout the world, small boats are used for exploring wilderness areas and observing wildlife without disturbance. Small boats without engines have great advantages for anyone wishing to explore rivers and canals because they cause no erosion, noise or pollution and they leave no trace of their passing.

Though organisations responsible for conservation of wildlife (such as those listed in Appendix III) campaign and work for the conservation of wildlife, it is the responsibility of every individual river or canal user to minimise their impact on, and disturbance to, wildlife. The best way not to disturb the river or canal environment more than is absolutely necessary is to follow the code of conduct in Appendix I.   The code is designed to try to ensure that recreational river and inland waterway users come into conflict with one another and with river wildlife as little as possible.

Specifically in terms of river wildlife, river and canal users should note the following:

- it is illegal to uproot any wild plant as this would prevent the plant from reproducing;
- do not paddle, row or sail too close to birds (e.g. moorhens or ducks) which have their young in tow as you may split the family group;
- do not approach nesting colonies of birds too closely, as the adults in fright may leave their eggs or young exposed to the dangers of hungry gulls or other such predators;
- try to disturb birds as little as possible in winter. Disturbance causes them to lose precious energy and fat reserves which they have no way of replenishing until spring;
- do not remove fish - it is illegal to do so even if you have a licence;
- do not disturb spawning fish or walk on gravel beds where there are unhatched eggs. For game fish this is typically between October and March;
- do not disturb sites used by breeding mammals (e.g. otter, water vole, etc);
- where possible, do not urinate or defecate within 100 m of a watercourse as **pathogens** from your faeces can easily enter the water. They can reside in the soil for long periods of time and later be washed into the watercourse, so the further away you can urinate or defecate, the better. Faeces should, at the very least be buried 15-20 cm below the soil surface.

1.4.5 Managing Recreation and Navigation

'River management is the art of resolving conflicting demands upon a natural resource and at the same time attempting to define and conserve features of that resource'

(Wood, 1981)

Space on rivers and inland waterways is ultimately limited. There is only a certain 'capacity' for recreational use of this space before which the experience of individual users will be spoiled by the fact that there are so many others using the same resource. However, as Table 1.4.2 shows, not all recreational users wish to use the same parts of a river at the same time. For example, people wanting to sail or windsurf will most likely choose to use the lowland open stretches of a river on windy days (Plate 1.12). On the other hand, a white water slalom canoeist would want to use the upper reaches of a river (Plate 1.13), preferably after rain when water levels are high. So, these two user groups are unlikely to conflict in terms of space or time. However, there may be other examples of where small boat users may have a clash of interests or may conflict with other non-boat users of rivers or canals.

Table 1.4.2: The Spatial Distribution Of Recreational Small Boat Users.

upstream		downstream
Upper reaches: white water, narrow, overhanging trees, numerous boulders, rapids, waterfalls, waves	Middle reaches: occasional rapids, may be overhanging trees, occasional rocks/boulders	Lower reaches: flat slow moving water, >10 m wide, exposed to wind (includes canals)
	Inland Canoe Touring	
		Marathon Racing
Slalom Racing		
Rodeo/Playboating (at specific waveforms only)		
		Canoe Sailing
Wild Water Racing		Placid Water Canoeing
		Canoe Polo
		Sprint Racing
White Water Recreational Canoeist		
		Rowing
		Sailing/windsurfing
Rafting		Canal Boating/River Cruising

In some areas management has become necessary to protect the interests of one user group or another. This may involve designating particular areas or certain times when particular activities are permitted.

On non-tidal rivers and lakes, the Crown is regarded as having in the long distant past, transferred the bed of the watercourse to the owners of the adjoining land, known as the riparian land owner. The riparian owner therefore has property rights over the land covered by water up to the centre line of the river (unless they have been sold to a new owner). Whilst there is no automatic right for the public to navigate, some public rights of navigation do exist, such as on the River Severn above Stourport and on the River Wye below Hay-on-Wye. Though the landowner does not own the water, s/he may use it so long as it does not interfere with the rights of the owners downstream to use it when it reaches them. The use of the bank for access to and egress from the water is a separate property right and unless the owner expresses dedication to public use, the right to use it for recreational boating purposes must have been negotiated. One of the major roles of Governing Bodies of Sports that use rivers and inland waterways, such as the British Canoe Union for example, is to establish access agreements between the riparian owner and boat users. If agreed, certain stretches of river can only be used at certain times of the year, or only on certain days, often in return for payment. The recreationalists are then expected to follow a code of conduct such as that in Appendix I. The former right of navigation on British Waterways owned canals was repealed by the Transport Act of 1968, so permission for use is now granted through a licence issued by the British Waterways Board. This does not apply to canals under the ownership of other navigation authorities, but again the purchase of a license will allow use by small boats.

However, on the sea and tidal waters up to the limit of high water mark ordinary spring tides (marked on Ordnance Survey maps), the land covered by water is regarded as belonging to the Crown. This permits public navigation (and fishing), so far as physical conditions allow, unless the Crown has conveyed the bed of the river to someone else. On many rivers, the limit of high water mark can reach several miles upstream from the point where the river reaches the sea. For example, on the river Dee the tidal limit is at Farndon some 14 km upstream of Chester, itself a long way from the open sea. However, the limit of navigation rights may not be the tidal limit if locks, weirs or other structures have been built which have affected the tidal limit. Recreational boaters and their responsible organisations, though continuing to seek a change in the law so that they can enjoy a fairer share of the possible boating opportunities as of right, generally press ahead with a policy of seeking access agreements by negotiation.

In conclusion, managing a river for such a wide range of purposes is clearly a difficult and complicated business. Figure 1.4.5 illustrates some of the aims that river basin managers would like to achieve. Any potential conflicts of interest must be 'managed' to allow the range of activities to be carried out in harmony.

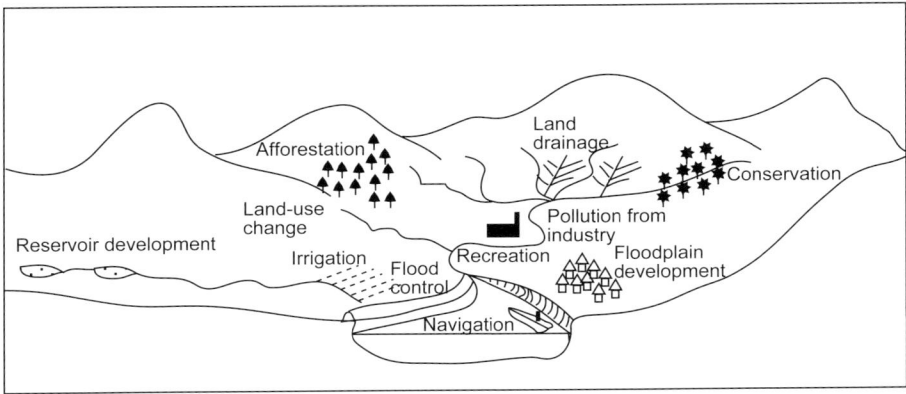

Figure 1.4.5: Some of the activities and interests that need to be managed in a river basin.

Part 1: Further Reading

Angel, H. (1976) *'The World of a Stream'*, Faber and Faber, London.

Angel, H. and Wolseley, P. *'The Family Water Naturalist'*, Michael Joseph.

British Canoe Union (1989) *'Canoeing Handbook'*, British Canoe Union, Nottingham.

Bunnett, R. B. (1988) *'Physical Geography in Diagrams'*, Longman, Essex.

Clegg, J. (1974) *'Freshwater Life'*, Warne.

Countryside Recreation Network (1996) *'UK Day Visits Survey 1994'*, CRN, Cardiff, June 1996.

Doherty, A. and McDonald, M. (1992) *'River Basin Management'*, Hodder and Stoughton, London.

Fitter, R. & R. Manuel, R. (1980) *'Collins Guide to Freshwater Life'*, Collins.

Forestry Authority (1993) *'Forests and Water Guidelines'*, 3rd edition, HMSO, London.

Hayman, P. (1979) *'The Mitchell Beazley Birdwatcher's Pocket Guide'*, Mitchell Beazley, London.

Heinzel, H., Fitter, R. and Parslow, J. (1979*) 'The Birds of Britain and Europe'*, Collins, London.

Inland Waterways Association (1994*) 'Recreational Value of Inland Waterways'*, Factsheet 5, IWA, London.

Inland Waterways Amenity Advisory Council (1996*) 'Britain's Inland Waterways: An Undervalued Asset'*, Consultative Report. IWAAC, London, March, 1996.

Mackean, D. G. (1982) *'Life Study: A Textbook of Biology'*, John Murray, London.

Manuel, R and Shields, C. (1991) *'Ponds and Streams'* (Collins Gem), HarperCollins Publishers, Glasgow.

Moore, P. D. (1980) *'The Mitchell Beazley Pocket Guide to Wild Flowers'*, Mitchell Beazley, London.

More, D. and Fitter, A. (1980) *'Collins Gem Guides: Trees'*, Collins, London.

National Rivers Authority (1995) *'Space to Live, Space to Play: A Recreation Strategy for the River Thames'*, NRA/Sports Council.

Orton, R., Bebbington, A. and Bebbington, J. (1995*) 'Freshwater Invertebrates'*, Field Studies Council, Freshwater Investigations Pack.

Parker, S. (1990) *'Pond & River'* (Eyewitness Guide), Dorling Kindersley/Natural History Museum.

Phillips, R. (1980) *'Wild Flowers of Britain'*, Pan Books, London.

Phillips, R. (1980) *'Grasses, Ferns, Mosses and Lichens of Great Britain and Ireland'*, Pan Books, London.

Richards, S. (1990) *'Living with the Physical Environment'*, Unwin Hynman, London.

Smith, V. and Quigley, M. (1986*) 'A Key to Invertebrate Animals in Freshwater'*, Blackwell Habitat Field Guides.

Swallow, S. (1978) *'Ponds & Streams'* (Nature Trail Guide), Usborne.

Thornes, J. (1979) *'River Channels', Aspects of Geography*, T. H. Elkins and Keith Clayton (General Editors), Macmillan Education.

Wildfowl and Wetlands Trust. (1980) *'Pondwatch Pack'*, WATCH / Shell Better Britain Campaign, Birmingham.

Plate 1.1: The Nant Ffrancon valley in Snowdonia is a good example of a U-shaped valley enlarged by glaciers and now occupied by the River Ogwen (taken by the author).

Plate 1.2: Using an orange to estimate the speed a river is flowing (taken by the author).

Plate 1.3: V-notch weir structure used to measure stream discharge (taken by the author).

Plate 1.4: Crump weir structure measuring discharge of a small river (taken by the author).

Plate 1.5: Baseflow flume for accurate measurement of low flows in a small river (taken by the author).

Plate 1.6: Spore
containing capsules
of moss.
(Taken by the author).

Plate 1.7: (a) Students
using nets and white
trays to sample and
examine invertebrates.
(Taken by the author).

Plate 1.7: (b) The white tray with the contents of net emptied (taken by the author).

Plate 1.8: (a) The River Severn at Newtown in mid-Wales looking downstream from the Long Bridge before construction of the flood alleviation scheme in 1970.

Plate 1.8: (b) The River Severn at Newtown looking upstream from the Long Bridge in 1900 before the flood alleviation scheme was constructed in 1970.

Plate 1.8: (c) The same view as in Plate 1.8 (b) taken in 1999.

Plate 1.8: (d) The River Severn at Newtown in mid-Wales looking downstream from the Long Bridge after construction of the flood alleviation scheme in 1970.

Plate 1.8: (e) View of Long Bridge at Newtown on R. Severn in 1960s (prior to construction of flood alleviation scheme in 1970).

Plate 1.8: (f) Same view of Long Bridge during severe floods in 1964.

Plate 1.8: (g) Broad Street, the main street in Newtown, December 1964 as the flooding recedes.

Plate 1.9: The River Brent in London heavily polluted with rubbish (source: Bunnett, 1988)

Plate 1.10: An algal bloom can turn water into a 'green pea soup' (taken by the author).

Plate 1.11: Afforestation of an upland catchment is preceded by ploughing and ditching to help the young trees to get established (taken by the author).

Plate 1.12: Sailing in lowland rivers: the Norfolk Broads (taken by the author).

Plate 1.13: Whitewater kayaking on the upper reaches of the river Dee at Llangollen, Wales (taken by the author).

Plate 2.1: The Tees Barrage artificial whitewater course was opened near Middlesborough in 1993 (taken by the author).

Plate 2.2: Canalfan Tryweryn Whitewater slalom course where reservoir releases from Llyn Celyn Dam provide reliable water suitable for World Championship Canoeing Events (taken by the author).

Plate 2.3: Recreational rowing craft in the River Avon (photograph by Alan Meegan, ARA).

Plate 2.4: A typical V-shaped valley on a tributary of the River Severn in mid-Wales (taken by the author).

Plate 2.5: High Force waterfall on the River Tees in Co. Durham.

Plate 2.6: Thornton Force in Kingsdale near Ingleton, North Yorkshire (taken by the author).

Plate 2.7: The Allt Mhor in the Cairngorms, a typical Scottish river in its upper course (taken by the author).

Plate 2.8: Rapids at Grand Tully on the River Tay in central Scotland are used as a canoe slalom training venue. (taken by the author).

Plate 2.9: A meander on the River Forth near Stirling in central Scotland (taken by the author).

Plate 2.10: Cuckoo Flower *(Cardamine pratensis)* (taken by the author).

Plate 2.11: Marsh Marigold *(Caltha palustris)* (taken by the author).

Plate 2.12: Common Reed *(Phragmites australis)* on the Norfolk Broads (taken by the author).

Plate 2.13: White Water Lily *(Nymphaea alba)* (taken by the author).

Plate 2.14: Ragged Robin *(Lychnis flos-cuculi)* in water meadow (taken by the author).

Plate 2.15: Mute Swan *(Cygnus olor)* (taken by the author).

Plate 2.16: Sand Martin *(Riparia tipalia)* nest tunnels in the bank of the River Beauly, NE Scotland (taken by the author).

Part 2:
Further Explorations into the River and Waterway Environment

Part 2: Further Explorations

Part 2 of this book is intended for those readers who have read Part 1 and now wish to delve deeper into some of the topics and issues raised so far. Though the Chapters follow the same basic headings, much more detail is given in Part 2 and issues are explored and discussed more fully. It is intended that this part will also be more suited to adults who are involved in the teaching or coaching of recreational sports and activities on rivers and inland waterways and who wish to broaden their knowledge of the environment in which they may be operating. Much of the material in this section will be relevant to the environmental aspects of coaching award syllabi and therefore will form essential reading to both aspirant and established coaches.

2.1 The Development of Recreation on Rivers and Canals

Over the last fifteen years there has been an increased emphasis on leisure time. In some sectors of society there seems to have been a shift away from earning money for the sake of it, towards a recognition of the importance of quality leisure time for releasing stress, recuperation and even as a form of therapy. This emphasis on leisure time has seen an increase in sporting activities, an explosion in the number of leisure and health clubs, gymnasia and sports halls, and a slower but nonetheless parallel trend in outdoor and recreational sports. Watersports and the use of rivers and inland waterways are firmly on the increase.

2.1.1 Case Study 1: Trends in Recreational Canoeing

The British Canoe Union (BCU) is the governing body responsible for canoeing. The BCU currently divides canoeing into two sections: competition and recreational canoeing. At present recreational canoeing is classed as canoe touring of around 12 miles or more. Competition canoeing comprises slalom, sprint racing, marathon racing, wild water racing, canoe polo and rodeo. Since only around a quarter of serious canoeists are members of the BCU it is extremely difficult to keep abreast of trends and changes in the numbers of participants engaging in the various sections of this sport.

Recent developments in canoeing such as Rodeo or Freestyle paddling may well have shifted the sport away from the traditional slalom competitions which helped earn canoeing a 'competitive' reputation in the 1960s and 70s. These new developments may have given the sport a slightly more appealing image, particularly to the younger generation. Television coverage of events and competitions has created interest and the variety of boats available along with their durability, the great variety of designs and the relative affordability of the modern plastic kayak may also have stimulated further interest in the sport. The vast range of disciplines within the sport means that there is something for all tastes, from steep upland white water rivers to leisurely summer paddles along lowland rivers, canals and lakes. This scope for diversity within the sport may also have led to an increase in its popularity. The increased number of car owners, the ability to transport small boats more easily and the relatively inexpensive cost of canoeing all add to its attraction.

In early 1998, under the supervision of the author, an undergraduate dissertation study was conducted at Liverpool John Moores University (Varey, 1998) to investigate participation in recreational canoeing with a view to providing some basic data for the BCU. The aim of the study was to find out what type of canoes people use, what type of water they paddled on, where and how frequently they paddled. As a background to the study Table 2.1.1 shows trends in British Canoe Union membership (1980-1997).

Year	Comprehensive				Basic			Total Ind.	Clubs/Association			Total
	Life	Adult	U-18	Family	Adult	U-18	Family		Senior	Junior	Assoc.	
1980		6554	1787	513				8854				8854
1985	69	7253	2807	427	821			11377				11377
1986	76	8703	2971	481	1132			12733	265	256	39	13293
1987	90	8775	3071	574	1063			12876	264	229	42	13418
1988	100	8385	2787	541	1062			13146	277	224	41	13673
1989	114	8766	2653	548	1065			13146	273	220	34	13673
1990	127	7831	1571	565	2507	755	589	13945	278	165	25	14413
1991	140	8195	1385	631	3209	756	767	15083	292	164	24	15563
1992	152	8539	1379	632	3216	784	872	15574	306	142	14	16036
1993	168	9825	1419	753	3632	765	888	17450	325	153	13	17941
1994	198	10715	1413	801	3869	801	979	18720	323	131	14	19188
1995	218	11408	1353	701	3892	809	1083	19464	339	129	13	19945
1996	233	11751	1316	670	4063	816	1171	20020	336	121	11	20488
1997	248	11869	1214	647	4227	865	1256	20320	340	105	8	20773

Table 2.1.1: Trends in British Canoe Union Membership (1980-1997) (source: BCU Headquarters)

Though some data for the early 1980s are missing, it is still clear that there has been a significant increase in the number of BCU members since 1980. The table shows an increase of 60% in individual membership between 1986 and 1997 whilst club affiliation fell from 560 to 453, a fall of around 19%. It has been estimated that BCU membership accounts for between 20 and 25% of all canoeists, so it would not be unreasonable to conclude that the total number of individual canoeists will have doubled from around 50000 in 1986 to around 100000 in 1997.

In order to gain information from both BCU members and also non-members, questionnaires were used to sample canoeists both by post and in person (at recreational tour events). There were 67 questionnaires returned by males and 25 by females. Figures 2.1.1 and 2.1.2 summarise the results for both kayakers and open canoeists respectively.

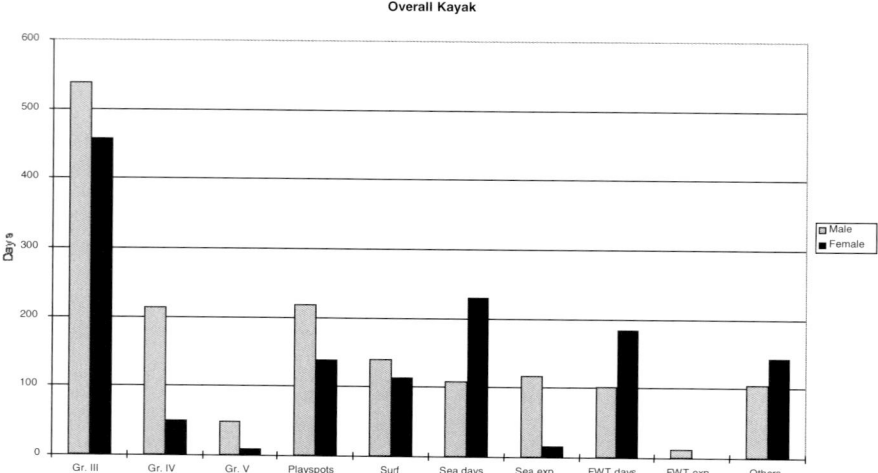

Figure 2.1.1: Summary of days spent recreational paddling in kayaks (after Varey, 1998)

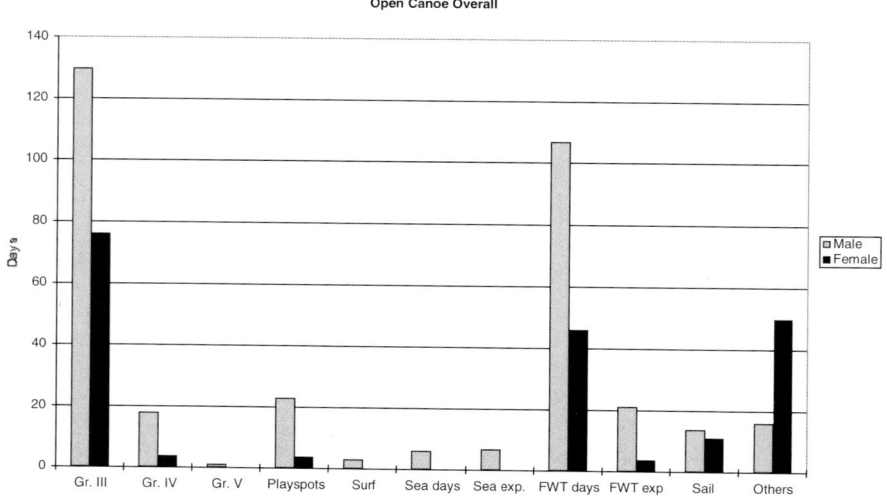

Figure 2.1.2: Summary of days spent recreational paddling in open canoes (after Varey, 1998)

Canoeists grade rivers on a scale of I-VI, I being the easiest, VI being barely passable and very rarely attempted.

Terms used.

Gr. III = up to grade III white water
Gr. IV = grade IV white water
Gr. V = grade V white water

Play = Playboating or Rodeo, using a specific site, i.e. a weir to perform tricks etc.
Surf = Surfing
Sea day = Single days spent on the sea
Sea exp. = Two or more days expeditioning at sea
F.W.T. = Flat water touring, single days paddling on flat water, i.e. a canal trip.
F.W. exp. = Two or more days flat water expeditioning
Sail = Canoe sailing
Other = Other activities, is either coaching or club nights unless stated otherwise.

Recreational kayaking far outweighs open canoeing in popularity by about five times and even when the results were weighted to take account of the fewer questionnaires returned by females, the total number of days out taken male participants still far outnumbered those taken by females.

In terms of the type of water used, it can be seen that moving water up to and including Grade III is most popular with both kayakers and open canoeists alike, with a rapid fall off in popularity with a move into the higher (more difficult) Grades IV and V. Excluding use of the sea, playboating featured as the next most popular activity with kayakers, while for open canoeists it was flat water touring.

Although this study was based on a relatively small sample of recreational canoeists it does highlight some trends which are worthy of further investigation if the right kind of provisions are to be made for recreational water users in future. For example, there has been a trend towards the development of 'artificial' or designated moving water venues over the past decade. In terms of purpose built artificial courses, the first was built during the 1980s on the Trent at the Holme Pierrepont National Water Sports Centre outside Nottingham (established in 1972). In 1993 the Tees Barrage artificial white water course was opened near Middlesborough (Plate 2.1). There are plans in store for a third on the Clyde at Glasgow, and ultimately one somewhere in the south-east of England would satisfy the needs of that part of the country with the greatest population.

The recently modernised White Water Centre (Canolfan Tryweryn) on the Tryweryn outside Bala in North Wales probably offers some of the most challenging white water which can be dependable due to releases from Llyn Celyn Dam on pre-determined dates throughout the year (Plate 2.2). Though this venue is a natural river, many of its features have been enhanced and engineered to make it the world famous international slalom course it has become as well as a popular venue for white water rafting. Another North Wales venue which has seen a tremendous increase in popularity since it was leased in the late 1980s by J. Jayes, is a half kilometre section of the River Dee at Mile End Mill, just upstream of Llangollen. This reach of the River Dee is bounded by two natural rapid sections and contains a natural stopper wave. The provision of changing facilities, a cafe and equipment shop have added to the attraction of this as a canoeing and rafting 'honeypot' within the last ten years.

One interesting development which is highlighted by all four 'venues' mentioned so far, and is perhaps the most important development which has come about over the past decade, is the preparedness of recreational canoeists to pay for the use of such venues. Payment ranges from £4-10 for a session on these venues (sometimes with reductions for BCU members, season ticket holders, etc). All four sites provide parking and changing facilities as well as dependable water features that are designed to test the skills and techniques of the user in some way or other. Now that the concept of recreationalists paying for the use of an established resource is becoming accepted, the way ahead to creating further such venues to meet the demands of future recreationalists may be clearing. The BCU is currently campaigning to raise funds to purchase the Symonds Yat rapids on the River Wye near Monmouth, and thereby ensure the future of this much needed recreational moving water venue in the south of the country.

2.1.2   Case Study 2: Uses of Inland Waterways for Recreation

The Countryside Commission, British Waterways (BW) and five other agencies commissioned the UK Day Visits Survey in 1994 (CRN, 1996). Data were gathered about leisure day visits from home and holiday bases; this included the main activities undertaken, the expenditure incurred and the general destination (i.e. town, countryside or coast). These destination categories also included the subsets of wood/forest and canal/river for which details of leisure and non-leisure day visits were also collected.

Data analysis was undertaken by the Market Research Unit of BW (British Waterways, 1996). The overall estimate for the annual number of visits to water recreation resources for all purposes made by adults and children, is 408 million. Of these 159 million were to BW waterways, 29 million to EA rivers, 77 million to estuaries, 45 million to other navigable inland waterways and 98 million to non-navigable waters. For non-estuary waterways this represents an average of 49000 visits per km per year; the average for BW waterways is 57000 visits/km/year. The visits to BW's navigable waterways have been estimated by BW and are shown in Table 2.1.2. The figures in Table 2.1.2 are dominated by the informal visitors who make up 91.5% of all visits to these waterways, and 83.3% of leisure visits. However the distribution of use on a visitor-hour basis would give somewhat less emphasis to informal users: the average informal visit lasts a few hours whereas all other activities are of longer duration; a holiday hire cruise, for example, typically lasts a week. Excluding non-leisure trips, the overall average visit duration was 3.75 hours.

Table 2.1.2: Visits to BW navigable waterways (source: Inland Waterways Association, 1997).

Activity	Visits (millions/ year)	Visit rate (number/ km/year)
Holiday hire boating	0.2	72
Private powered boating	0.9	322
Restaurant/trip boats	1.5	536
Canoeing/unpowered boating	1.5	536
Fishing	2.6	930
Cycling	7.2	2570
Other informal leisure trips	67.5	24100
Non-leisure trips	78.0	27900
TOTAL	159.0	57000

The Survey shows that visits to waterways occur all year round with the highest numbers in early summer: May, June, July and August receive 16%, 11%, 13% and 7% respectively of annual visits. These figures are, of course, dominated by the informal visitors. The distribution of boating use is more concentrated in summer: based on a sample from 35 locks throughout the country in 1992 (British Waterways, 1996) the same months have, respectively, 12%, 11%, 16% and 18% of annual boat movements.

Informal visitors tend to be concentrated at "honey pot" sites whereas other types of users tend to be more evenly spread. The visit rate to a particular waterway will vary according to its attractiveness and to the population within its catchment. For example, the Kennet & Avon Canal (139 km in length) has well developed trip boat businesses with 550 visits/km/year in 1990, higher than the average BW figure of 460 visits/km/year in 1989. However other boating use was lower than average because the canal was not fully restored at the time of the survey (British Waterways, 1991).

Some evidence of the catchment area for informal visits to waterways is given by the distances travelled by visitors from home in the 1994 Day Visits Survey. The average round trip distance travelled was 32 km (20 miles), with 50% travelling less than about 10 km (6 miles) and 9% travelling more than 64 km (40 miles). A BW survey in 1995 (British Waterways, 1995) gave an average distance of 30 km (19 miles) with 41 % travelling less than 10 km (6 miles) and 9% travelling more than 64 km (40 miles). Both surveys give similar results although based on slightly different samples: the former excludes non-leisure visitors and visits by holiday makers, but includes leisure day visitors, boaters and anglers; the latter excludes boaters and anglers, but includes leisure day visitors, non-leisure visitors and holiday makers. Both results emphasise that waterways are largely local recreational resources for informal visitors, as are most public parks. BW point out that about half the country's population lives within 8 km (5 miles) of a BW waterway. The British Waterways (1996) analysis shows that 53% of all visits from home to waterways are made by car, demonstrating the need to provide car parking facilities, especially at honey pots; 34% travelled by foot and 6% by bicycle, again indicating the local nature of the majority of visits.

The numbers of boats licensed in 1995/96 by BW on its canals and rivers, by the Broads Authority on the Broads, and by National Rivers Authority (now replaced by the Environment Agency) on the non-tidal Thames are shown in Table 2.1.3. Short-term licenses are excluded so the figures are a good measure of the numbers based on the various waterways. On the Thames, exempted craft and crown vessels are also excluded.

Table 2.1.3: Boat use on waterways in Britain (source: Inland Waterways Association, 1997).

	BW Waterways		Broads		Thames	
Length of waterways (km)	2790		160		202	
Boat type	Nos	No/km	Nos	No/km	Nos	No/km
Powered: private	21410	7.17	7407	46.3	10080	49.9
Powered: hire	1533	0.55	1902	11.9	511	2.5
Business	417	0.15	16	0.1	49	0.2
Unpowered: private & hire	481	0.17	3760	23.5	5450	27.0
TOTAL	23841	8.55	13085	81.8	16090	79.6

The table shows that there are over nine times more boats per kilometre on the Thames than there are on the waterways of British Waterways which are generally narrower and have water resource limitations. Unpowered craft make up only 2% of the total in these waterways. To the best of the author's knowledge, no equivalent figures are available for rivers.

92

It is particularly difficult to measure the rate of growth in recreational use of waterways because of the dominant effect of weather on outdoor activities and the margin of error in the survey data. Comparing the 1984 and 1989 figures in a survey commissioned by British Waterways (M & S Research Marketing Consultancy, 1991) gives an approximate annual growth rate of 2.5%, but it should be remembered that this was a period of strong economic growth when personal incomes were rising relatively rapidly. Considering other related activities, those walking a distance of 2 miles or more at least once a month increased by 1.2%/year between 1977 and 1986 and has continued to grow by 1.3%/year since then.

Since the early 1980s the number of licenses for privately-owned powered boats on BW waterways has increased by about 2%/year, although better enforcement accounts for some of the growth. Licenses for private boats on the Broads have increased at about the same rate. Licenses on the Thames and EA Anglian region rivers also increased, but more recently license fees have been increased by significantly more than inflation and the number of licensed private boats has fallen to levels below those in the early 80s. Numbers of licensed hire boats have remained about constant on BW waterways and the Anglian rivers, but have reduced on the Broads and the Thames. Taking account of the greater use made of hire boats, it is likely that there has been an overall growth of boat movements on BW waterways of about 1% per year but none on the other waterways.

2.1.3   Case Study 3: Current and Future Participation in Rowing

The Amateur Rowing Association (ARA) is the governing body for the sport of rowing in Great Britain (GB). It was founded in 1882 and is affiliated to the Federation Internationale des Societies d'Aviron (FISA). The ARA represents GB's interests to FISA and is responsible for the preparation, training and selection of GB teams in competitive rowing. The ARA is also responsible for the organisation and development of rowing in England, whereas the Scottish Amateur Rowing Association (SARA) and Welsh Amateur Rowing Association (WARA) are responsible for the organisation and development of rowing in Scotland and Wales respectively.

The ARA has carried out a recent survey of its membership which is summarised in Table 2.1.4. This shows the breakdown of rowing clubs, membership and coaches on a regional basis (data provided by ARA, survey date 30/6/97). Slightly over 43% of registered members are based in the Thames Region, with the Thames and Eastern Regions together having over 56% of the membership. Clearly, the geographical spread of clubs and members is a significant factor in the development of the sport. Almost all clubs are river or coast based, on sites which they have occupied since the end of the last century. The location of virtually all clubs is dictated by the availability of good rowing water (i.e. the combination of sufficient width and depth for rowing boats). Rowing on rivers is complemented by four specialist rowing courses at: Holme Pierrepont, Nottingham (2000 m); Strathclyde Park (2000 m); London Docklands (1750 m) and Peterborough (1000 m). As Table 2.1.4 shows, there are over 500 clubs affiliated to the ARA which represents approximately 30000 committed rowing competitors, coaches, officials and supporters. It is also recognised by the ARA, that there are many thousand more rowers who row on a recreational and participation basis in universities and health and fitness centres.

Rowing activity in clubs is separated between traditional sweep oared rowing (single oar) and sculling (two oars). Activity takes place in single boats, doubles, fours and eights. In competition there is a further categorisation by weight, gender and status. Whilst regional activity is mainly based upon coaching and competition, recreational rowing forms another, though much smaller, branch of the sport. The record of achievement in international rowing is impressive with Britain having won medals at every Olympic Games since 1976. Britain has consistently featured in the top five rowing nations in the world.

The ARA has plans to increase participation in their sport beyond the millennium. 'Project Oarsome', for example, is a young people and coaching programme that aims to increase the number of young people participating in rowing by 35% and to increase the number of qualified coaches by 300% by the year 2001. This will build on an already increasing trend in the number of coaches which rose from 397 in 1993 to 515 in 1997. Plate 2.3 shows recreational rowing craft on the River Avon.

Table 2.1.4: Breakdown of rowing clubs, membership and coaches on a regional basis as at 30 June 1997 (source: Amateur Rowing Association)

Region	Number of Clubs			Number of Members									% of Total	No. Reg. Heads	No. of Coaches
	Open Clubs	Colls and Univs	Schs.	Sen.	New	Stud.	Junior	Jun. U-13	Recrea-tional	Ass.	Pat.	TOTAL			
Northern	10	20	8	181	42	537	197	25	4	22	5	1013	6.4	21	20
Yorks & H	7	7	5	162	34	250	139	45	6	35	6	677	4.3	11	18
North W	16	8	6	360	57	341	363	23	16	49	8	1217	7.7	17	62
East Mids	15	5	3	354	77	318	71	4	3	48	8	883	5.6	11	62
West Mids	18	3	8	487	131	142	400	12	16	66	1	1255	7.9	21	44
Eastern	33	34	14	567	129	712	526	14	17	87	6	2058	13.0	27	77
Thames	84	65	46	2325	497	1407	2038	21	74	466	37	6865	43.3	75	166
South E	20	2	5	184	18	21	207	2	8	42	1	483	3.0	24	21
WAGS	8	5	6	189	49	131	305	7	7	26	1	715	4.5	14	20
Wessex	18	4	4	48	11	95	247	0	14	61	2	478	3.0	14	17
West	15	1	-	68	8	62	4	0	8	36	1	187	12.0	16	15
Totals	244	154	105	4925	1053	4016	4497	153	173	938	76	15831		251	515

Yorks & H = Yorkshire & Humberside; WAGS = Wiltshire, Avon, Gloucestershire and Somerset

Sen. = Seniors; Ass. = Associate Members; Pat. = Patrons

2.1.4 The Impacts of Water Based Recreation on The River and Inland Waterway Environment

Water plants and animals are likely to be affected by many human activities, including sewage disposal, land drainage and various land use practices (as discussed in earlier sections), which, in turn, may be influenced by an influx of visitors to an area for recreation (Liddle and Scorgie, 1980).

The effects of recreational activities on aquatic animals are less well understood than the effects on plants, partly because animals react to the presence of humans, and to the results of their activities, in very different ways. They may be disturbed by sight and sound, as well as by pollution or other changes in the environment. Animals are often very dependent on plants for food, shelter, breeding sites, or simply for somewhere to hide, so that they may suffer indirectly if plants themselves are affected. This applies equally to zooplankton in the open water and to birds and mammals at the margins of rivers and inland waterways.

Sometimes the effects of recreational activities are clear, for example when groups of birds feeding or roosting on the water take flight at the approach of a boat (Ward, 1990). However, unless an animal or plant is particularly conspicuous, or the subject of special interest (e.g. angling), the effects may not be noticed. When more than one factor is involved, as in the case of an enclosed water body used for multi-recreational activities, it may be virtually impossible to isolate the cause of any observable effect, except in the clear-cut instance of wildfowl being disturbed by boats or fishermen.

The many possible ways of classifying the impacts of recreation will be influenced by the amount and quality of information available. A useful distinction can be made between shore- and water-based activities (between fishing from the bank and boating, for example) and this type of user-orientated system, which has been widely used (e.g. Liddle, 1997).

2.1.4.1 Impacts of Water Based Activities

The physical forces associated with water-based activities originate mainly from motorised boats and include wash, turbulence, propellor action (cutting effects), direct contact and also disturbance by sight and sound. The effects of unpowered boats such as canoes, rowing boats, yachts and windsurfers are generally deemed to be minor in comparison with powered boats (House of Commons Environment Committee, 1995). Likewise, activities such as swimming are insignificant except where particularly concentrated in space and/or time. The impacts of wash will be greatest from high speed motorboats and most navigable waterways therefore enforce speed limits. Wash can damage bankside plants (Haslam, 1978) and increase bank erosion. Propellor action may create turbulence in the water which can disturb the bed and increase turbidity sufficiently to restrict light supply for photosynthesis (Croft, 1975; Hilton and Phillips, 1982; Murphy and Eaton, 1983; Liddle, 1997).

Moss (1977) reported that in the Norfolk Broads, the turbidity of the waters was not strongly correlated with the amount of use by boats. The amount of clay in the sediment, the depth of the water and the size and horsepower of the craft are likely to be just as important. Boats propelled by oars or paddles impart relatively little energy but it is still possible for oars or paddles to uproot plants in shallow water.

The edges of propellers can act as a set of rotating knives. Liddle and Scorgie (1980) found that an outboard motor attached to a boat driven through a patch of yellow water lily (*Nuphar lutea*) will cut through the petioles, leaving a very jagged end. On a run of 50 m, 15 leaves were detached and many more were overturned. Lagler *et al.* (1950) found that prolonged use of an outboard motorboat, operating in water 75 cm deep, with the propeller 35 cm from the bottom, removed all plants from a strip 1.5 m wide; and that the silt had been washed to the sides of the strip, leaving sand and gravel in the centre.

Boats may cause damage by direct collision with the marginal vegetation or a bank. Damage to emergent macrophytes by boats running into them at right angles to the shore line, and by boats turning, leaving isolated patches of plants, was recorded by Sukopp (1971). He also noted that gaps caused in this way were then enlarged by moored boats being moved to and fro by wash from other craft. Boat berthing, launching and beaching are reported by Rees and Tivy (1977) to have an abrasive action on the beds and shores of Scottish lochs. This activity can eliminate extensive areas of emergent vegetation where heavy use occurs. However, Rees and Tivy (1977) considered that floating leaved plants are relatively immune to damage because boat users tend to avoid these communities where oars, fishing lines and even propellers can become entangled.

In some areas the intensity of recreational boating has become so great that vessels have to be treated like road traffic in order to minimise impacts. Jackson (1988) developed a technique for scoring potential impact based on vessel speed (slow = 1 or fast = 2), number of visualised traffic lanes used (1-3), wake (small = 1 or large = 3) and operation (stop = 1.5 and U-turn = 2). The scores ranged from 1 to 24, but the interesting result was that water-skier speedboats had over two times the impact score of the runabout cruiser category and nearly four times the impact of canoes and kayaks.

2.1.4.2 Impacts on River and Canal Banks

Recreational activities that take place on the banks of rivers and inland waterways include angling, bird watching, swimming, camping, picnicking and walking. Also, the banks are used by small boat users for access to and egress from the water. Since these activities produce broadly similar physical effects on aquatic plants and animals, they are considered together. The effects of management for recreation and the effects of disturbance on animals are treated separately.

Walking in and out of the water is an activity associated with many forms of aquatic recreation. The forces exerted by walking have been described in detail by Harper, Warlow and Clarke (1961), who resolved them into vertical, horizontal and tangential components and showed that the force of the impact is partly determined by the hardness of the substratum. Some forms of recreation produce additional effects as people deliberately clear marginal vegetation to gain access to the water. At one site on the river Ouse near Huntingdon, Liddle and Scorgie (1980) found that 30% of the area of the bank vegetation had been changed in this way near an access track, and that 20% was changed 300 m further away. This may increase the diversity of the river bank vegetation but it breaks up a continuous habitat into a series of small units.

Marginal vegetation may also be damaged by people walking parallel the water's edge or seeking access to the water for activities such swimming, scuba diving, fly fishing or the launching of small boats. The damage may be extensive, changing whole communities, as Sukopp (1971) observed at the margins of the Havel River in West Berlin. The vegetation fringing the Havel River was subjected to wear by as many as 350000 people on 1 day on 95 km of shore, which, because of restricted access, resulted in 9 people m^{-1} of usable shoreline. Slight disturbance at first allowed room for annual and short lived species, especially where the margins were a managed meadow, but the reed stands vanished with intensive use, especially for bathing, and this was followed by erosion of the bank. Sukopp (1971) recorded that a total 31% of the reed swamps disappeared from the shores of part of the Havel River in the 5 years between 1962 and 1967.

At the other extreme, Rees (1978) noted that paths made by fishermen and wildfowlers were usually between 30 and 45cm wide, and they were typically parallel to the shore at the junction of two different plant communities. The substratum on which these pathways develop beside Scottish lochs (lakes) was usually silty with a high organic content and often with stands of reeds, reed grasses and sedges. This author observed that on little used pathways the dominant emergent species were still present.

They were replaced on pathways of intermediate use by harder wearing species, including bent grasses and meadow grasses, with amphibious periscaria, common knot grass or forget-me-not in the margins; the heavily used pathways largely consisted of bare mud with occasional invading species. The introduction of members of the common path flora was restricted to common knot grass in this case, but the often observed increase in species number under conditions of light trampling was recorded. Sukopp (1971) commented that common reed (see Plate 2.13) is able to stand wave action caused by boats but not mechanical damage caused by trampling.

2.1.4.3 Recreational Release of Sewage

Sewage resulting from water based recreational activities may be discharged directly into the water, particularly from boats, or, in the case of visitors based ashore, it may undergo some form of treatment before being discharged. Both the quantity and quality of effluent discharged are dependent on several factors, including the type, extent and location of activity, and whether refuse from visitors can be processed by existing sewage works (Liddle and Scorgie, 1980).

The amount of sewage and other pollutants released into waters by land based and water based recreation activities varies from the low levels of leaching from shallowly buried faeces to the urban levels of discharge from large tourist developments. The major constituents of whole and settled sewage are identified by Liddle and Scorgie (1980), and indicate that a potentially large amount of nutrients, especially nitrogen and phosphorus, may be released into waters where overnight stays by visitors occur. In camping, and to some extent boating, the amount released will be reduced, but the large amounts may be released from any form of accommodation development. The release of sewage into freshwater areas can clearly cause serious problems, but the nature and extent of the damage depends to some extent on the 'natural' status of the water body receiving the effluent, as well as the quality and quantity of the effluent itself (Liddle and Scorgie, 1980). The sources of sewage along rivers and waterways was discussed in Section 1.4 and the harmful effects to recreatoinal users are discussed further in Section 2.4.

2.1.4.1 Release of Petrol and Oil

Outboard motors are probably the most common means of propulsion for motorboats used for recreation, the majority are now of the four-stroke cycle type. These are much 'cleaner' than the two-stroke engines in common use until the early 1980s. The following discussion is adapted from Liddle and Scorgie (1980).

The substances emitted by outboard motors are derived from petrol and lubricating oil. Both petrol and oil consist mainly of hydrocarbon compounds with small amounts of additives. Oils contain elements such as zinc, sulphur, phosphorus and other unspecified additives (Jackivicz and Kuzminski, 1973a). There is little quantitative information on what substances actually appear in the aquatic environment during the operation of outboard motors. Jackivicz and Kuzminski (1973a) working with two-stroke motors suggested that water vapour, carbon oxides, nitrogen and sulphur are emitted from the combustion chamber, in the unburned fuel mixture and partial oxidation products are discharged below the water surface. Various investigators have reported values for the volatile and non-volatile fractions of oil, phenols, lead, chemical oxygen demand (COD) and biological oxygen demand (BOD) in two-stroke outboard motor-exhausted water (Jackivicz and Kuzminski, 1973a). They have estimated that the total discharge of hydrocarbons from one two-stroke outboard engine, running for 1 day, would be equivalent to the waste material (sewage) produced by a population of 400 people, assuming that the products contain 85% degradable carbon.

Lagler *et al.* (1950) reported no effects on populations of fish in experimental ponds, that could be attributable to outboard motor exhausts. Jackivicz and Kuzminski (1973b) reviewed the available information and concluded that while pollution from outboard motors can exhibit a toxic effect in sufficiently high concentrations, and may affect reproduction of fish, under the conditions of normal use there is nothing to suggest that there is a problem. They called for more research to relate laboratory and field observations. As Tanner (1973) pointed out, pollution can pose a serious threat to wildlife, but the pollution from recreational activities is generally small compared to other sources.

According to the Dartington Amenity Research Trust (1974), the effects of pollution from outboard motors and fuel spillage are likely to be lost in a river like the Yorkshire Ouse, which carries large volumes of water to dilute the 'relatively small' quantities of discharged material. They consider that pollution caused by the discharge of crude sewage and litter directly into the river is more serious. The available evidence suggests that, as far as effects on plants are concerned, this appears to be the case. Lagler *et al.* (1950) concluded that if no oil pollution could be discerned in their experimental ponds, it is probable that this is 'almost never an item of concern from ordinary outboard use in natural waters'. Oil from outboard motors may affect plants indirectly, particularly phytoplankton, by lowering the oxygen content of the water, particularly of the first few centimetres of a lake.

2.1.4.5 Impacts of Management For Recreation

The increased use of freshwater areas for recreation has led to a demand both for more space and for better management of existing facilities. Aquatic plants and animals are thus threatened by the development of marinas (Sidaway, 1991) and the restoration of canals, as well as by routine dredging and weed control operations. While the creation of large areas of solid substrata, such as wooden or steel piles, may benefit certain organisms, piling a previously sloping bank removes the normal habitat of marginal plants. The creation of 'landing holes' and the laying out of 'wild animal bays' to overcome this problem was suggested by von Schneider and Wolfel (1978). Mechanical weed control and dredging appear to have only minimal long-term effects (Pearson and Jones, 1975, 1978; Scorgie, 1978), although animals living at the margins and on the water surface may be severely affected by management programmes that cause disturbance and wholesale changes in the habitat.

In summarising this section, the physical impacts of water based recreation can be very intense, although not as widespread as those of pollution. Macrophytes and shore vegetation may be destroyed by trampling from shore based fishermen, campers and people gaining access to the water, either for swimmmg or launching boats.

The physical damage may be the result of trampling, sliding boats (on or off trailers) down banks or the collision of boat hulls and keels with the plants. High speed propellers may act as rotating knives cutting floating macrophytes, and the turbulence created by motor driven craft may increase the suspended material and hence the turbidity of the water column. Wash from powerboats will also erode unprotected banks in lakes and rivers.

The amounts of pollution released by recreators are generally low, but it can become a significant factor where there is any form of development, which includes running water leading to normal quantities of sewage being produced. In remote areas, perhaps when camping, the location of latrines is crucial as water passing through these human faeces into a river or stream may be significant and they should be as far from water bodies or streams as possible. The release of petrol and oil from outboard motors does have an impact on water quality, though seems to be relatively insignificant as compared to other sources of pollution.

2.2 Drainage Basins and How Rivers Work

2.2.1 Precipitation Generation

In the British context, and even in Scotland, snowfall makes up a relatively small proportion of the total precipitation input to the typical drainage basin system. So, in terms of causing river levels to rise, we are usually concerned with rainfall. There are, however, some notable occasions when snowmelt has generated significant rises in river levels. These have, in the past, resulted in flooding (e.g. snowmelt flooding on the River Tay in Spring 1990; snowmelt resulted in severe flooding in York in 1992 caused by prolonged rises in the River Ouse and its tributaries). In countries where high mountainous areas store water in the form of snow and ice, then glacier fed streams and rivers will respond to temperature changes and thus control river levels almost entirely, usually on a seasonal basis. This situation is relatively uncommon in the British context and will not be discussed further here.

As a basic principle, rainfall results from cooling (usually by uplift) of moist air. Such uplift may be caused in three main ways, after which the three main mechanisms for rainfall generation are named. Figure 2.2.1 illustrates these:

i.   Relief or orographic rainfall
ii. Convectional rainfall
iii. Frontal or cyclonic rainfall

Relief or orographic rainfall is that associated with, or caused by, mountains. Moist air is forced to rise over mountain barriers and sheds its moisture once the air cools and condenses above the cloud or **condensation level**. Most rain falls on the windward slopes and summit of the mountain giving rise to a rain shadow effect on the leeward side. This type of rainfall is common over the mountains of north and west Britain.

Convectional rain is the type we associate with thunderstorms on hot summer afternoons. In this case the sun heats the ground and causes the air in contact with it to warm. The warm air rises and when it reaches the **condensation level**, it cools and condenses to form heavy, thundery clouds which can deliver very intense storms.

The third mechanism by which rainfall is generated is that we get from depressions, known as cyclonic or frontal rainfall. This type of rainfall results from the meeting of warm and cold air masses. The warm unstable air rises over the cold, stable air, and in so doing, it cools and condenses to form clouds which bring rain associated with warm and cold fronts. For more details of rainfall generation see Thomas (1995) or Langmuir (1984).

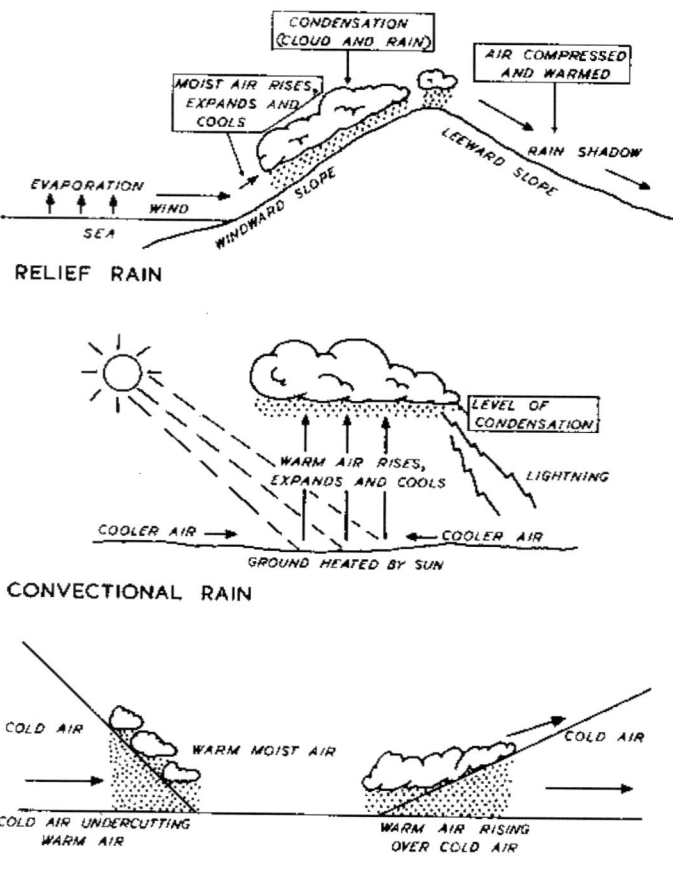

RELIEF RAIN

CONVECTIONAL RAIN

CYCLONIC RAIN - Cross section of a depression

Figure 2.2.1: Mechanisms of rainfall generation (after Dobson & Virgo, 1964).

2.2.2   The Drainage Basin As A System

The drainage basin may be described as an open system and it forms part of the water cycle described in Part 1.2. When viewed as a system it has:

• inputs (in the form of precipitation like rain and snow);

- outputs (where water is lost to the system by the river carrying it to the sea or by **evapotranspiration** (the loss of water directly from the ground, water surfaces or through vegetation).

Within the system some of the water:
- is stored either in lakes or in the soil, or
- passes through a series of transfers (e.g. infiltration, percolation,
- throughflow).

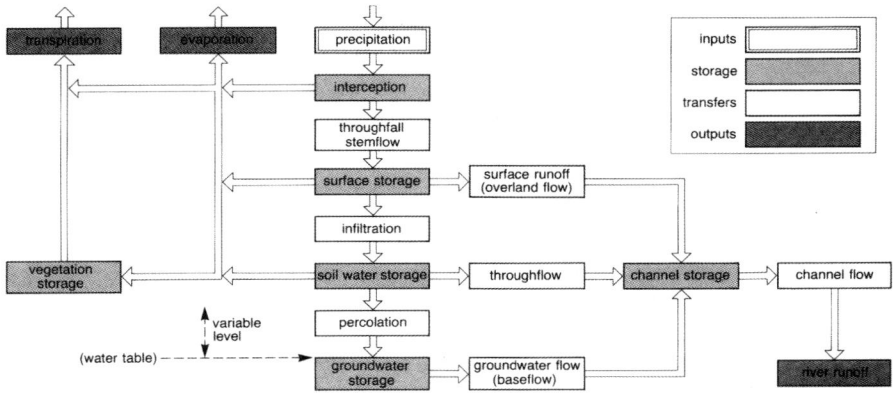

Figure 2.2.2: The drainage basin system for a region such as the British Isles (after Waugh, 1990).

Precipitation. This forms the major input into the system, though the amount of input varies depending on the intensity and duration of rainfall. Usually the more intense the storm, the shorter the duration. Convectional thunderstorms are short, heavy and may be confined to small areas, whereas the passing of a warm front will probably give a longer period of more steady rainfall extending over the whole drainage basin.

Evapotranspiration. The two components of evapotranspiration contribute to form an output from the system. **Evaporation** is the physical process by which moisture is directly lost into the atmosphere from various water surfaces and the soil due to the effect of air movement or the sun's heat. **Transpiration** is a biological process by which water is lost from a plant through the minute pores (stomata) in its leaves. Evaporation rates are affected by temperature, wind speed, humidity, hours of sunshine and other climatic factors. Transpiration rates depend on the time of year, the type and amount of vegetation, and the length of the growing season. It is also possible to distinguish between the potential and the actual evapotranspiration of an area. For example, in deserts there is a high **potential evapotranspiration** because the amount of moisture that could be lost is greater than the amount because the amount of moisture that could be lost is greater than the amount of water that is actually available. On the other hand, in Britain, the amount of water that is available for evapotranspiration usually exceeds the amount that actually takes place, hence the term **actual evapotranspiration.**

Interception. The first raindrops of a storm will fall on trees or plants which shelter the underlying ground. This is called interception storage, and naturally will be greater in a woodland area than over grassland. If the precipitation is light and of short duration, much of the water may never reach the ground, and may be quickly lost to the system through evaporation. Estimates suggest that in a woodland area up to 30 per cent of the precipitation may be lost because of interception, which helps to account for reduced soil erosion in forests. In an area of deciduous trees, both interception and evapotranspiration rates will be higher in summer. If a storm persists, then water begins to reach the ground by three possible routes: dropping off the leaves as **throughfall;** flowing down the trunk as **stemflow;** or by undergoing **secondary interception** by any undergrowth. Following a warm or dry spell in summer, the ground may be hard, so that at the onset of a storm, water lies on the surface as soil surface storage until the upper layers become wet and soft enough to absorb the moisture. If precipitation is very heavy at the beginning of the storm, then the ground may be incapable of absorbing all of the rain. As a result, excess water flows away over the surface, a transfer known as surface runoff or **overland flow.**

Infiltration. In most environments overland flow is relatively rare except in urban areas, which have impermeable coverings of tarmac and concrete, or during exceptionally heavy storms. Usually the ground rapidly becomes soft and sufficiently absorbent for water, gradually, to infiltrate vertically through the pores in the soil. The speed at which water can pass through the soil is called its **infiltration capacity** and is expressed in mm/hour. Table 2.2.1 shows some typical infiltration rates for agricultural land.

Table 2.2.1: Some typical infiltration capacities for agricultural land.

Land use	Infiltration rate (mm / hr)
Old permanent pasture	57
Moderately grazed pasture	19
Heavily grazed pasture	13
Weeds or cereals	9
Bare ground (baked hard by sun)	6

The rate of infiltration depends upon the amount of water already in the soil, the **porosity** and structure of the soil and the type, amount and seasonal changes in vegetation cover. On slopes, water in the soil may flow horizontally as **throughflow.** On reaching valley sides this throughflow can give rise to springs which provide a constant supply of water to a river even in dry spells. During drier periods, some water may be drawn up towards the surface by **capillary action** while at all times plant roots are likely to take up moisture from the soil (vegetation storage) which may later be lost from the system by transpiration.

Percolation. As the excess water reaches the underlying soil or rock layers, which tend to be more compact, its progress is slowed. This constant movement, called percolation, creates **groundwater storage.**

Groundwater. Water eventually collects above an impermeable rock or fills all pore spaces, creating a **zone of saturation.** The upper level of saturated material, i.e. the upper surface of the groundwater layer, is known as the **water table.** Water may then be slowly transferred laterally as groundwater flow or **baseflow.** Groundwater levels usually respond slowly to surface storms or droughts. During a lengthy dry period some of the groundwater store will be utilised as river levels fall. In a subsequent wetter period, groundwater must be re-placed before the level of the river can rise appreciably. If the water table reaches the surface it means that the ground will be saturated and excess water forms a marsh where the land is flat, or becomes surface runoff if the ground is sloping.

Channel flow. Although some rain does fall directly into the channel of a river, most water reaches it by a combination of three transfer processes: surface runoff (overland flow), throughflow, or groundwater flow (baseflow). Once in the river as channel storage, water flows towards the sea where it is lost to the drainage basin system.

2.2.3   The Water Balance

The water balance shows the state of equilibrium in the drainage basin between the inputs and the outputs. It can be expressed as:

$$P = Q + E \pm \text{changes in storage}$$

where:
         P = precipitation (measured using rain gauges),
         Q = runoff (measured by weirs or flumes in the river channel),
         E = evapotranspiration (this is more difficult to measure).

In Britain the annual precipitation is almost always greater than evapotranspiration. The situation can become reversed during drought summers (e.g. 1975, 1976, 1984), especially in the SE of England. When evapotranspiration exceeds precipitation, any surplus soil moisture will be used to leave a **soil moisture deficiency**. When it next rains, there will be a period of **soil moisture recharge** until the water in the soil is replenished to its **field capacity**.

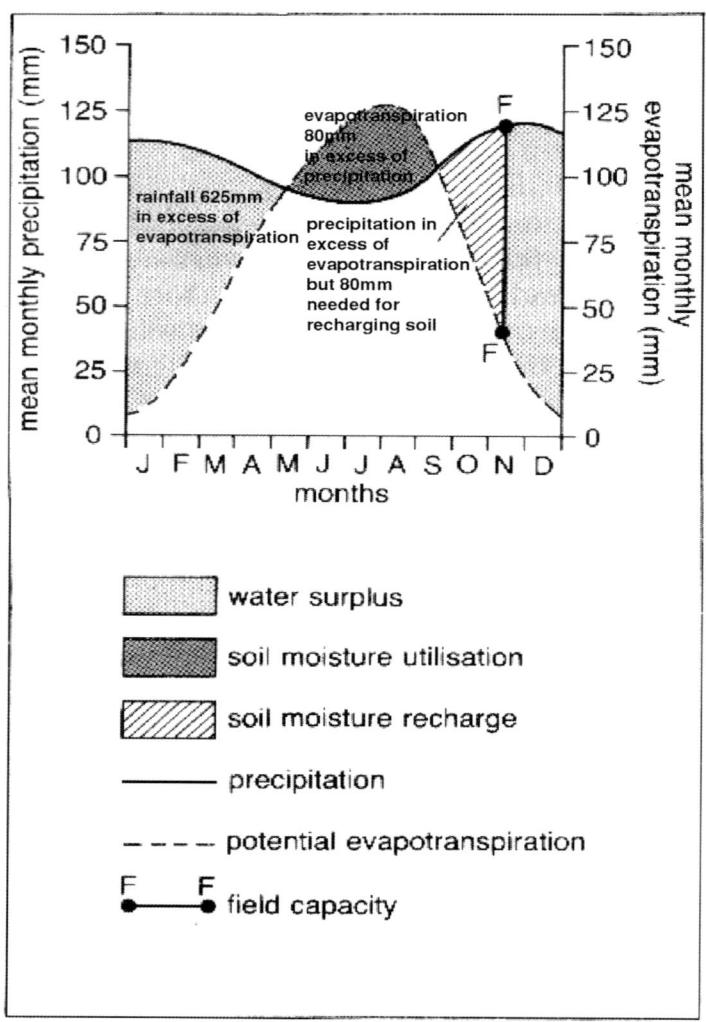

The figure contains the following labels:

- mean monthly precipitation (mm) [left y-axis]
- mean monthly evapotranspiration (mm) [right y-axis]
- months [x-axis: J F M A M J J A S O N D]
- evapotranspiration 80mm in excess of precipitation
- rainfall 625mm in excess of evapotranspiration
- precipitation in excess of evapotranspiration but 80mm needed for recharging soil
- F F [field capacity points]

Legend:

- water surplus
- soil moisture utilisation
- soil moisture recharge
- precipitation
- potential evapotranspiration
- F——F field capacity

Figure 2.2.3: A model showing the water balance (after Waugh, 1990).

Figure 2.2.3 is a water balance model typical of SE England. During winter precipitation is greater than evapotranspiration (P > E) which produces a water surplus and plenty of runoff - the soils will be wet and river levels high. In summer, E > P and so plants and humans use water from the soil store, leaving it depleted and causing river levels to drop. By autumn, P will again become greater than E although the first part of the rain has to be used to recharge the soil store.

2.2.4 The Storm Hydrograph and The Effects of Changing Landuse

2.2.4.1 Interpreting The Storm Hydrograph

Figure 2.2.4. shows a typical river hydrograph.

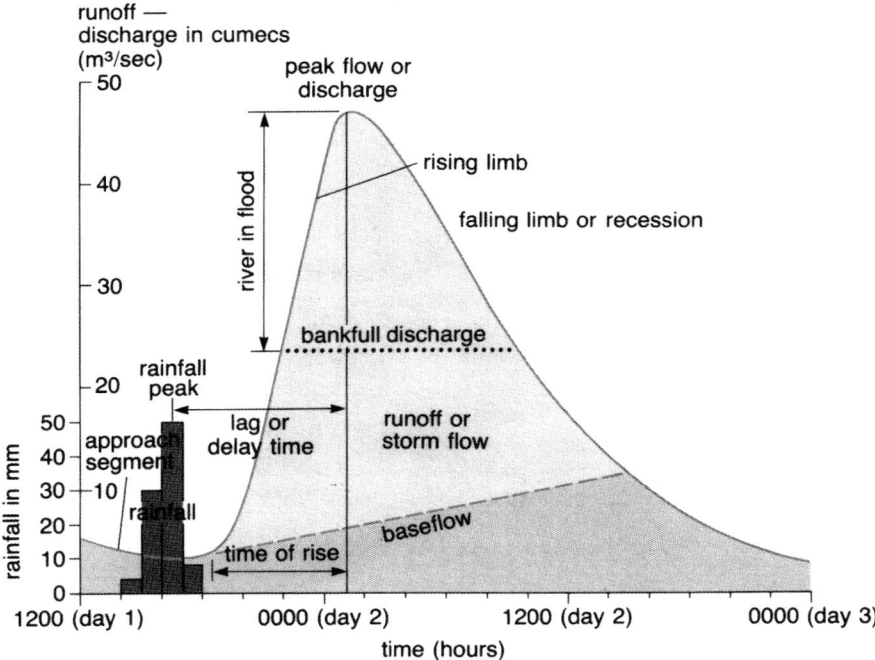

Figure 2.2.4: The storm hydrograph (after Waugh, 1990).

The hydrograph in Figure 2.2.4 includes the approach segment which shows the discharge of the river before the storm. At the time when the storm begins, the river's response is negligible for although some of the rain does fall directly into the channel, most falls elsewhere in the basin and takes time to reach the channel. However, when the initial surface runoff, and later the throughflow, eventually reach the river there is an increase in discharge. The **rising limb** shows this increase in discharge. The period between maximum precipitation and peak discharge is referred to as the **lag time.** Lag time varies according to conditions within the drainage basin, e.g. soil and rock type, slope, size of the basin, drainage density, type and amount of vegetation and water already in storage. The **falling** or **receding** limb is the segment of the graph where discharge is decreasing and the level of the river is falling. This segment is usually less steep than the rising limb because throughflow is still being released into the channel. By the time all the water from the storm has passed through a given point in the channel, the river will have returned to its baseflow level, unless there has been another storm within the basin. Baseflow is very slow to respond to a storm, but by continually releasing water from the lower ground, it maintains the river's flow during periods of low precipitation. Indeed, baseflow is more significant over a longer period of time than an individual storm, and reflects seasonal changes in precipitation, snow melt, vegetation and evapotranspiration. Finally, on the hydrograph, **bankfull discharge** is the point when the level of water has reached the top of the channel banks and any further increase in discharge will result in flooding of the surrounding land.

2.2.4.2 Effects of Land Use Changes on The River Hydrograph: Case Studies

It could be argued that the job of the hydraulic engineer is to modify the flood hydrograph to reduce the steepness and sharpness of the discharge peak, thereby reducing the flood hazard. Unfortunately, the effects of two of Britain's major land use changes this century: afforestation and urbanisation, have been to reverse this aim and increase in the steepness of the hydrograph. Figure 2.2.5 shows examples of the effects of urbanisation and afforestation on the river hydrographs.

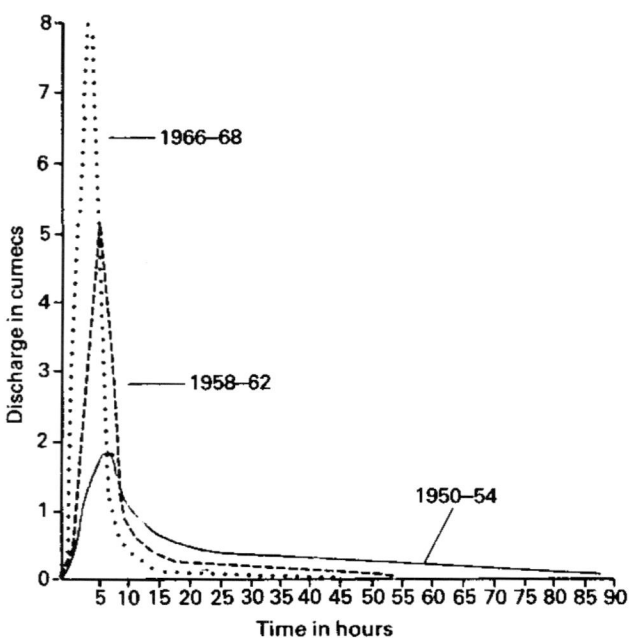

Figure 2.2.5: The impact of building Harlow New Town on the mean unit hydrograph of Canon's Brook, Essex (after Collard, 1988).

108

During the building of Harlow New Town, the changing nature of the hydrograph of Canon's Brook during the 1950s and 60s is illustrated. The lag time has been reduced and the peak discharge considerably increased. This increase will be as a result of the building of roads, buildings and paved areas which are designed to divert rainwater into drains as quickly as possible so as to avoid the build up of flood water in the town. The diverted water quickly enters the local watercourses, such as Canon's Brook, which are now more prone to flooding.

Figure 2.2.6 shows the impact of ditch excavation (in preparation for planting a commercial forest) on the stream hydrograph of a catchment at Coalburn in the North Pennines

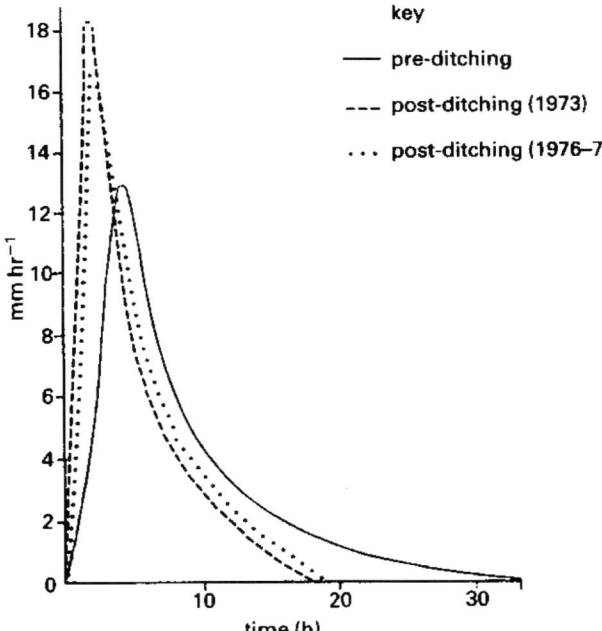

Figure 2.2.6: The impact of ditch excavation on a forested catchment at Coalburn in the North Pennines (after Collard, 1988).

Drainage ditching is carried out on wet upland catchments in order to drain the land to make it more suitable for planting coniferous trees. As with urbanisation, the effect of such drainage ditching is to reduce the lag time and increase the peak discharge. Water landing on the catchment following drainage ditching finds its way into the ditches easily and runs off into the stream channel rather than being stored in the soil or on vegetation. More water enters the ditches and leaves the catchment.

Figure 2.2.7 shows the effect of mature coniferous plantations in upland Britain on the storm hydrographs of the River Wye (moorland land use) and the River Severn (mature coniferous forest); geology and precipitation are the same in both basins. The peak flow is delayed and is lower in the Severn, and runoff is less rapid due to interception and evaporation by the trees. The effect of harvesting the trees is the focus of recent research studies. Preliminary findings suggest that with the trees removed, interception will be considerably reduced and there will be a temporary return to a more rapid stream response (reduced lag time and increased peak discharge).

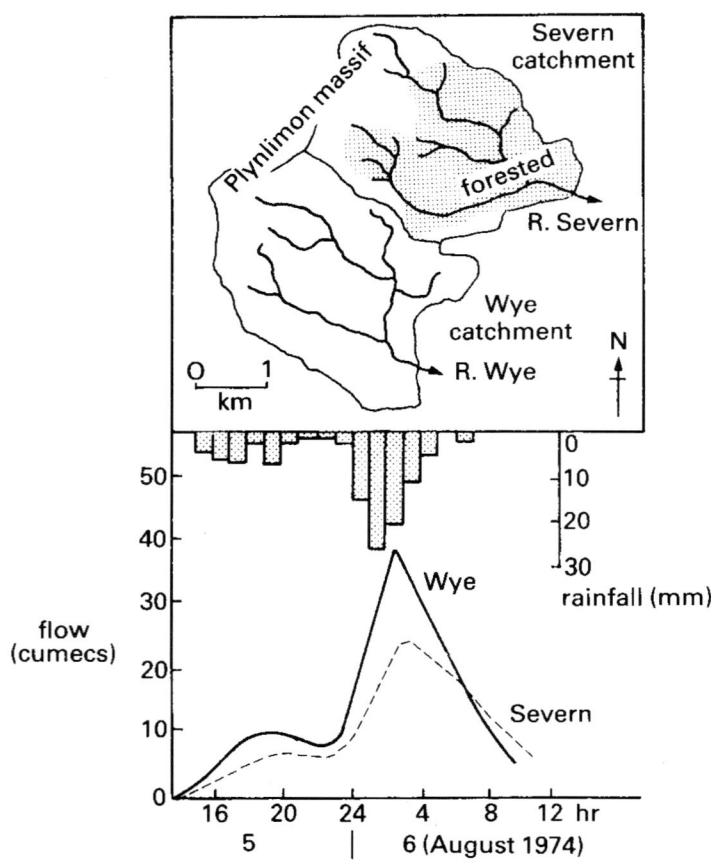

Figure 2.2.7: The effect of mature coniferous plantations in upland Britain on the storm hydrographs of the River Wye (moorland land use) and the River Severn (mature coniferous forest) (after Collard, 1988).

110

2.2.5 River Regimes

The **regime** of a river describes the annual variation in discharge. The average regime, which can be shown by either the mean daily or the mean monthly figures, is mainly determined by the climate of an area, e.g. the amount and distribution of rainfall together with the rates of evapotranspiration and snowmelt. Local geology may also be significant. There are few rivers flowing today under wholly natural conditions, especially in Britain. Almost all rivers are managed, regulated systems resulting from human activity. Regimes of rivers, which are used to demonstrate any seasonal variations, may be either simple, with one peak period of flow, or complex with several peaks.

Figure 2.2.8 shows the rainfall and runoff figures for the River Don (South Yorkshire) from October 1964 to September 1965. (Note that the Water Authority's year begins in October).

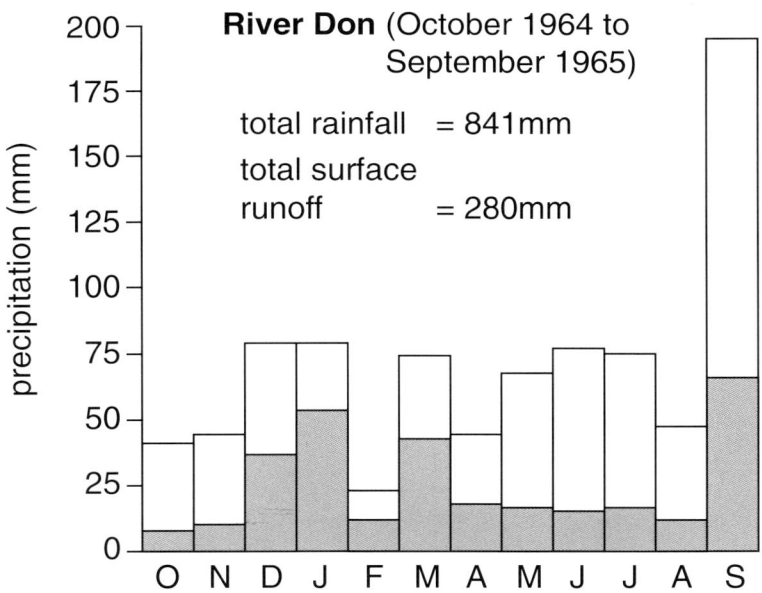

Figure 2.2.8: Rainfall and runoff figures for the river Don (after Waugh, 1990).

The discharge is usually at its highest in winter when Britain receives most of its rain and snowfall and when temperatures are low, limiting the amount of evapotranspiration. Early spring may also show a peak if the source of the river is in an upland area liable to heavy winter snowfalls. In the case of the River Don shown in Figure 2.2.8 the river drains part of the

Pennines. In contrast, river levels are lowest in summer when most of Britain receives less rainfall and when evapotranspiration rates are at their highest.

2.2.6   River Form

A river will try to adopt a channel shape that best fulfils its two main functions: transporting water and transporting sediment. It is important to understand the significance of channel shape in order to identify the controls on the flow of a river.

2.2.6.1 Types Of River Flow.

As water flows downhill under gravity it seeks the path of least resistance, i.e. a river possesses potential energy and follows a route which will maximise the rate of flow (velocity) and minimise the loss of this energy caused by friction. Most friction occurs along the banks and bed of the river but the internal friction of the water, and air resistance on the surface, are also significant. There are two patterns of flow, **laminar** and **turbulent.** Laminar flow (Figure 2.2.9 (a)) is a horizontal movement of water so rarely experienced in rivers that it is usually discounted. Such a method of flow, if it existed, would travel over sediment on the river bed without disturbing it. Turbulent flow, which is the dominant method, consists of a series of erratic eddies, both vertical and horizontal, generally in a downstream direction (Figures 2.2.9 (b)). Turbulence varies with the velocity of the river which, in turn, depends upon the amount of energy available after friction has been overcome. It is estimated that under 'normal' conditions about 95 per cent of a river's energy is expended in order to overcome friction.

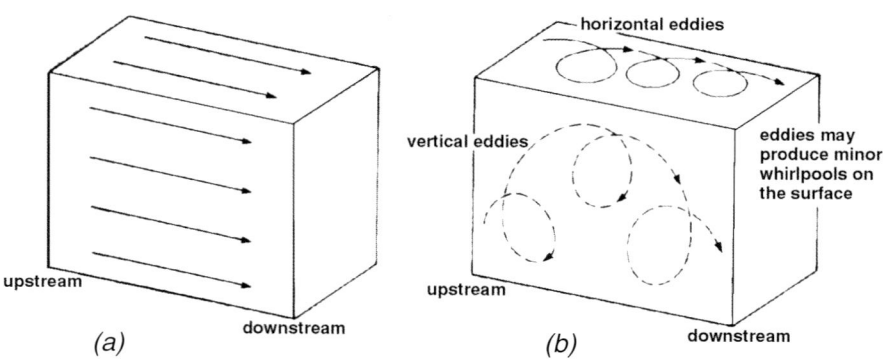

Figure 2.2.9: Types of flow in a river (a) laminar flow, (b) turbulent flow (after Waugh, 1990).

112

The influence of velocity on turbulence is as follows:

- If the velocity is high, the amount of energy still available after friction has been overcome will be greater, and so turbulence increases. This results in sediment on the bed being disturbed and carried downstream. The faster the flow of the river, the larger the quantity and size of particles that can be transported. This transported material is referred to as the river's **load.**

- When the velocity is low there is less energy to overcome friction. Turbulence decreases and may not be visible to the human eye, and sediment on the river bed remains undisturbed. Indeed, as turbulence maintains the transport of the load, a reduction in turbulence may lead to deposition of sediment.

2.2.6.2 Factors Affecting River Speed.

The velocity of a river is influenced by three main factors:

1   Channel shape

This is best described by the term **hydraulic radius,** i.e. the ratio between the area of the cross-section of a river channel and the length of its wetted perimeter. The cross section area is obtained by measuring the width and the mean depth of the channel (as shown in Part 1, Figures 1.2.6 and 1.2.7).

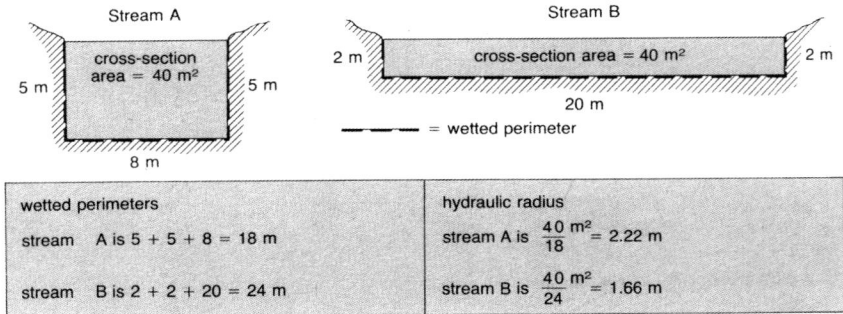

Figure 2.2.10: The wetted perimeter, hydraulic radius and efficiency of two differently shaped channels with the same cross-sectional area (after Waugh, 1990).

The **wetted perimeter** shown in Figure 2.2.10 is the length of the bed and banks which is in contact with the water in the channel. Figure 2.2.10 shows two channels with the same cross-sectional area but with different shapes and hydraulic radii. Channel A has a larger hydraulic radius, meaning that it has a smaller amount of water in its cross-section in contact with the wetted perimeter. This creates less friction, and allows greater velocity. Channel B has a smaller hydraulic radius, meaning that a relatively large amount of water is in contact with its wetted perimeter. This results in greater friction and reduced velocity. The river with channel A is therefore the more efficient of the two.

The point of maximum velocity is different in a river with a straight course, where the channel is likely to be approximately symmetrical (Figure 2.2.11 (a)), compared to a meandering channel where the shape is asymmetrical (Figure 2.2.11 (b)).

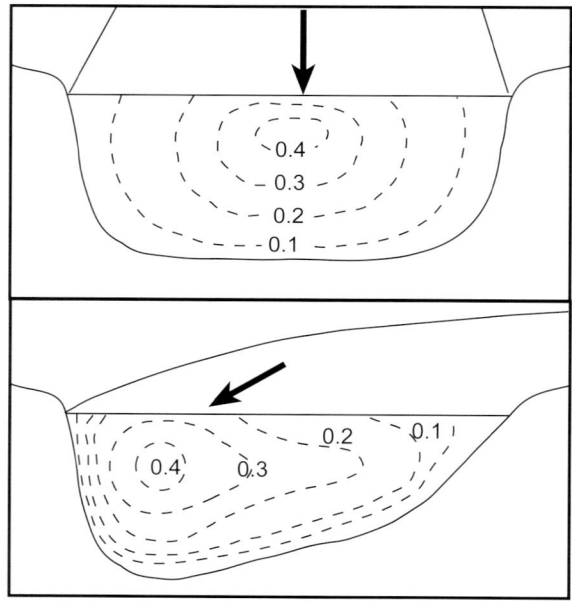

Figure 2.2.11: Velocities in a straight symmetrical channel (top), and an asymmetrical channel (bottom) showing velocities through the cross-section of a typically meandering river.

2 Roughness of channel bed and banks

A river flowing between banks composed of coarse material, with numerous protrusions (with a bed of large, angular rocks) meets with more resistance than a river with cohesive clays and silts forming its bed and banks (Figure 2.2.12).

114

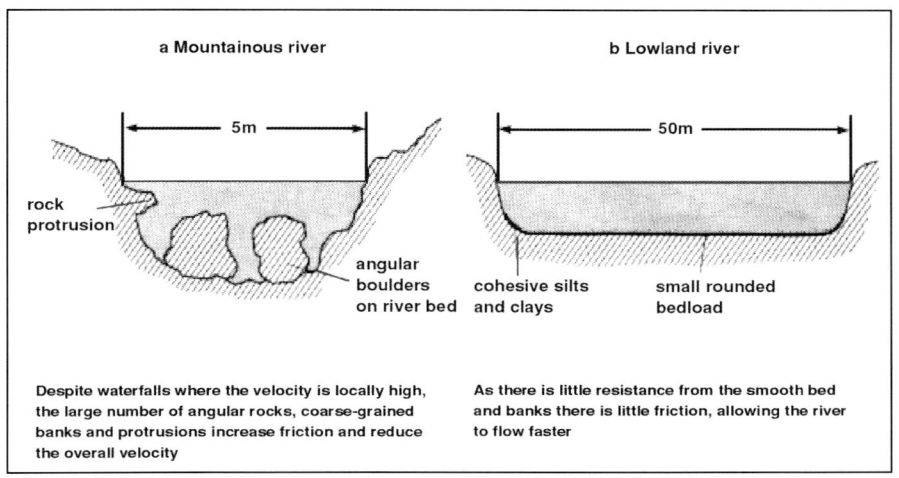

a Mountainous river

b Lowland river

5m

50m

rock
protrusion

angular
boulders
on river bed

cohesive silts
and clays

small rounded
bedload

Despite waterfalls where the velocity is locally high,
the large number of angular rocks, coarse-grained
banks and protrusions increase friction and reduce
the overall velocity

As there is little resistance from the smooth bed
and banks there is little friction, allowing the river
to flow faster

Figure 2.2.12: Why a river increases in velocity towards its mouth, (a) mountainous or upper course of a river, (b) lowland or lower course river (after Waugh, 1990).

Compare the photographs of the Allt Mhor in the Cairngorms, eastern Scotland (Plate 2.7) which has a very coarse bed with large boulders, to the relatively smooth bed of silt and mud of the lower River Forth (Plate 2.9) near Stirling in lowland central Scotland.

Figure 2.2.12 explains why the velocity in a mountain stream is less than that of a lowland river. As bank and bed roughness increase, so does turbulence. Therefore a mountain stream is more likely to pick up loose material and carry it downstream.

Roughness is difficult to measure but Manning, an engineer, calculated a **roughness coefficient** in which he interrelated the three factors affecting the velocity of the river. His formula is known as 'Manning's *N*':

$$v = R^{0.67} S^{0.5} / n$$

where:
v = mean velocity of flow,
R = hydraulic radius,
S = channel slope,
n = boundary roughness.

The formula gives a useful approximation for velocity. The higher the value of *n*, the rougher the bed and banks.

3   Channel slope

As more tributaries and water from surface runoff, throughflow and groundwater flow join the main river, the discharge, the channel cross-section area and the hydraulic radius will all increase. At the same time, less energy will be lost through friction and the role of bedload material will decrease. As a result, the river flows over a gradually decreasing gradient which, in profile shows a characteristic concave **long profile** as shown in Figure 2.2.13.

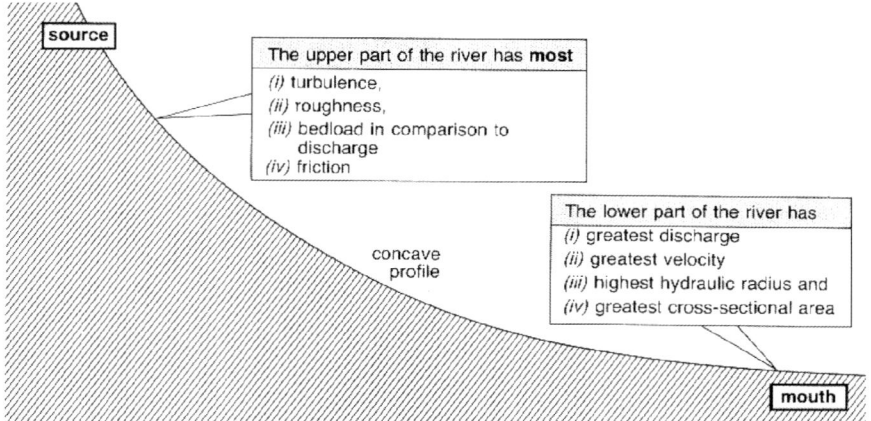

Figure 2.2.13: A typical long profile of a river (after Waugh, 1990).

In summarising this section it should be noted that:

- A river in a deep, broad channel, often with a gentle gradient and a small bedload will have a greater mean velocity than a river in a shallow, narrow, rock and boulder filled channel, even if the gradient of the latter is steeper,
- The velocity of a river increases as it nears the sea,
- The velocity increases as the depth, width and discharge of a river all increase,
- As roughness increases, so too do turbulence and the ability of the river to pick up and transport sediment.

116

2.2.7   Transport of Materials in Rivers

Any energy remaining after the river has overcome friction can be used to transport sediment. The amount of energy available increases rapidly as the discharge, velocity and turbulence increase, until the river reaches flood levels. A river in flood has a large wetted perimeter and the extra friction that it has to overcome is likely to cause it to deposit sediment on the flood plain. A river at **bankfull stage** can carry large quantities of soil and rock (its **load**) along the channel.   The load is transported by three main processes: **suspension, solution** and as **bedload** (Figure 2.2.14).

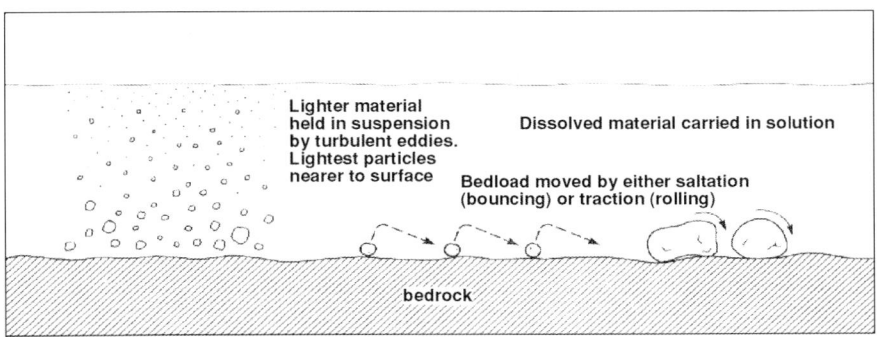

Figure 2.2.14: Transport processes in a river or stream (Source: Waugh, 1990).

Suspended load.   Very fine particles of clay and silt are dislodged and carried by turbulence in a fast flowing river. The greater the turbulence and velocity, the larger the quantity and size of particles which can be picked up. The material held in suspension usually forms the greatest part of the total load and the amount increases towards the river's mouth and gives the water its brown, grey or black colour.

Dissolved or solution load.   Water flowing within a river channel contains acids (e.g. carbonic acid from precipitation). If the bedrock is readily soluble, like limestone, it is constantly dissolved in the running water and removed in solution. Except in limestone areas, the material in solution usually forms a moderate to small proportion of the total load.

Bedload.   Larger particles (pebbles, cobbles and boulders known as clasts) that cannot be picked up by the current may be moved along the bed of the river in one of two ways: (a) **saltation** is when pebbles, sand and gravel are temporarily lifted up by the current and bounced along the bed in a hopping motion, and (b) **traction** is when the largest cobbles and boulders roll or slide along the bed. Some of these may be moved only during times of extreme flood.

It is much more difficult to measure the bedload than the suspended or dissolved load. Its contribution to the total load may be small unless the river is in flood. For example, it has been estimated that the proportion of material carried in one year by the River Tyne is: 57 per cent in suspension, 35 per cent in solution and 8 per cent as bedload. This is the equivalent of a ten tonne lorry tipping its load into the river every 20 minutes throughout the year. In comparison, the Amazon's load is equivalent to four ten tonne lorries tipping every minute of the year!

Two further terms should be noted at this point: the competence and the capacity of a river. The **competence** of a river refers to the maximum size of material the river is capable of transporting. The **capacity** is the total load actually transported. When the velocity is low, only small particles such as clay, silt and fine sand can be picked up. As the velocity increases then larger material can be moved. Because the maximum particle mass which can be moved increases with the sixth power of the velocity, it means that rivers in flood can move considerable amounts of material. For example, if the stream velocity increased by a factor of four, then the mass of boulder which could be moved would increase by 4^6 or 4096 times; if by a factor of five then the maximum mass it could transport would be multiplied 15 625 times.

The relationship between particle size (competence) and water velocity is shown in Figure2.2.15.

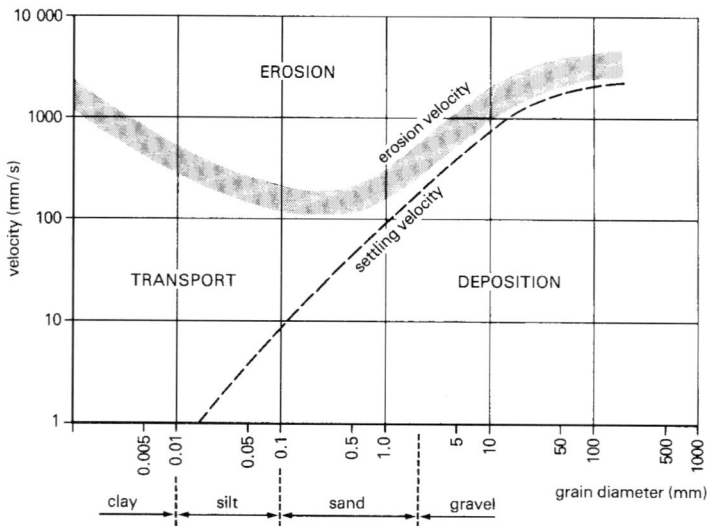

Figure 2.2.15: The relationship between velocity and particle movement (after Hjülstrom, 1935) (Source: Clowes & Comfort, 1982).

The **mean,** or **critical erosion velocity** curve gives the approximate velocity needed to pick up and transport, in suspension, particles of various sizes from clay to boulders. The material carried by the river (capacity) is responsible for most of the subsequent erosion. The **mean fall,** or **settling velocity** curve shows the velocities at which particles of a given size become too heavy to be transported and so will fall out of suspension and be deposited.

The graph shows two important points:

•   Sand can be transported at lower velocities than either finer or coarser particles. Particles of about 0.2 mm diameter can be picked up by a velocity of 20 cm/sec whereas finer clay particles, because of their cohesive properties, need a similar velocity to pebbles to be dislodged.

The velocity required to maintain particles in suspension is less than the velocity needed to pick them up. Indeed, for very fine clays the velocity required to maintain them is virtually nil - at which point the river has presumably stopped flowing! This means that material picked up by turbulent tributaries and lower order streams can be kept in suspension by a less turbulent, higher order main river. For coarser particles, the boundary between transportation and deposition is narrow, indicating that only a relatively small drop in velocity is needed to cause sedimentation.

2.2.8   Erosion by Rivers

The material carried by a river can contribute to the wearing away of its banks and bed. There are four main processes of erosion:

Corrasion. This is when the river picks up material and rubs it along its bed and banks, wearing them away by **abrasion,** rather like sandpaper. This process is most effective during times of flood and is the major method by which the river erodes both vertically and horizontally. If there are hollows in the bedrock of the river bed, particularly if it is limestone, pebbles are likely to become trapped. As the current produces turbulent eddies the pebbles will be swirled around in the hollows and enlarge them to form **potholes.**

Attrition. As the bedload is moved downstream, boulders collide with other material and the impact may break the rock into smaller pieces. In time these angular rocks become increasingly rounded in appearance.

Hydraulic action. The sheer force of the water as the turbulent current hits river banks, e.g. on the outside of a meander bend. This force may mean that water is forced into cracks. The air in the cracks is compressed, pressure is increased and, in time, the bank may collapse. **Cavitation** is a form of hydraulic action caused by bubbles of air collapsing. The resultant shock waves hit and slowly weaken the river banks. This is the slowest, least effective erosion process.

Solution or corrosion. This erosion mechanism works by dissolving the rock in the river water. This occurs continuously and is independent of river discharge or velocity. It is affected by the chemical composition of the water, e.g. the concentration of carbonic and humic acid.

2.2.9   Deposition in Rivers

When the velocity of a river begins to fall, the flow no longer has the competence or capacity to carry all of its load. So, starting with the largest particles, material begins to be deposited (Figure 2.2.15).

Deposition occurs where:

- a river broadens out and therefore has a larger wetted perimeter which, assuming the volume of water remains constant, results in increased friction and a reduction of velocity,
- a river enters the sea or a lake and therefore velocity is reduced,
- discharge is reduced following a period of low precipitation,
- the river is shallower on the inside of a meander,
- the load is suddenly increased, e.g. by debris from a landslide.

As the river loses energy the following changes are likely:

- the heaviest clasts are deposited first. It is for this reason that the channels of mountainous streams are often filled with large boulders. These increase the size of the wetted perimeter,
- gravel, sand and silt, transported either as bedload or in suspension, will be carried further to be deposited over flood plains or in the channel of rivers as they near their mouth,
- the finest particles of silt and clay, which are carried in suspension, may be deposited where rivers meet the sea either to infill estuaries or to form a **delta**.

The dissolved load will not be deposited but will be carried out to sea where it will help to maintain the saltiness of the oceans.

2.2.10   Fluvial Landforms

As the velocity of a river increases, surplus energy becomes available which may be harnessed to transport material and cause erosion.   Where the velocity decreases, an energy deficit is likely to result in depositional features.

2.2.10.1 Features Caused by Erosion

V-shaped valleys and interlocking spurs. In its upper course the channel of a river is often choked with large, angular boulders (as seen in Plate 2.7 in the Allt Mhor, Cairngorms). This bedload produces a large wetted perimeter and the friction that the river has to overcome to flow uses up much of the river's energy. Erosion is minimal because little energy is left to pick up and transport material. However, following periods of heavy rainfall or after snowmelt, the discharge of the river may rise rapidly. As the water flows between the boulders turbulence increases and may result either in the bedload being taken up into suspension or, as is more usual because of its size, in it being rolled or bounced along the river bed. The result is intensive **vertical erosion** which enables the river to create a steep sided valley with a characteristic 'V' shape (see Plate 2.4).

The steepness of the valley sides depends upon several factors. These include: (a) **climate**: is there sufficient rain to instigate mass movement on the valley sides and to increase discharge sufficiently for the river to generate enough energy to move its bedload ?, (b) **rock structure:** a resistant rock with vertical jointing, such as carboniferous limestone, will tends to produce almost vertical valley sides, and (c) **vegetation:** which may help to bind the soil together and keep the hillslope more stable. **Interlocking spurs** form because the river is forced to follow a winding course around the protrusions from the surrounding highland. As these spurs interlock, the view up or down the valley is restricted.

A process characteristic at the source of a river is **headward erosion,** or **spring sapping.** Here, where throughflow reaches the surface, the river may erode back towards its watershed as it undercuts the overlying rock, soil or vegetation.

Waterfalls. A waterfall forms when a river, after flowing over a relatively hard band of rock, meets a band of less resistant rock. As the water approaches the brink of the falls, velocity increases as the water in front of it loses contact with its bed and so is unhampered by friction. Plate 2.5 shows High Force waterfall on the River Tees in Co. Durham where the river breaks through the resistant Whin Sill igneous dolerite intrusion which is underlain by less resistant limestone.

The underlying softer rock is worn away as water falls on to it. This may lead to the harder rock becoming undercut, unstable and eventually it will collapse. At High Force, some say that divers searching for a missing person in the **plunge pool** below the waterfall discovered a cave cutting back many metres under the waterfall. As this undercutting process is repeated, the waterfall retreats upstream leaving a deep, steep-sided gorge. High Force is reputed to be England's largest waterfall in terms of it having the greatest discharge flowing over it, though at 21 m high it is not the highest. Plate 2.6 shows another of England's classic waterfalls. At Thornton Force in Kingsdale near Ingleton, North Yorkshire (see Plate 2.6), the River Greta cuts down through thick beds of limestone through a geological unconformity to the Silurian shales below.

At Niagara, it has been estimated that the falls are retreating by one metre per year. The rock, which collapses to the foot of the falls, is swirled around by the turbulence, usually in times of high discharge, and carves out a deep **plunge pool.**

Rapids. Rapids develop where the gradient of the river bed increases without a sudden break of slope as in a waterfall, or where the stream flows over a series of gently dipping bands of harder rock. Rapids increase the turbulence of a river and hence its erosive power. The rapids at Grand Tully on the River Tay in central Scotland (see Plate 2.8) are used as a canoe slalom training venue.

2.2.10.2   Effects of Fluvial Deposition

Deposition of sediment takes place when there is a decrease in energy or an increase in capacity. This makes the river less competent to transport its load and can occur anywhere from the upper course, where large boulders may be left, to the mouth, where fine clays may be deposited. Features which are formed by fluvial deposition are described next:

Flood plains. Rivers have most energy when at their bankfull stage. Should the river continue to rise, then the water will cover any adjacent flat land. This flat or gently sloping land adjacent to the river channel which is susceptible to flooding is known as the **flood plain.** At this point there will be a sudden increase in both the wetted perimeter and the hydraulic radius which in turn will produce an increase in friction and a corresponding decrease in velocity which results in the river depositing some of its load. The thin veneer of silt deposited over the flood plain often increases the fertility of the land. Successive floods mean that the flood plain builds up in height. The edge of the flood plain most distant from the river channel is often marked by a prominent break in slope known as the **bluff line** (see Figure 2.2.16).

Levees. As we have seen, when a river overflows its banks, the friction produced by the flood plain causes material to be deposited. The coarsest material is dropped first to form a small, natural embankment alongside the channel called a **levee** as seen in Figure 2.2.16.

If, later on, the river bed is raised by deposition of material, these embankments are sometimes artificially strengthened and heightened to try to contain the river. Some rivers flow above the level of their flood plains which means that if the levees collapse there can be serious danger to life and property.

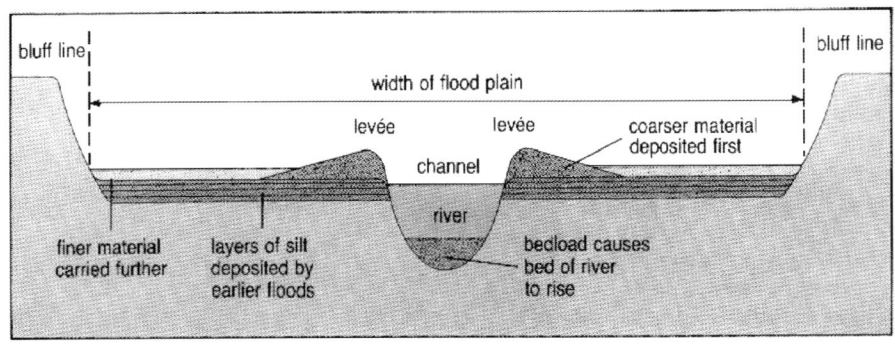

Figure 2.2.16: Cross-section of a flood plain showing levees and bluffs (after Waugh, 1990).

Braiding. For short periods of the year some rivers carry a very high load in relation to their velocity, e.g. during snowmelt periods in Scotland, or in Alpine or Arctic regions. When river levels fall rapidly, competence and capacity are reduced, and the channel may become choked with material which causes the river to divide into a series of diverging and converging segments. Small islands called **bars** can form in mid-channel, but bars can also be attached to banks and are most frequently found on the inside of river bends (**meanders**).

Deltas. A delta is usually composed of fine sediment which is deposited when a river loses energy and competence on flowing into an area of slow moving water such as a lake or the sea. When rivers like the Mississippi or Nile reach the sea, the meeting of fresh and salt water produces an electric charge which causes clay particles to coagulate and to settle on the sea bed, a process called **flocculation.** Deposits are laid on the ocean bed in a threefold sequence (Figure 2.2.17).

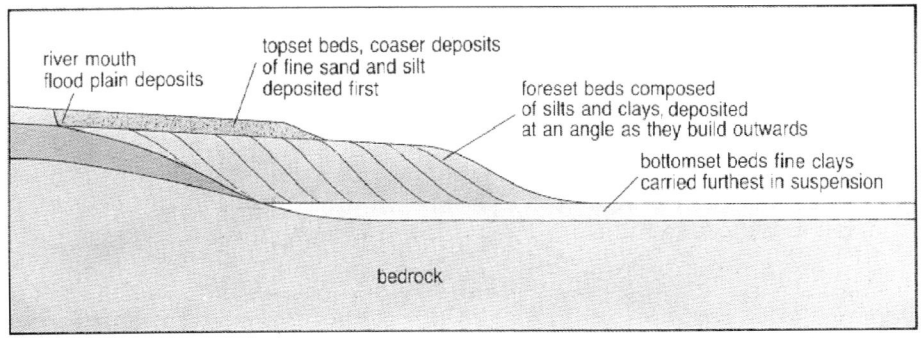

Figure 2.2.17: The structure of a delta (after Waugh, 1990).

123

`The finest materials are carried furthest and form the **bottomset beds** which are composed of fine clays. These will be covered by slightly coarser materials which are deposited to form a slope and make up the foreset beds. The upper layers, nearest to the land and composed of still coarser deposits, are the horizontal topset beds. Deltas were named because it was thought that their shape resembled that of the fourth letter of the Greek alphabet. In fact, deltas vary greatly in shape but geomorphologists have grouped them into three basic forms:

- **arcuate:** which has a rounded, convex outer margin, e.g. the Nile,
- **cuspate:** where the material brought down by a river is spread out evenly on either side of the channel, e.g. Tiber,
- **bird's foot:** where the river has many distributaries bounded by sediment and which extend out to sea like the claws of a bird, e.g. Mississippi.

In the British context rivers tend not to be large enough to exhibit classic deltas and tidal currents in estuaries do not often allow sediment to build up.

2.2.10.3 Effects of Combined Erosion and Deposition

Pools, Riffles and Meanders. Rivers rarely flow in a straight line. Indeed, testing under laboratory conditions suggests that a straight course is abnormal and unstable. How bends in rivers called **meanders** begin to form is uncertain, but they appear to have their origins in relatively straight sections where pools and riffles develop (see Figure 2.2.18). The usual spacing between pools, areas of deeper water, and **riffles,** areas of shallower water, is five to six times the bed width. The pool is an area of greater erosion where the available energy in the river builds up because of reduced friction. Hence, velocity and erosive capacity increase. Across the riffle area a higher proportion of total energy is used in overcoming friction. Thus velocity and erosive capacity are reduced and further deposition may take place.

In order to avoid the riffles, the main current swings from side to side in a sinuous course. Consequently, the maximum discharge and velocity are directed towards one side of the channel, which will be eroded, while on the opposite bank, where volume and discharge are at a minimum, deposition occurs. In time, this process increases the **sinuosity** of the meander.

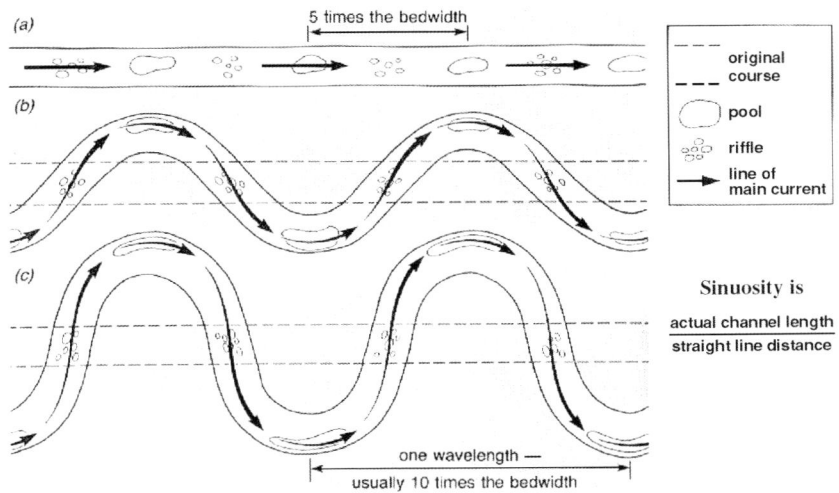

Figure 2.2.18: Sequence in the development of a meander through time (after Waugh, 1990).

Meanders, Point Bars and Oxbow Lakes. Plate 2.9 shows a meander on the River Forth near Stirling in central Scotland.

A meander has an asymmetrical cross-section shape (see Figure 2.2.19).

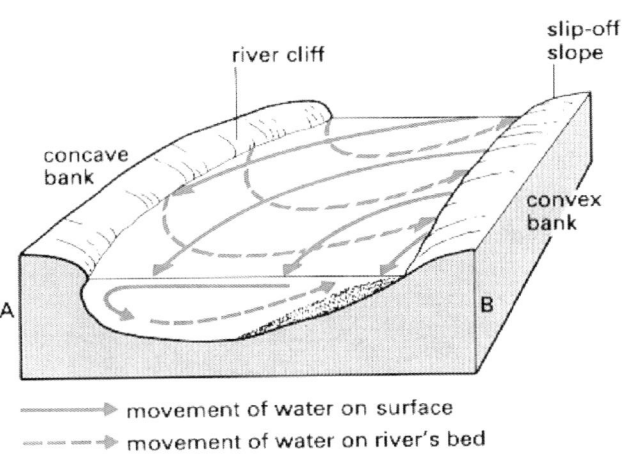

Figure 2.2.19: Flow patterns on a meander bend showing how sediment builds up on the inside of a river bend to form a point bar (after Bunnett, 1988).

125

It is thought that the material eroded from the outside of one bend is moved downstream by a corkscrew flow pattern known as **helicoidal flow**, and that much of this material is deposited on the inside of the next bend. The remainder is carried, mainly in suspension, towards the river mouth. Sediment deposited on the convex slope on the inside of the bend may take the form of a curving **point bar** (Figure 2.2.19), and its particles are usually graded in size, with the largest material being found highest up the slope. As erosion continues on the concave outer rim of the meander, the whole feature tends to migrate slowly downstream. Over time, the **sinuosity** may become so pronounced that during a flood the river cuts through the narrow neck of land in order to shorten its course. Having achieved a temporary straightening of its channel, the main current flows in the centre of the channel and deposition occurs near to the banks. This means that the old curve of the river will be cut off. The remaining crescent-shaped feature is an **oxbow lake** or **cutoff** (see Figure 2.2.20).

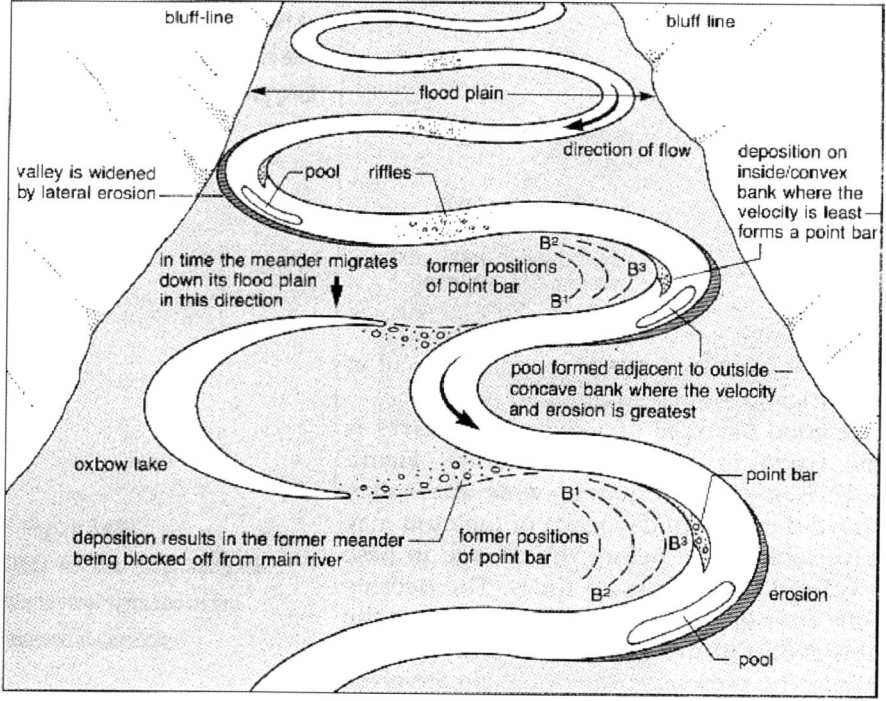

Figure 2.2.20: Meanders, point bars and oxbow lakes showing changes in the position of the point bar over time (after Waugh, 1990).

2.2.11 Base Level and the Graded River

Base Level. This is the lowest point to which erosion by running water can take place. In the case of rivers, the ultimate base level is sea level. Exceptions are when the river flows into an inland sea or there happens to be a temporary, local base level, such as where a river flows into a lake, where a tributary joins the main river or where there is a resistant band of rock crossing a valley.

Grade. The concept of grade supports the idea that a river is capable of existing in a state of balance, or **dynamic equilibrium**, with the rate of erosion being equal to the rate of deposition. In its simplest interpretation, a graded river has a gently sloping long profile with the gradient decreasing towards its mouth (Figure 2.2.21 (a)).

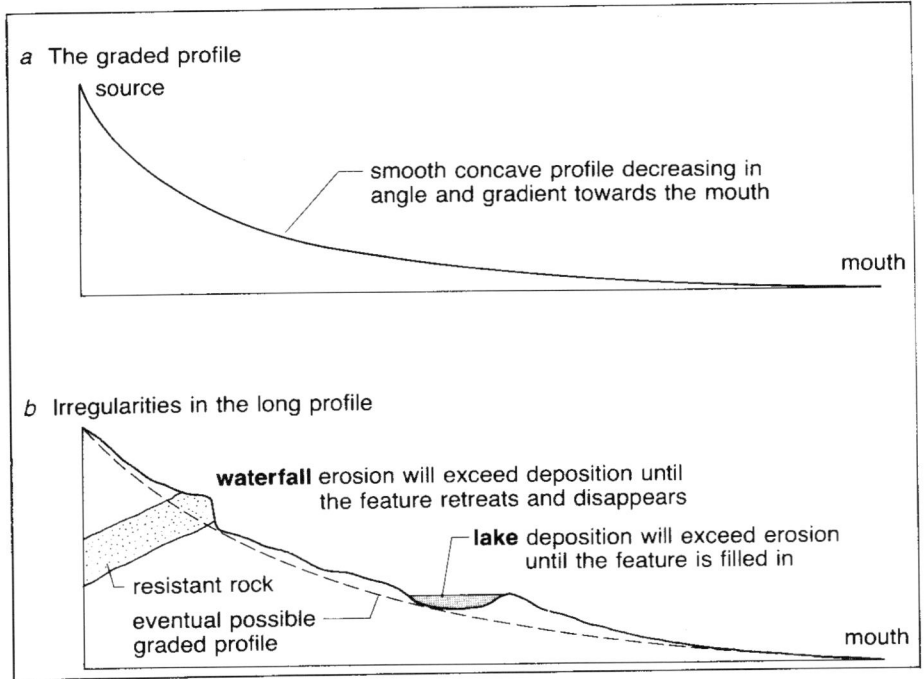

Figure 2.2.21: Graded river profiles (after Waugh, 1990).

This balance is always transitory as changes in volume, velocity and load increase either the rate of erosion or rate of deposition until a state of equilibrium has again been reached. This may be illustrated by two examples:

- if the long profile of a river happens to contain a waterfall and a lake (Figure 2.2.21 (b)), erosion is likely to be greatest at the waterfall, while deposition slowly fills in the lake so that in time both features are eliminated.

- there is a lengthy period of heavy rainfall within the river basin. As the volume of water rises and consequently the velocity and load of the river increase, so too will the rate of erosion. Ultimately the extra load carried by the river leads to extra deposition further down the valley or out at sea.

In a wider interpretation, grade is a balance not only in the long profile, but also in the river's cross section and the roughness of its channel. In this sense, balance or grade is when all aspects of the river's channel (width, depth and gradient) are adjusted to the discharge and load of the river at a given point in time. If the volume and load change then the river's channel morphology must adjust accordingly.

Changes in base level. Factors which influence changes in base level can be divided into two groups:

- **Climatic:** the effect of glaciation and changes in rainfall (either an increase or drought),
- **Tectonic:** crustal uplift following plate movement, and local volcanic activity.

Changes in base level affect coasts as well as rivers. There are two types of base level movement: positive and negative. **Positive** change is when sea level rises in relation to the land (which also means that land can sink in relation to the sea). This results in a decrease in the gradient of the river with a corresponding increase in deposition and potential flooding of coastal areas. **Negative** movement is when sea level falls in relation to the land (or the land rises in relation to the sea). This movement causes land to emerge from the sea, increasing the gradient of the river and therefore increasing the rate of fluvial erosion. This process is called **rejuvenation.** A negative change in base level increases the potential energy of a river enabling it to revive its erosive activity and so upsetting any possible graded long profile. Beginning in its lowest reaches, next to the sea, the river will try to regrade itself. During the Pleistocene glacial period, Britain was depressed by the weight of ice. Following deglaciation, the land slowly and intermittently rose again **(isostatic uplift)**, so that rejuvenation took place on more than one occasion: many rivers today show several partly graded profiles as illustrated in Figure 2.2.22.

Should the rise in the land be rapid, the river does not have sufficient time to erode vertically to the new sea level, and so rivers may descend as waterfalls over recently emerged sea cliffs.

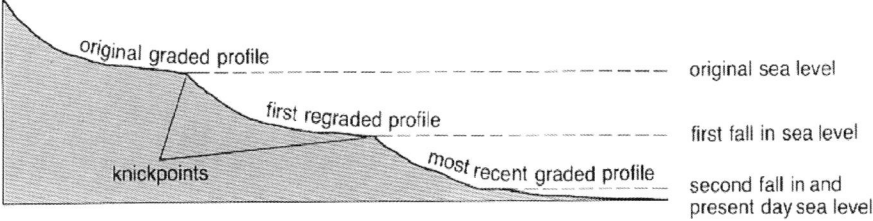

Figure 2.2.22:The effect of rejuvenation on the long profile of a river (after Waugh, 1990).

In time, the river cuts downwards and backwards and the waterfall, or **knickpoint,** retreats upstream and marks the maximum extent of the newly graded profile (see Figure 2.2.23). Should a river become completely regraded, which is unlikely because of the timescale involved, the knickpoint and all of the original graded profile will disappear.

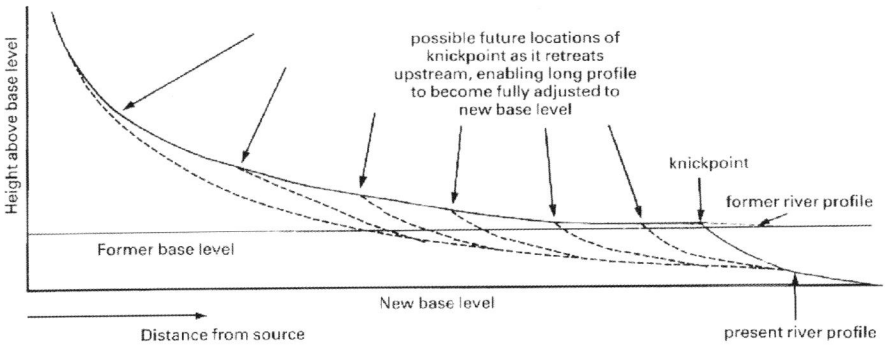

Figure 2.2.23: The adaptation of a river's long profile to an increase in energy (after Collard, 1988).

A good example of a rejuvenated river is the Greta in northwest Yorkshire. Figure 2.2.24 is a construction of what the valley above the village of Ingleton may have looked like before the change in base level and how it appears today. The Beezley Falls are a knickpoint, while below these the new 'profile forms a **valley in valley** feature. Plate 2.6 shows Thornton Force on the same river, another classic knickpoint.

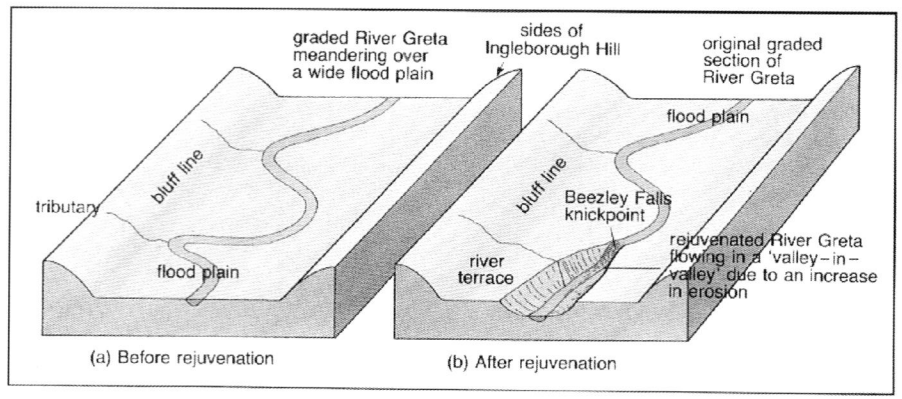

Figure 2.2.24: The River Greta, Yorkshire Dales National Park (a) before and, (b) after rejuvenation (after D. S. Walker, source: Waugh, 1990).

If the uplift of the land, or fall in sea level, continues for a lengthy period, the river may cut downwards to form **incised meanders** (e.g. the Wear at Durham). There are two types of incised meanders: entrenched and ingrown (Figure 2.2.25).

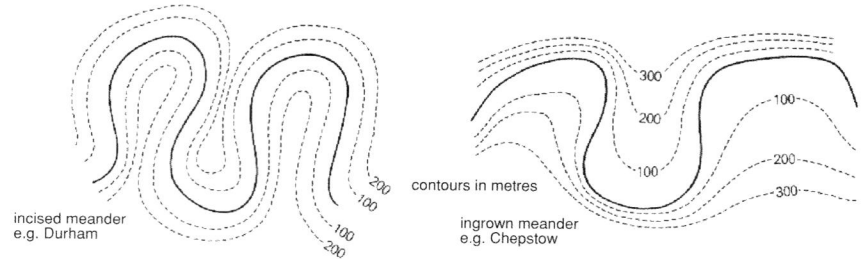

Figure 2.2.25:   *Incised and ingrown meanders (after Clowes & Comfort, 1982).*

Entrenched meanders have a symmetrical cross-section and result from either a very rapid incision by the river or the valley sides being resistant to erosion (e.g. the River wear near Durham). **Ingrown meanders** occur when the uplift of the land, or incision by the river, is less rapid, allowing the river to have time to shift laterally and to produce an asymmetrical cross valley shape (e.g. the River Wye at Chepstow). As with meanders in the lower course of a normal river, incised meanders can also change their channels to leave an abandoned meander with a central meander core. Above the present small flood plain are **river terraces.** A terrace is an area which was once the flood plain of the river but which, following vertical erosion, is now left high and dry above the maximum level of flooding.

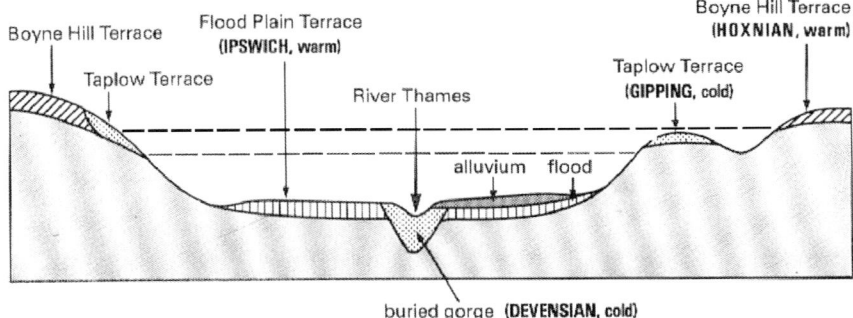

Figure 2.2.26: Cross section of the Lower Thames terraces (after Waugh, 1990).

River terraces offer excellent sites for the location of towns (e.g. London, Figures 2.2.26). Above the present flood plain of the Thames are two earlier ones forming the Taplow and Boyn Hill terraces. If a river erodes rapidly into its flood plain, a pair of terraces of equal height may be seen flanking the river. However, more often than not, the river cuts down relatively slowly, enabling it to meander at the same time. The result is that the terrace to one side of the river may be removed as the meanders migrate.

In conclusion, this chapter has described a number of fluvial processes and landforms that should be of interest to the small boat user. An understanding of the processes, and being able to give names and explanations to the landforms, should add interest to any trip made in a small boat along the course of a river.

2.3 Further Explorations into Life in Rivers and Inland Waterways: The Common Plants and Animals

The wealth of animal and plant life in freshwater, and particularly its diversity, is astounding. As such it would be impossible to do justice to the identification of freshwater life, even that found in Britain, in this book. There are many field guides currently available which will help you (see Further reading). In this section I have tried to select and describe briefly, only the most common and distinctive plants and animals which you are likely to come across. This should form a basis for your interest in the practical art of watching and understanding the living creatures you might encounter on rivers and canals. Table 2.3.1 (next page) gives many of the plants and animals you are likely see, with those in bold described in this section. They are described in order, starting with those you are most likely to see, the trees, followed by flowering plants, then birds, mammals, fishes and finally ending with the cold-blooded creatures.

2.3.1 Plants found in and around Rivers and Inland Waterways

Plant species in rivers and canals can range from truly aquatic plants that live in the water, to wet-loving but terrestrial plants which live around the edges. Canals, like ponds and lakes, if left unmanaged are doomed to fill in eventually; rivers too are subject to change as a result of natural processes and human activities.

2.3.1.1 Waterside Trees

River and canal landscapes are enhanced by the variety of shapes, sizes and seasonal colours of their waterside trees. The canopy of such waterside trees attracts feeding insects and other invertebrates in their hundreds during summer, and when the leaves fall to the water in autumn, they become the source of food for a totally different world of minute animal life. The roots and branches also act as a home to a range of creatures.

The **Alder** (*Alnus glutinosa*) illustrated in Figure 2.3.1 can be a shrub or a proper tree and is Britain's most characteristic waterside tree. Its maximum height is about 40 m but when conditions are not ideal it is often much shorter. Its root system is highly branched and spreads like minute fingers into the water, creating a habitat that is a haven for aquatic invertebrates. It lives on wet ground and can be recognised from a distance as it tilts slightly over the water. It lines the banks of rivers and streams and in fact, grows anywhere its roots can bathe in water and absorb rich minerals. Its leaves are rounded and prominently serrated. Male flowers are firm scaly catkins, borne in small clusters; female flowers are green cones, which ripen to brown with a woody texture and last through winter.

Table 2.3.1: Common Plants and Animals of British Rivers and Inland Waterways (those in **bold** are described in the text).

COMMON PLANTS AND ANIMALS OF BRITISH RIVERS AND INLAND WATERWAYS

TREES
Alder, Black Poplar, White Willow, Crack Willow, Goat Willow, Grey Willow

FLOWERS
Brooklime, Butterbur, Canadian Pondweed, Common Water Plantain, Cuckoo Flower, **Hogweed, Giant Hogweed**, Great Yellow-Cress, **Hemlock**, Horse Radish, **Himalayan Balsam**, Japanese Knotweed, Marsh Bedstraw, Marsh Bird's-Foot Trefoil, **Marsh Marigold**, Marsh Thistle, Nodding Bur-Marigold, **Ragged Robin**, **Common Reed**, Sedge Species, Small Teasel, Snake's Head Fritillary, Trifid Bur Marigold, **Water Crowfoot Species**, Water Forget-Me-Not, **Water Lily Species**, Water Speedwell, **Yellow Flag Iris**

BIRDS
Common Sandpiper, **Coot, Dipper**, Garganey, **Goosander, Great Crested Grebe, Grey Heron, Grey Wagtail, Kingfisher,** Little Grebe (Dabchick), **Mallard, Moorhen, Mute Swan, Sand Martin, Teal**

MAMMALS
<u>Water Dwellers</u>: **Water Shrew, Water Vole, Otter, Mink**
<u>Visitors</u>: Daubenton Bat, Fox, Mole, Polecat, Rat, Weasel

FISHES
Barbel, Bream, Bullhead, **Chub**, Dace, **Eel**, Grayling, Gudgeon, Lamprey, Loach, Minnow, **Perch, Pike**, Rudd, **Trout**, **Salmon,** Sticklebacks

COLD-BLOODED CREATURES
<u>Amphibians</u>: **Common Frog**
<u>Insects</u>: **Caddisflies, Damselflies, Dragonflies, Gnats, Great Diving Beetle, Greater Water Boatman, Mayflies, Midges,** Mosquitos, **Pond Skaters, Springtails, Stoneflies, Water Beetles, Water Boatmen, Water Cricket, Water Scorpion, Water Stick Insect, Whirligig beetle**
<u>Molluscs</u>: **Swan Mussel, Pearl Mussel, Freshwater Limpet**

Figure 2.3.1: Common Alder (Alnus glutinosa) showing tree shape, leaf shape, male and female catkins) (illustration by Philippa Mitchell).

Trees growing in wet places may find difficulty obtaining sufficient nutrients which may be lost in water. To overcome this many have evolved associations with other organisms (symbioses). Alder has root nodules containing nitrogen-fixing bacteria.

The **Black Poplar** (*Populus nigra*) is illustrated in Figure 2.3.2 and is usually regarded as being native to Britain. The leaves are broad and roughly triangular in shape. They are yellow-green, turning bright yellow in the autumn, and about 5-10 cm long. The buds are reddish-brown and pointed and like the leaves, they are arranged alternately along the twigs which is typical of poplars and willows. The male catkins mature in March before the leaves come out. At first they are grey, but turn crimson-red as they release their pollen. It is confined mostly to central and eastern England. It grows on river banks, since it likes moist soil but it will not tolerate stagnant water. This is because the roots breathe. From a distance they often have a characteristic lop-sided trunk which is caused by the prevailing wind and this can allow for easy identification.

Figure 2.3.2: Black Poplar (Populus nigra) showing general tree shape, the shape of the leaves, and female and male catkins (illustration by Philippa Mitchell).

Willows (*Salix spp.*) are illustrated in Figure 2.3.3. They range from creeping shrubs to large trees like (the white willow shown on the left). Their leaves are oval (like the goat willow leaves illustrated) to lanceolate (like the osier leaves shown), usually with serrated edges. The flowers are usually erect catkins (males are often yellow, females are green, ripening to fluffy white, with trees usually only bearing one sex) or 'pussy willow'. The willow, along with the alder, are perhaps the dominant tree species associated with the water's edge, yet the willow's abundance today is related more to the influence of man than to natural development. The most interesting for wildlife is the 'pollard' created by regular cutting. Larger willows are often pollarded (the branches cut back as shown in the illustration of the pollarded crack willow) producing characteristic club-shaped trunks with a spray of slender branches radiating from the crown. The timber is of limited value but some is ideal for cricket bats, walking sticks etc. It is now being developed as a sustainable source of energy.

Figure 2.3.3: Willows (Salix spp.): White Willow tree, pollarded Crack Willow, White Willow leaves and female catkins, Goat Willow leaves and female catkins and Osier leaves (unserrated) and female (illustration by Philippa Mitchell).

Goat Willow (also known as Great Sallow, or **Pussy Willow)** (*Salix caprea*) has more rounded leaves than others which are dark green above and whitish downy undersides. It is the commonest of the sallows. It gets its name because the young spring foliage was fed to goats. Its full potential height is around 10 m. **Grey Willow** (*Salix cinerea*) or common sallow, is a smaller bushy tree which grows on limey as well as acid soils. Its leaves are narrower than those of the goat willow, harder to the touch and downy on the upper side. The Latin name *cinerea* means ashen or cindery. **White Willow** (*Salix alba*) is the largest (up to 20m) and probably most common and familiar willow, with soft green lanceolate leaves which are silky grey beneath. **Crack Willow** (*Salix fragilis*) has slightly darker leaves and brittle shoots that snap cleanly rather than bend.

Osiers (*Salix viminalis*) are smaller plants with very narrow unserrated leaves. They have for centuries been managed to produce long flexible branches used to make baskets and fencing; beds of these tall shrubs still occur in some marshy areas. Hybrids are frequent where different species grow together and can cause confusion but the graceful **Weeping Willow** is a hybrid known as (*Salix x chrysocoma*) is well known and unmistakable, yet it is not native to the British Isles, being introduced here less than 200 years ago. Alder and sallow in particular are important food plants for many insects and are vital members of the freshwater ecosystem.

Many more trees are also found along streams, rivers and canals, yet it is a tragedy that there are not more. Many riverside trees were lost during river 'improvements' carried out to help agriculture. Once, virtually every river below 500m was lined with native trees. In the water-logged sections of carr and fen, alders and willows thrived, and in drier sections trees such as ash, beech and maple, together with shrubby dogwood, spindle or guelder rose, grew where the soil was calcareous, with rowan, silver birch, oaks and Scots pine flourishing alongside rivers flowing over the more acidic rocks. Although millions were removed, not all were lost and pockets of the natural riverine tree fauna can fortunately still be found.

2.3.1.2 Flowers of Rivers and Canals

The flowers of aquatic plants form a tapestry of colour floating on the water surface of rivers and canals, while emergent reeds growing along the channel margins provide a subtle green backcloth. For the riverbank and water-dwelling community of animals, the success of this plant community is vital to their survival.

One of the major benefits water plants give to rivers and canals is a cleansing service. They oxygenate the water and help to purify and nullify the effects of noxious substances. The plant life also determines the variety of habitats available for invertebrates and fish. A marginal reed bed, for example, will shelter an animal community which is in total contrast to that of a lily bed. Whatever the habitat, however, the animal variety increases as plant diversity develops.

Emergent and floating-leaved plants also perform one other major service for the animals: they link the underwater world with the air. For many insects this is vital since the juvenile stages are spent under water while the adults live in the air. Like all forms of life, particular plant species are adapted to specialised conditions. In the centre of a river channel grow submerged and floating species (crowfoots, starworts and water lilies) while at the shallower margins may be found **amphibious** and emergent species such as Amphibious Bistort, Great Yellow Cress and Water Forget-me-not. The interface between water and land might be abrupt, dry and inhospitable, or it might be shallowly sloping, constantly wet and ideal for marshland and fen plants such as Marsh Orchids, Fritillaries and Ragged Robin. The margins, too, are alive with colour. The reds of Hemp Agrimony, Great Willowherb and Purple Loosestrife contrast with the paler flowers of Water Plantain, Meadowsweet and Water Cress, all creating subtle variations that make one section of river different from another.

Brooklime (*Veronica beccabunga*)

Spikes of Brooklime and Water Speedwell in summer make conspicuous splashes of blue on the banks of streams, rivers or canals. As with many plants of wet and muddy places, the fleshy stems of Brooklime creep along the ground, and each stem has a hollow centre. These air spaces allow oxygen and other essential gasses to be transferred from the surface parts of the plant to the roots, which depend on the oxygen for their growth.

Both the common name and the botanical *(beccabunga* comes from the German *beck*, 'a stream') refer to the watercourses in which Brooklime is found; 'lime' comes from the Latin *limus,* meaning 'mud'.

Figure 2.3.4: Brooklime (Veronica beccabunga) (illustration by Philippa Mitchell).

In the 17th century diet drinks made from Brooklime were taken to purge the blood. The herbalists John Gerard and Nicholas Culpeper prescribed the plant as a cure for scurvy. Fried with butter and vinegar, full of 'hot and biting properties', it was said to relieve 'all manner of tumours, swellings and inflammations'. The plant's young, leafy shoots were also widely used in in in Britain and northern Europe, even though the taste was rather bitter.

Butterbur (*Petasites hybridus*)

According to tradition, the large leaves of this liver-coloured plant (Figure 2.3.5) were used for wrapping butter, which is how it got its English name. The leaves can grow to almost 90 cm across and have a dense felting of hairs underneath. The genus name, *Petasites,* comes from the Greek *pettusos,* a broad-brimmed hat, and the 16th-century herbalist John Gerard wrote that the leaf "is bigge and large inough to keepe a man's head from raine, and from the heat of the sunne'.

Figure 2.3.5: Butterbur (Petasites hybridus) (illustration by Philippa Mitchell).

The male Butterbur is common throughout Britain, but the female plant is usually only found in Yorkshire, Lancashire, Cheshire, Derbyshire and Lincolnshire. Occasionally, however, single female flowers occur on an otherwise male plant, and it is presumably from these that sufficient seed is produced to assist the Butterbur's spread to new localities. But it also spreads to cover large areas by means of its creeping, underground roots.

139

In the Middle Ages, the plant's roots were powdered and used to remove spots and skin blemishes. The herbalist Nicholas Culpeper thought that rich gentlewomen should preserve the roots for their poor neighbours, who 'cannot help themselves'.

Canadian Pond Weed (*Elodea canadensis*)

Figure 2.3.6: Canadian Pond Weed (Elodea canadensis)   (illustration by Philippa Mitchell).

This invader from Canada illustrated in Figure 2.3.6 spread so luxuriantly when it first gained a foothold in Britain that it blocked the Thames in several places. It first appeared in Europe in 1836, when it was recorded in Ireland, and by 1842 it was spreading across the lake of Duns Castle in Berwickshire. Thereafter, its progress was aided by botanists, who had no idea of how explosive its growth would be. In 1849 a small scrap of this pondweed was introduced into an aquarium in the Oxford Botanic Garden; it soon escaped to thrive and proliferate in the ditches and ponds around the city, and nine years later the plant was growing profusely in the Thames as far downstream as Reading. When the river started to become blocked with long stems, alarm was felt about the damage that might be caused, but in fact, the danger was almost over.

By the late 1860s the plant's remarkable expansion was coming to an end; nobody knows why. Nowadays it is widespread in ponds, streams, rivers, canals and ditches all over the British Isles, but seldom in such quantities as to cause a serious nuisance. Nevertheless its formidable reputation lives on in the name it won in Worcestershire -'drain devil'.

Common Water Plantain (*Alisma plantago-aquatica***)**

The Common Water Plantain grows on mud, in or beside water. When in flower, from June to August, the Water Plantain makes an impressive show, its tall, graceful flowering stems growing up above the leaves and bearing a pyramid of numerous delicate, pale lilac blooms.

Figure 2.3.7: Common Water Plantain (Alisma plantago-aquatica) (illustration by Philippa Mitchell).

141

The flowers remain closed all morning, opening at the beginning of the afternoon and shutting again in the early evening. Each flower secretes several tiny droplets of nectar in a ring at the base of the stamens. Flies, attracted by these, become covered with pollen as they move from drop to drop, helping to pollinate the flower as they do so. In spite of its name, this plant is no relative of the plantains; it is so called because of the similarity of its leaves to those of some species of plantains. The base of the stem appears almost bulblike, because of the thick, fleshy stalks of the broad, oval leaves which arise from it. It grows to a height of around 60 cm.

Cuckoo Flower (*Cardamine pratensis*)

According to John Gerard, the 16th-century herbalist, this pretty springtime flower was called Cuckoo Flower because it blooms 'for the most part in April and May, when the Cuckoo begins to sing her pleasant note without stammering'. Another 16th-century explanation relates the name to 'cuckoo-spit', the foamy substance with which the plant is often covered. This foam has actually nothing to do with cuckoos, but is produced by the nymphs of a bug called the frog hopper. The cuckoo flower is shown in Plate 2.10.

The spring blooming of Cuckoo Flower has led to folklore associations with milkmaids, their smocks and the Virgin Mary; 'milkmaid' and 'lady's smock' are alternative names. There are other, less pleasant associations. In Austria, it was thought that anyone who picked the plant would soon be bitten by an adder; and in Germany some people believed that bringing the plant indoors would cause the house to be struck by lightning.

Probably because of its more sinister connections in folklore, the Cuckoo Flower was little used in medicine. It is, in fact, safe enough; the leaves may be eaten in salads as a substitute for watercress, as may those of hairy bittercress, a close relative which grows on waste ground.

Hogweed (*Heracleum sphondylium*)

Children have long used the hollow stems of Hogweed as pea-shooters. The plant is the most common species of the parsley family, and its flowers often have bright orange soldier beetles on them. The insects are especially common in July, when the large, flat flower-heads, called umbels, provide a feeding and mating ground for the insects. The flowers (see Figure 2.3.8), with their rather unpleasant scent, also attract the less desirable carpet beetles, which may move on into houses and live in rugs and carpets.

Until fairly recently, Hogweed was gathered for pig fodder, which gave rise to its common name. As well as providing food for swine, the young leaves were once considered a delicacy fit for humans as, when boiled, they taste very much like asparagus. The plant's generic name of *Heracleum* comes from the legendary Greek warrior-hero Heracles, known to the Romans as Hercules, who believed it had medicinal value. It grows to 60-180 cm high and flowers in June - September.

Figure 2.3.8: Hogweed *(Heracleum sphondylium)* and Giant Hogweed (*Heracleum mantegazzianum*) (illustration by Philippa Mitchell).

Its close relative, the Giant Hogweed (*Heracleum mantegazzianum*) and, to a lesser extent, Common Hogweed, are species to be wary of. Their sharp poisonous hairs can easily sting anyone who accidentally comes into contact with the plant. It contains a volatile substance which sensitises the skin. If the infected skin is then exposed to sunlight a reaction occurs and a painful blister is formed which usually takes a long time to heal., especially in hot weather. Both plants should therefore be treated with caution. Giant Hogweed seems to be spreading. For example in County Durham, until 1960 only two colonies of Giant Hogweed were known, one along the River Tees, first sighted in 1944, and the other along the River Wear, sighted ten years later. Then in 1960, a colony was discovered growing alongside the River Wear in Durham and since then more than 50 colonies have been recorded in the county. Giant hogweed sometimes has purple-blotched stems reaching 4 m, with flower-heads up to 60 cm across.

Hemlock (*Conium maculatum*)

In the year 399 BC the Greek philosopher Socrates was accused of impiety on two counts: 'corruption of the young' and 'neglect of the gods whom the city worships and the practice of religious novelties'. He was found guilty, sentenced to death and drank a cup of hemlock, the poison used for judicial executions in ancient Greece.

Figure 2.3.9: Hemlock Water Dropwort (Conium maculatum) (illustration by Meike Stephenson).

Hemlock contains several poisonous alkaloid chemicals, the chief being coniine which derives its name from the Latin name of the plant. All parts of the plant are poisonous, but the seeds contain particularly high concentrations of coniine. Nicholas Culpeper, the 17th-century herbalist, recommended pure wine as an antidote to hemlock poisoning, but this was not to be relied upon. Shakespeare's witches in Macbeth used a 'root of hemlock digg'd i' the dark' in their brew.

Hemlock resembles in appearance many other, harmless members of the parsley family, like the hogweeds already described. There have been several recorded deaths among children who, by using the hollow stems for

144

whistles and pea-shooters, have absorbed enough **poison** to kill them. **If you were to eat hemlock by mistake, respiratory problems or death by paralysis can result**. Hemlock can, however, be fairly easily identified by its smooth, purple-blotched stems and unpleasant, foetid smell. It grows to 90 - 210 cm high and flowers in June-July.

Himalayan Balsam (*Impatiens glandulifera*)

Also called Indian Balsam (Figure 2.3.10), a fusillade of exploding seed capsules may shower the walker who pushes through a thicket of Himalayan Balsam in a moist valley or beside a river bank. For when the green seed capsules of the plant have ripened, their sides spring back, throwing seeds violently for considerable distances. Himalayan balsam also has a foolproof method of ensuring its pollination. When a bumble-bee visits the purplish-pink or white flowers for the nectar contained in the lower sepal, this broad, deep cup closes completely round the insect.

Figure 2.3.10: Himalayan Balsam (Impatiens glandulifera) (illustration by Philippa Mitchell).

As the bee comes into contact with the male and female parts of successive flowers, the flowers are pollinated and the fruits start to form. The plant is often called 'policeman's helmet' because of the shape of the flower, or 'jumping jack' because of the way in which the ripe seed capsule explodes, due to the tensions set up in the fleshy fruit wall. The 4-12 seeds in a capsule may be thrown as far as 2 m, a medium sized plant producing as many as 800 seeds. Nearly all the balsams are naturalised 'foreigners'. Himalayan Balsam was introduced from Asia in 1839, and grown in greenhouses before it escaped into the wild. Within 60 years it had become naturalised in many areas. Orange Balsam was brought from North America. Only the rare yellow-flowered 'Touch-me-not' Balsam *(Impatiens nolitangere)* is native to the British Isles; both its names arise from the effect of touching the explosive seed capsules.

Marsh Marigold *(Caltha palustris)*

As early as March, with snow still on the ground, Marsh Marigolds (see Plate 2.11) may often be seen lighting up windswept marshes and damp woods with their brilliant golden flowers and bright green, glossy leaves. The plants continue flowering well into summer, and are grow best in partial shade.

Some Marsh Marigold flowers are as much as 2 in. (5 cm) across, with as many as 100 stamens. Numerous insects, including many species of fly, visit the flowers for their nectar and pollen; an insect crawling over the stamens becomes covered with pollen and so pollinates the flower. Plants growing on high land in the north of England and in Scotland have smaller flowers, growing from stems sprawling on the ground.

The plant's common name of kingcup is derived from the Old English *cop*, meaning a 'button' or 'stud' such as kings once wore. In many parts of the British Isles, farmers used to hang Marsh Marigolds over the bytes of their cattle on May Day to protect them from the evil-doings of fairies and witches.

Common Reed (*Phragmites australis*)

Britain's tallest grass, the Common Reed (seen in Plate 2.12) has tough, stiff stems which persist throughout the winter. These make ideal thatching material, and plants growing in brackish water produce the best, most durable stems. The wide, tough leaves are also used. In the Norfolk Broads, reeds for thatching are cut between Christmas and early April, as cutting later destroys new shoots. On the other hand, the clearing of waterways choked by reeds takes place in July and again before mid-August to prevent the plants building up stores of food for next year's growth.

The plant's huge feathery heads stand erect, but they may droop as their seeds ripen. Each floret has a dense fringe of silky white hairs which catches the wind and takes the seed with it. Pampas Grass (*Cortaderia selloana)*, a garden species, has similar heads and is closely related.

Tough rooting stems of the Common Reed form tangled networks over the mud on which they grow. The stems are often so long that they stretch right across a waterway, and once established, a reed bed is difficult to get rid of. This is the major plant responsible for the silting-up of freshwater habitats, as its wide branching root system traps particles of silt. Stems die back each winter and new growth builds on the remains the following year, creating a higher and higher reed bed. Numerous insects feed on it, such as larvae of wainscot moths. It provides shelter for nesting birds such as bitterns and marsh harriers and small passerines, such as reed warblers and bearded tits, nest in it.

Water Crowfoot species (*Ranunculus spp.*)

With their summer blaze of flowers, water crowfoots are one of the most characteristic plant groups of our rivers, yet telling the species apart can tax even the expert. To the casual observer, buttercups which grow in water and which have white leaves are, simply, Water Crowfoot.

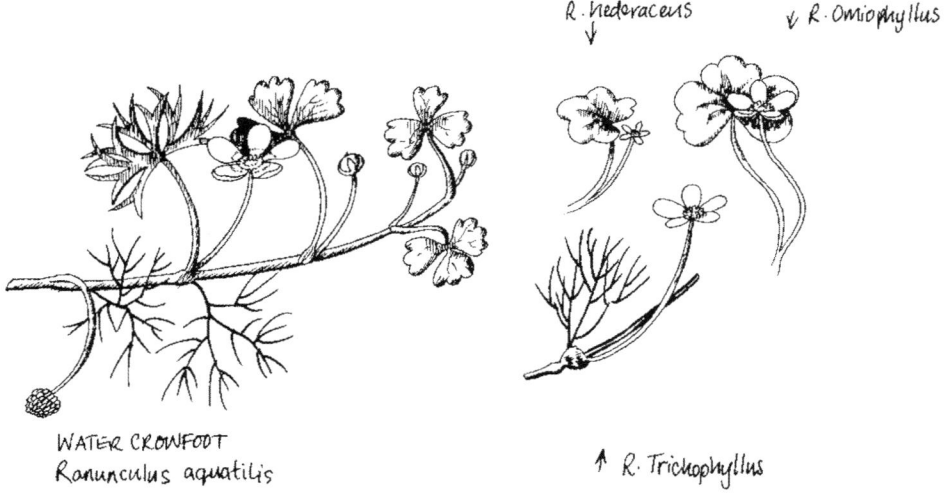

Figure 2.3.11: Water Crowfoot species (Ranunuculus spp.) (illustration by Philippa Mitchell).

To the botanist, however, Water Crowfoot is a collective name for a group of nine very similar plants which, when looked at very closely, are found to be quite different from each other. For example, if a random handful of Water Crowfoot is taken from the water the chances are that it will have two sets of leaves. There are the round ones that float on the surface, and the much-divided, feathery ones which are submerged. In three plants of the Water Crowfoot group: Ivy Leaved Crowfoot (*R. hederaceus*), Three Lobed Crowfoot and Round Leaved Crowfoot (*R. omiophyllus*) the submerged leaves are usually absent. In three others: Thread Leaved Water Crowfoot (*R. trichopyllus*), River Water Crowfoot (*R. fluitans*) and Fan Leaved Water Crowfoot (*R. circinatus*) , the floating leaves are missing. The three remaining Crowfoots have both kinds of leaves. One of them, Brackish Water Crowfoot, grows only in brackish coastal water. The other two: Shield Leaved Water Crowfoot and Common Water Crowfoot, are much alike. But the flowers of Shield Leaved Water Crowfoot are almost an inch across, twice the size of those of the Common Water Crowfoot. The plants are 2.5 - 120 cm long and it flowers in May-June.

Water Lilies

Water Lilies are a characteristic feature of many slow-moving rivers, canals, lakes and ponds, and a wide variety of forms and colours occur. Although only four species are native to Britain, producing either white or yellow flowers, a very large number of alien species and their horticultural cultivars have been introduced to artificial habitats. Many have escaped, adding red, violet and pastel pink water lilies to the range we already have in the wild. Other than the White Water Lily (*Nymphaea alba)* described below, the other three species native to Britain include the Yellow Water Lily (*Nuphar lutea*), Fringed Water Lily (*Nymphoides peltata*) and Least Yellow Water Lily (*Nuphar pumila*).

White Water Lily (*Nymphaea alba)*

To Elizabethan poets and apothecaries, the Water Lily (see Plate 2.13) was 'nenuphar', a word corrupted from the Sanskrit *nilotpala,* describing another water plant, the Indian blue lotus. For poets, the bloom of the White Water Lily, the largest flower in the British flora, was a symbol of purity of heart. For apothecaries, the plant was the source of oils and distillations of nenuphar, used in the treatment of skin blemishes and sunburn, baldness and feminine disorders.

The underwater stems are fleshy and grow as deep as 1.8 m below the surface of ponds and slow-moving rivers. These stems were once eaten as a delicacy, and are sometimes still served as a food in parts of northern. Europe. Some local English names for the White Water Lily approach the beauty of its bloom. In Cheshire it is called 'lady of the lake', and in Wiltshire and Dorset it is known as 'swan among the flowers'. But the beauty is transient. The flowers, on stems up to 2.75 m long, open only towards midday and close again, sinking partly below water, as evening approaches. There are usually more than 20 petals; those nearest the centre of the flower are stamens.

Yellow Flag Iris (*Iris pseudaconis*)

Yellow Flag Iris is a plant of wet ground or shallow water. It grows in marshes, woods and near rivers, canals and streams. According to legend, the first person to wear the iris as a heraldic device was Clovis, who became king of the Franks in the late 5th century. He drove the Romans out of northern Gaul, was converted to Christianity, and changed the three toads on his banner for three yellow irises. Six centuries later, the iris was adopted by Louis VII in the *fleur-de-lys* which he wore in crusade against the Saracens - 'lys' is a corruption of 'Louis'.

Figure 2.3.12: Yellow Flag Iris (Iris pseudaconis) (illustration by Meike Stephenson).

The word *iris* is Greek for 'rainbow', and the plants are grown in gardens for their showy flowers in various shades of yellow, violet, blue and white. Another name for the Yellow Flag Iris is the Sword Flag, as its leaves are sharp-edged and can cut if handled carelessly. The plant is mainly pollinated by bees, which crawl inside the flowers to reach the nectar at the base of the petals. After pollination, the petals fall off to reveal a huge, green capsule. The capsule stalk begins to bend, and the capsule eventually splits to reveal a mass of yellowish-brown seeds.

By the 19th century, the yellow flag was a source of inspiration to English poets, including Gerard Manley Hopkins, who wrote in his journal of 'Camps of Yellow Flag flowers blowing in the wind, which curled over the grey sashes of the long leaves'. The plants grow to a height of 40-152 cm and it flowers in May-June.

Ragged Robin (*Lychnis flos-cuculi*)

The colourful flowers of Ragged Robin resemble those of the Red Campion, but the petals are deeply cut into four narrow lobes at the margin, creating the ragged look described by the common name. This is a plant often found in river-side meadows as seen in Plate 2.14. In spring and early summer, river-side meadows are ablaze with a profusion of colourful flowers: golden yellow marsh marigolds, rich blue scabious, deep pink ragged robin, white sneezewort and sometimes the rare chequered purple fritillary.

Some of Britain's richest areas of grassland, in terms of the number of species that grow there, are those found on the moist alluvial soils of river valleys. Like most areas of grassland in this country, these valley meadows are artificial in the sense that they were originally created by man and, if left completely untended, would eventually revert to the woodland that once covered much of our islands.

Changing meadows. During recent years there have been many changes in traditional agricultural methods, and one casualty has been the river meadow. It was formerly flooded in winter, then left during the spring to allow grasses and herbaceous plants to flower, but better drainage of the land today has led to the demise of many water-loving species as their habitat is destroyed.

Once the land has been drained, it is suitable for ploughing. What was previously summer cattle pasture may make way for grain crops or grasses. If the farmer chooses to cut the existing meadow early for a silage crop, then the developing flowers or fruit are removed. The plants will often try to produce a second crop of flowers, but these too will probably be removed by a second mowing or by grazing. The plant's limited resources are thus rapidly used up and it may not even have sufficient food reserves to survive until the next year. Sometimes meadows, and water meadows in particular, are abandoned as being uneconomical to maintain and the land is soon invaded by more vigorous perennials, scrub and saplings which displace the smaller herbaceous species. In recent years, in some parts of the country, farmers have been encouraged to preserve water meadows by means of Government grants and subsidies.

2.3.2   The Common Birds of Rivers and Inland Waterways

The majority of breeding birds found using our rivers, streams and canals depend not only on the linear watercourses themselves, but also to a vital extent on the mosaic of habitats which flank them. One without the other is rarely good enough.

A walk along open stretches of a river or canal interspersed with sections bordered by reed beds or woodland and scrub, will show you the importance of these hinterland areas for the birds of our waterways. In the open areas, your eyes may be drawn to a stately family of Mute Swans or a young brood of Mallard, while among the reeds and thickets the calls of Buntings, Whitethroats, Tits, Warblers and a host of others, sound from all sides. You may also be rewarded by the sight of a silent, shimmering blue dart as a Kingfisher disappears downstream.

Upland rivers, which tumble over boulders and have rocks instead of emergent vegetation flanking their sides, attract different birds altogether. You can expect to see the bobbing Dipper, but the Grey Wagtail is equally at home here too. The two contrast markedly, however: the dumpy dipper swallows stones to weigh itself down as it feeds submerged in the torrent, while the wagtail flits over stones, snapping up insects as it goes. The Common Sandpiper is also almost restricted to upland rivers in summer.

The differences between a canal and a lowland river can be very important for a bird. Although most prefer the undisturbed tranquillity of a river miles from the beaten track, the threats to raising a family here may be greater from sudden flash floods than from the seasonal hustle and bustle of the canal with its stable water level. Almost any bird may turn up near or over water, so this section has been limited to those which are commonly seen on Britain's rivers and canals. Many of these birds feed in or under water, others feed on insects which breed in the water, or on the seeds of aquatic plants.

Coot *(Fulica atra)*

The Coot is about the size of a small duck and is a relative of the Moorhen, both belonging to the rail family. The Coot is all black, with a white shield above its white bill, and a faint whitish wing bar (but as it does not fly very much it is difficult to see the wing bar). A characteristic habit is the jerking of its head back and forth as it swims. It upends and dives for its food, but its buoyancy makes it cork-like as it resurfaces. It is widespread on lakes, slow rivers, reservoirs, lagoons and even ornamental waters in urban situations, and can become totally accustomed to humans. They are omnivorous, taking mainly plant material, including terrestrial plants, insects, aquatic invertebrates and, to a lesser extent, small fish, mammals and amphibians. The adult bird is around 41 cm long.

Figure 2.3.13:   Coot (Fulica atra) *(illustration by Philippa Mitchell).*

The nest-site is usually in shallow water, often concealed by reeds or other vegetation. The nest is a bulky cup of reed stems and other plant material, built by both sexes, though the male brings most material for the female to add to the structure. Both sexes share incubation and care of the young. Outside the breeding season, the species is gregarious and is often seen in flocks during the winter, but becomes aggressively territorial in the breeding season. Large numbers concentrate on suitable waters in winter which may include brackish or even sheltered marine waters.

Dipper (*Cinclus cinclus*)

Dippers nest beside fast-flowing streams and flit low over the water, landing on favoured stones and boulders. They stand bobbing and bowing for a while, and then plunge into the rushing water to hunt aquatic creatures. They can even walk beneath the surface, gripping the stream bed with their powerful claws.

Figure 2.3.14: Dipper (Cinclus cinclus) (illustration by Philippa Mitchell).

With its bold plumage and strong association with rivers and streams, the dipper is normally an easy bird to identify. Perhaps best likened to a 'thrush-sized wren' (about 18 cm long), it has a familiar, tail-cocked posture, and as it stands on some stone or boulder, it usually bobs up and down. Its legs are strong and look similar to those of a starling, while its beak is like that of a thrush in both colour and size. The upper parts are a rich, plain chocolate brown, and the wings and tail look short in proportion to the distinctly plump body. By far the most conspicuous feature is the large, strikingly white 'bib' extending across the throat and breast, and down on to the belly. The Welsh name for the Dipper, 'Bronwyn a Dwr', literally means white breast of the water.

In the case of English and most Scottish breeding birds, this white bib has a broad chestnut margin which merges gradually into the near-black of the flanks and belly. Irish breeding dippers (and also those in the Hebrides) have considerably less chestnut, and birds of the Continental race (which sometimes stray into east and south-east England in spring and autumn) have almost no chestnut at all. The Continental race of dipper is in fact known as the black-bellied dipper.

It is a streamside bird in all seasons and is seen away from water only when taking a short cut to avoid a loop in the river. It has a territory that may be up to 2 km long, but only a few metres wide. They are reluctant to cross the border with adjacent territories, and prefer to double back when they reach this invisible line. Not only do they have a home reach of water, but also a number of favourite boulders within this, from which they hunt. These are often in mid-stream, and the dipper stands on them, bobbing up and down continuously. Before diving, the bird draws down its 'third eye lid' or nicitating membrane, which is thought to protect its eyes when hunting underwater. The angle of its body when feeding head-down forces the water over its back and helps to keep it submerged.

Goosander (*Mergus merganser*)

Goosanders have the typical long, thin serrated bill of the sawbill ducks, ideally suited to grasping slippery fish, and bright coral-red in colour. It is larger than a Mallard, up to 65 cm long with a wingspan of up to 95 cm. It frequents inland waters ranging from fast-flowing rivers to large lakes. Unlike the Red Breasted Merganser, it is rarely seen on marine waters. It feeds largely on fish, though other aquatic creatures such as crustaceans and insects are also taken.

Figure 2.3.15: Goosander (*Mergus merganser*) (illustration by Philippa Mitchell).

Goosanders nest along the upper reaches of fast flowing rivers and streams, or beside freshwater lakes but in winter they descend to the broad lower reaches. The nest site is usually in a hole in a tree, or in a bank or amongst rocks, and it frequently uses nestboxes. The nest is usually near water but may be up to 1 km away. Little nesting material is used other than down. The pair bond is formed during the winter or early spring and the males desert the females during incubation. The female broods and rears the young alone, and may leave the young before they fledge. The principal food is fish, which they catch by diving, though they may first locate their prey by swimming on the surface with just the head and neck submerged. Underwater, they use only their feet to propel themselves, keeping their wings closed tightly.

The species is gregarious outside the breeding season with large flocks wintering on suitable waters. Some populations are largely resident whilst others migrate to winter in southern England and much of northern Continental Europe.

Great Crested Grebe (*Podiceps cristatus*)

The Great Crested Grebe is a magnificent, conspicuous, and fascinating bird. The back is dark grey, the flanks buff, the belly and foreneck white. It is, however, the beautiful head plumes, for which they were hunted in the nineteenth century, that formerly endangered the species. In winter the plumes are lost.

Figure 2.3.16: Great Crested Grebe (Podiceps cristatus) (illustration by Philippa Mitchell).

During the breeding season Great Crested Grebes frequent shallow inland waters, ranging from large lakes to small ponds and slow flowing rivers. During the spring its noisy territorial squabbles and courting displays can hardly be missed. Food, which is mainly fish, is obtained by diving; some aquatic invertebrates and plant matter are also taken. Their courtship display is quite remarkable. The pair perform an elaborate series of movements, many of which make great use of the head plumes. They shake their heads, swim towards each other with necks low on the water surface, bow, present weed to each other and so on. Hostility is shown to sexual and territorial rivals, though in colonial sites the territory is reduced to the immediate environs of the nest.

The nest is a large structure of aquatic vegetation with a shallow cup to contain the eggs. It is concealed in reeds or other plants and may be free floating, tethered or built up from the bottom. Nests are usually solitary, though colonies are found where conditions are favourable. The adult birds are around 48 cm long. Great Crested Grebes show some winter movements, especially away from smaller lakes. Birds then gather on reservoirs and large estuaries, and are particularly numerous in the southeast.

Grey Heron (*Ardea cinerea*)

The Grey Heron is a timid creature, in spite of its size, and the slow, powerful beat of its retreating wings, is often the only sight most of us are allowed.

Figure 2.3.17: Grey Heron (Ardea cinerea) (illustration by Philippa Mitchell).

However, occasionally you may get a glimpse of this tall, stately bird posing motionless in the shallows, waiting for some unfortunate fish, frog, water vole or large insect to wander within range of its long neck and sword like bill. It is the top bird predator of the freshwater food pyramid, a status which affords it a wide range of diet, but also makes it most vulnerable to the build-up of toxic chemicals in the water. Despite this, and other threats, the number of heron pairs in England and Wales remains around a stable 10000. The large, stately and distinctive-looking grey heron (90-98 cm long) is generally found beside or in fresh water. You may also spot it flying with its long neck tucked in against its body and its legs stretching far beyond the tip of its tail. The harsh, honking 'fraank' call of the heron is a familiar sound on the marshes, instantly recognisable to birdwatchers and the many anglers who come across herons while they themselves are fishing.

Herons breed in colonies, preferring huge nests in trees; but sometimes they nest on cliffs, or at ground level on islands in lakes and lochs, especially in Scotland. Most colonies contain 10-30 nests; though occasionally the number of nests exceeds 100. Herons at a colony refurbish their old nests in January, or even December, ready for the early breeding season. Most colonies have traditional 'club' areas close by, where the 'off-duty' herons stand around. These gatherings are called 'sieges' and provide the sites where the birds begin their courtship display. The male chooses a site and then advertises himself and his site to the females. When one of the latter shows interest, both sexes display together; this leads to mutual preening and the start of nest-building.

Grey Wagtail (*Motacilla cinerea*)

The Grey Wagtail is somewhat confusingly named: although it is true that the upperparts of the bird are a bluish grey, the feature that most often catches the eye is the brilliant patch of lemon yellow on the under tail coverts and on the belly. In summer this yellow colouring often extends up on to the breast. It is at all times conspicuous, even in birds seen flying overhead. Thus it would seem sensible to call this the 'yellow wagtail'. However, the true yellow wagtail has yellow upper parts as well as underparts. Besides its difference in colour, the yellow wagtail is distinguished from the grey by the habitat in which it is seen, for it is a bird of damp meadows and marshes, only occasionally being seen on arable farmland, while the typical habitat of the grey wagtail is beside fast flowing water, in hilly regions in summer, in winter more widespread but never far from water. The adult bird is around 18 cm long. Unlike yellow wagtails which are migrants visiting us in summer from Africa, most grey wagtails remain in Britain or Ireland throughout the year. Their plumage, however, changes with the seasons. The nest is built by the female. She performs the bulk of the work of incubation, which takes 13 to 14 days. However, both sexes feed the young.

158

Figure 2.3.18: Grey Wagtail (Motacilla cinerea) (illustration by Philippa Mitchell).

In many lowland areas, two broods are raised, and the season usually starts early. Most pairs produce their first eggs in the second half of April. Natural nest sites include cavities between exposed roots, wall crevices and holes in the banks of streams.

Kingfisher (*Alcedo atthis*)

The Kingfisher is one of our most brilliantly coloured birds, but its small size and rapid flight can make it difficult to spot. However, once seen it is seldom forgotten. In flight, the kingfisher looks like a flash of bright blue light as it skims fast and low over the water. It is one of Britain's most beautiful birds, with upper parts of an iridescent cobalt blue or emerald green depending on the angle at which the light catches them, and there is a very noticeable paler blue streak stretching from nape to tail. The underparts and cheeks are a warm chestnut colour, which is most obvious when the bird is perching, and there is a patch of white on the throat and sides of the neck. The legs are a bright red. Juveniles generally have a duller plumage, shorter bills with a white tip and dark legs. The adult bird is around 16 cm long.

Figure 2.3.19: Kingfisher (Alcedo atthis) (illustration by Philippa Mitchell).

The nest is made at the end of a tunnel excavated by the birds (15-100 cm into a river bank, depending on how hard the soil is). The tunnel has a circular entrance hole, usually near the top of the bank, which slopes gently upwards and ends in chamber where the nest is built and the young are reared.

The Kingfisher's characteristic method of fishing is to perch on a convenient branch or tree stump, until it sights a small fish. Then it flies up and hovers directly above the spot where the prey is hiding, before diving straight down into the water to catch it with its open beak. The Kingfisher is seldom preyed upon by other birds who avoid it because of the unpleasant taste of its flesh.

Years ago this bird was persecuted for the crime of poaching hatchery fish, but now it is a fully protected species under the Wildlife and Countryside Act of 1981.

Mallard (*Anas platyrhynchos*)

The Mallard is the most common and best known wild duck. It is an ancestor of the farmyard or 'park pond' duck with which it may interbreed to produce colourful variants. The drake (male) has a glossy green-purple head and chestnut throat, divided by a white clerical collar. The duck (female) is mottled and streaked brown, broken only by a blue flash on each wing. Adult birds are around 58 cm long.

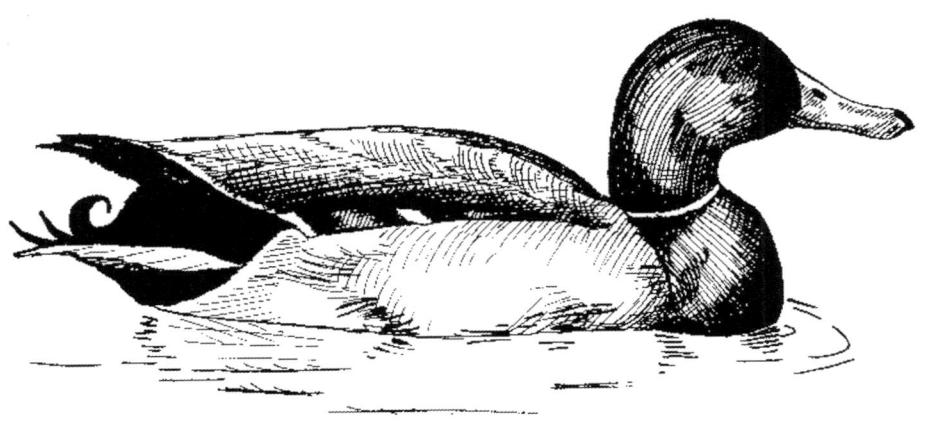

Figure 2.3.20: Mallard (Anas platyrhynchos) (illustration by Philippa Mitchell).

It is found on inland waters of all types and will tolerate human presence to the extent of living in city parks. Mallard are virtually omnivorous, taking a variety of plant material, seeds, aquatic creatures, small fish and even human leftovers. The choice of nest site is equally varied, mostly on the ground in thick cover, but also in hollow trees, among boulders or in nest boxes and baskets. The shallow nest is made of grass and leaves, and is lined with down. The female is responsible for building the nest, incubation and care of the young, though the male may assist in the early stages of incubation. The male loses interest once incubation is under way and may associate with other females. Large flocks of several thousand may occur on inland waters in winter. Sheltered coastal localities and river estuaries are also used. The British population is in the region of 100000 pairs.

Moorhen (*Gallinula chloropus*)

The Moorhen is one of the most characteristic birds of canals and ponds in particular, but is frequently seen on rivers too. It is a common inhabitant of inland waters and wetland of most types..

Figure 2.3.21: Moorhen (Gallinula chloropus) (illustration by Philippa Mitchell).
Sleek blackish brown, with a red forehead, yellow tip to its bill and a white flash on tail and wings, it is usually seen stepping warily around the water's edge or on lily pads, which can just bear its weight spread over the wide extent of its

enormously long toes. Its body is around 33 cm long. It requires less vegetation than the smaller crakes and rails and will nest in waterside trees. It swims freely and obtains much of its food while swimming. It eats a variety of plant matter including pond weeds, seeds and leaves. Animal matter is also taken (insects, aquatic invertebrates, small fish and amphibians). Nest sites are varied, ranging from reedbeds and similar emergent vegetation to floating nests, nests in trees and low bushes, or on branches in the water. The nest is built by both sexes and is a cup of leaves, stems, twigs and reeds. Incubation and care of the young is also done by both sexes and the young of the first brood may help to feed those of the second. When swimming, they often dip their heads under water, and even upend, but only very occasionally dive.

Mute Swan (*Cygnus olor*)

The Mute Swan seen in Plate 2.15 is our only resident swan and scarcely requires description, save to note its red and black knobbed bill. Other swans are winter visitors with yellow unknobbed bills. Europe's largest bird is arrogantly aware of its status: breeding pairs (they mate for life) vigorously defend their nest pile of broken reeds and water plants, bullying smaller birds and even snorting, hissing and flapping at humans.

The Mute Swan is frequently described as a royal bird, and in fact all swans were once said to belong to the Crown, just as forests were reserved for royal deer hunting. Noblemen and city guilds were also given a right to own swans; a marking system of cuts and nicks on the swan's bill was used to identify the ownership of each bird.

Today the Dyers and the Vintners City of London livery companies are the last lawful owners (apart from the Queen). The Dyers use a single nick on the side of the bill, while the Vintners use two. The Queen's birds are not marked at all. This ownership of swans is taken as applying only to the Thames; elsewhere swan populations are unmarked and are treated as wild birds.

Each July the colourful ceremony of swan upping, when the cygnets are rounded up and marked, takes place on the Thames. Three groups of swan uppers, one from each livery company and one led by the Queen's swanherd, row for four or five days up the Thames, from Maidenhead to Pangbourne, herding each brood of cygnets and marking them according to the marks found on their parents.

The swan has no serious natural predators, although foxes and pike will sometimes take unguarded cygnets; and pike have been known to drown adult swans by holding their heads under water. The only real threat to the swan comes from human encroachment on its natural habitats. Overhead power cables are a major hazard to swans in flight and a number also die

163

every year from oil pollution and mercury poisoning. Until the ban on the use of lead shot in angling, a common cause of death was lead poisoning. An adult swan that is fortunate enough to escape all those threats to its life, however, can live up to 15 years and sometimes even longer; but on average a swan that succeeds in fledging will only survive for two to three years. The adult mute swan is around 1.5 m long.

Sand Martin (*Riparia riparia*)

Sand Martins are summer visitors related to House Martins and Swallows, though are much smaller. You almost always find them near sandy cliffs, soft river banks or sometimes in sand quarries, for here they dig their long tunnels, often in colonies numbering hundreds of birds (see Plate 2.16).

Figure 2.3.22:   *Sand Martin (Riparia riparia) (illustration by Philippa Mitchell).*

The Sand Martin feeds on the wing and when seen in flight silhouette, they are very like their relative the House Martin, but their brown plumage is altogether distinctive. It is around 12 cm long. Because their flying insect food is missing in winter, the Sand Martin migrates to west Africa between September and March-April. The wintering area of the Sand Martin (the Sahel on the southern fringe of the Sahara desert in north Africa) was subjected to severe drought in the in the summer of 1968 when the rains failed completely. Trees died and the loss of foliage meant no insects were available for the Sand Martins to feed on. In Britain, the Sand Martin population had been at a high level through the early 1960s, but only around one third of the birds came back in the spring of 1969. The numbers are recovering, but in the early 1980s Britain's numbers of Sand Martins were still well below the levels of the early 1960s.

Teal (*Anas crecca*)

The Teal is a pigeon-sized duck, fairly common but secretive, often nesting away from water. The male has a chestnut brown head with large green eye patch bordered by a narrow line of yellow. The back and flanks are grey and the breast is buff speckled with brown. The female is mottled in browns and buffs like so many other surface feeding ducks. It frequents most inland waters, marshes and rivers, favouring shallow water, where it can dabble for animal material (mostly in summer) and plant material (mostly seeds) in winter.

Figure 2.3.23:   Teal (Anas crecca) (illustration by Meike Stephenson)

165

The nest site is on the ground in thick cover, rarely far from water. The nest is a hollow formed of grass and leaves lined with down. The female is responsible for building the nest, incubation and care of the young. The species pairs in the winter quarters or on migration to the breeding areas. The males are promiscuous and pay no attention to the females once incubation commences. It is around 35 cm long. The resident summer population is around 1500 to 2600 pairs, but this can rise to some 140000 in autumn when Britain receives a huge influx of Continental birds from Iceland, Scandinavia and parts of Russia. Flocks will inhabit sheltered coastal waters, salt-marshes and estuaries in winter.

2.3.3   Mammals of British Rivers and Inland Waterways

There are only three truly aquatic freshwater mammals in Britain: the Otter, the Water Shrew and the Water Vole. The rest are either: marine, like the seals; extinct, like the Beaver; or introduced, like the Mink. Several other mammals can certainly be seen along rivers and canals, but they rarely take to the water by choice. Moles, for instance, frequently feed near rivers where the damp soil is a prime source of succulent worms, and foxes are drawn seasonally to canals and river margins to feed on duck, Coot and Moorhen chicks, while the aggressive Weasel has been observed swimming in pursuit of fleeing Water Voles. Apart from land mammals, bats patrol the air over large rivers and canals to take advantage of the insect life above the water.

The three truly aquatic British mammals contrast so markedly with one another in lifestyles that they do not compete with each other.

Water Shrew (*Neomys fodiens*)

The diminutive Water Shrew is probably, for its size, the most ferocious animal in Britain. It is the largest of five species of shrew found in the British Isles. Even so, they weigh little more than a 50 pence piece. They are more active during the day than at night and will tackle prey larger than themselves with enormous relish and tenacity. Although they feed most during the day, they are very difficult to see.

The body size is up to 9 cm long with the tail up to 7 cm. They are a dark colour, almost black, but may have a brownish tinge and are usually white on their underside. They can live up to about 18 months and feed on invertebrates underwater as well as on land. They will also eat small fish or frogs which are paralysed or killed by a venomous saliva. Their coat is very water repellent, and the fur traps air bubbles so that the water shrew remains very buoyant when afloat.

166

Figure 2.3.24: Water Shrew (Neomys fodiens) (illustration by Meike Stephenson).

Water Vole (*Arvicola terrestris*)

Water Voles are frequently seen swimming across rivers and canals, leaving characteristic V-shaped ripples in their wake.

Figure 2.3.25: Water Vole (Arvicola terrestris) (illustration by Philippa Mitchell).

The reputation of the Water Vole has suffered through constant confusion with the Brown Rat. In fact the two are dissimilar in all important respects, for although the rat is quite common along urban and rural towpaths, the Water Vole is more often seen and is more often associated with slow water habitats.

The rounded nose, small ears and rather short tail of the vole are important features, but these are not always seen if the animal is disturbed. A walk along the canal bank can be punctuated at intervals by the abrupt 'plop' of voles diving from the water edge where they have been resting or feeding. Under these circumstances a good view is virtually impossible, since they will swim underwater until they are among vegetation or until they reach their burrows. The burrows often have entrances both on the bank and below water level, so the voles can reach safety without being seen, and can escape in times of danger.

Water Voles are territorial, and males in particular usually remain within their own section of water. Male territories are about 130 m, while females take up much shorter ranges and are more inclined to establish new breeding areas. On heavily used canals, vole numbers remain quite high, suggesting that the problems of burrow erosion, water turbulence and pollution are not significant. Certainly voles swim at about the same speed as most canal craft and are able to avoid any obvious danger. They feed on the leaves, stems and roots of waterside plants and are therefore by no means dependent on purely aquatic life.

Otter (*Lutra lutra*)

Our premier aquatic mammal is unquestionably the Otter, but unfortunately during the last 30 years it has declined drastically in abundance. The agility of this animal in water is incredible. Its smooth contours and the apparent bonelessness of its body allow it to execute underwater acrobatics which defy description. Other playful habits include tossing pebbles and sliding down muddy banks. The otter is a very streamlined strong swimmer, its five-nailed toes being webbed like a duck's foot. Its coat is made of two layers: the visible one is long and coarse, while the under-fur is fine, glossy and so thick that it is almost impossible to part. It is this under-fur which traps a layer of air bubbles when the otter submerges, which insulates the animal and prevents water getting to the skin.

Before diving, the otter takes a deep breath, and is able to stay under water for 3-4 minutes, during which time it can swim up to a quarter of a mile, using its powerful tail as a rudder. When hunting for eels (a favourite food) the otter will turn over stones at the bottom of the river with its paws.

168

Figure 2.3.26: Otter (Lutra lutra) (illustration by Meike Stephenson)

Contact with other otters is maintained chiefly by scent messages in the form of a special anal jelly, produced by a pair of anal glands under the tail, and droppings called spraints. The full significance of these messages is not known, but research has shown that the chemical character of the jelly is as individual as a signature, and that otters can distinguish between deposits left by different otters. The jelly may also be used by the dog otter to tell whether a particular bitch is 'on heat'. The spraints are much easier to find than the special jelly. They are left in places where other otters are most likely to find them: on ledges, under bridges or on rocks in mid-stream. Good sites for depositing spraints will be used year after year. The spraints are dark in colour and have a very distinctive, not unpleasant, musky smell, once smelt never forgotten. They can be any length up to 10 cm and any consistency depending on what the otter has been eating. Examination of their contents gives a good idea of the otter's diet as the hard parts of its prey, such as fish bones, pass through the gut without much change. Otters feed mainly on fish, and for centuries gamekeepers have waged war on them under the impression that otters damaged fish stocks. Otters certainly do take trout, and the occasional salmon, but they are just as likely to catch eels and more sluggish coarse fish, frogs, tadpoles and even water birds such as moorhens, which they catch by coming up underneath them as they swim, and pulling them under the water. The total length of the otter is 1 - 1.2 m.

It is clear that the European Otter is vanishing from many of its haunts, chiefly because of man made changes to its environment. Their distribution is mainly restricted to South West England, East Anglia and parts of Wales, but they are more numerous in Scotland. Polluted rivers, for example, will affect the food supply and detergents in the water can destroy the otter's indispensable waterproofing. Once its diving suit is damaged, the Otter can no longer resist the wet and cold and so succumbs to both and dies. Its numbers have

169

declined so much in England and Wales that it is now a protected species. Positive steps have been taken to protect its environment and promote its increase by the setting up of nationwide Otter haven projects. There is still a great deal of argument over whether the Mink, which escaped from fur farms and now lives in many areas in the wild, competes to a serious extent with the Otter. Scotland is undoubtedly the best place to see Otters today.

Mink (*Mustela vison*)

Mink were introduced from North America and bred wild for the first time in 1956 (on the River Teign in Devon).

Figure 2.3.27: Mink (Mustela vison) (illustration by Philippa Mitchell).

Many people have suggested that Mink are partly to blame for the decline of the Otter, but since the remains of Mink have been found in Otter droppings, any interference is likely to be the other way round. Certainly Mink have spread dramatically along river systems and have become pests in some places. They are very effective killers, as are all the Weasel family, and although fish are often taken, Moorhens and voles are equally important in their diet. Mink are mainly nocturnal and are dark brown in colour. As with Otters, the best method of discovering their presence is to look for footprints on the water's edge. It seems that canals are as suitable as rivers, and that Mink will tolerate a high level of disturbance. If numbers increase further, it may well prove necessary to control their numbers, but it is difficult to see how this can be achieved. The retraining of otter hounds to hunt for Mink is only likely to succeed in disturbing any Otters that are in the neighbourhood. Trapping has already been attempted in some places, but with only limited success.

2.3.4   Fishes of British Freshwaters

The size range of British fish is immense. Minute Stickleback weigh only a few grams while large Pike and Salmon may exceed 25 kg (55 lb). All but the most polluted of our fresh water areas are capable of supporting fish. About half the British species are large enough to be of interest to anglers, and this has frequently resulted in their natural range being increased by artificial means. The present day distribution of the smaller fish reflects more accurately their natural range, because they have not been introduced deliberately into new sites for commercial reasons.

The sporting fish which are caught on the fly (salmon, brown trout and grayling), prefer clear, cool, clean rivers with gravel beds. All spawn in oxygen rich substrates since their eggs would die immediately if they were smothered by fine silts. Other fish, such as Barbel, Chub, Minnow, Stone Loach and Brook Lamprey, also spawn in gravels, but their requirements are generally less exacting. These species can therefore breed in a greater variety of rivers at lower attitudes.

The majority of coarse fish, on the other hand, tend to spawn among the cover of water plants. Pike, Carp, Tench, Bream, Rudd, Roach, Ruffe, Perch and Bass are the most adept at this strategy. Weedy canals, with their muddy bottoms and sluggish flows, are thus frequented primarily by coarse fish such as Perch and Roach. Canals are intensively fished and they are usually stocked with commercially bred fish. Populations of fish popular to the angler have, certainly developed artificially in canals, whereas smaller fish, notably Gudgeon, Ruffe, Minnow and Stickleback, have probably established themselves naturally by migrating from streams connected to the canal network.

Chub (*Leuciscus cephalus*)

The Chub is a member of the Carp family, *Cyprinidae*, common in Europe and North America. The Chub is closely related to the Dace, but it is twice the size and has a much broader head. It is a large-mouthed fish with large, black-edged scales, and attains a maximum length and weight of about 60 cm and 7-8 kg. Chub are good bait fish, and large specimens are caught for sport or food. However, they are so boney that they are rarely eaten by humans. They are voracious and prey on insects, plants, and other fish. Some Chub will take a fisherman's artificial fly. Chub can often be seen from bridges, because the young fish live in close schools and often swim near the surface.

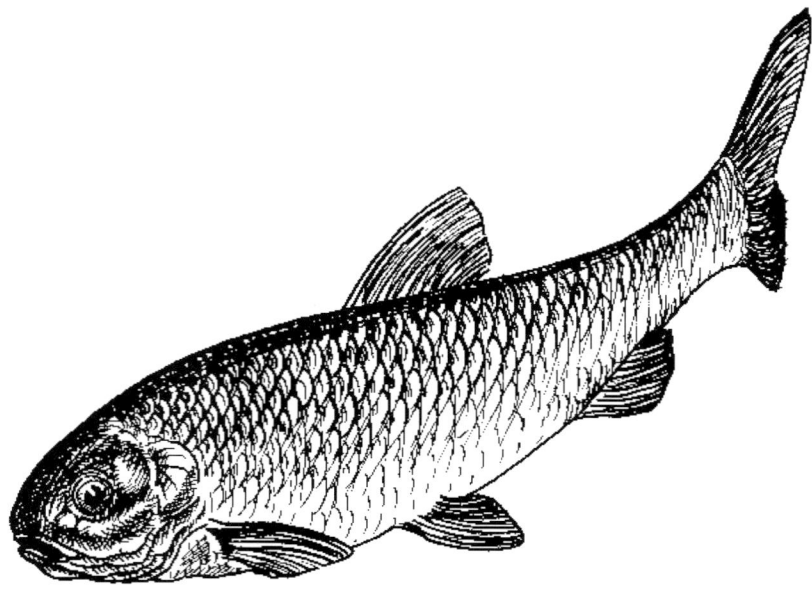

Figure 2.3.28:   Chub (Leuciscus cephalus) (illustration by Philippa Mitchell).

Eel (*Anguilla anguilla*)

The remarkable story of the Eel starts and finishes deep in the Atlantic Ocean for in March and April the adult Eels spawn in the deep water of the Atlantic Ocean including the Sargasso Sea north east of the Caribbean, and then they die. Meanwhile, the tiny larvae that hatch from the eggs start their amazing journey of over 3000 miles across the Atlantic to Europe. The young Eels move into rivers, streams and lakes to develop until, some years later, they are ready to leave their freshwater habitat and return to the sea to breed.

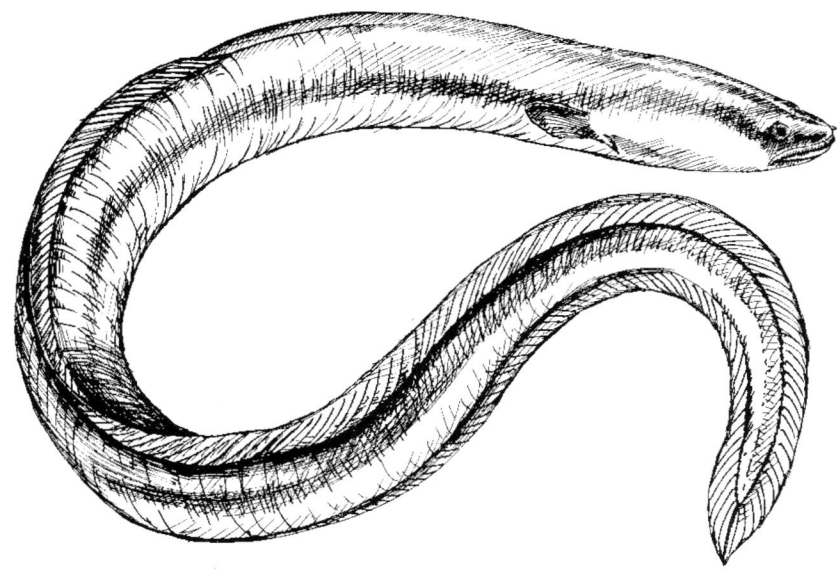

Figure 2.3.29: Eel (Anguilla anguilla) (illustration by Philippa Mitchell).

On their way to the sea they travel along rivers, streams, ditches and other waterways, even overland on dark wet nights, when their thick skin and narrow gill slits prevent them drying out. Little is known about how Eels navigate across thousands of miles of ocean, but they may be guided by the increase in temperature or saltiness of the water as they head towards the Sargasso Sea.

Perch (*Perca fluviatilis*)

The name 'Perch' is sometimes confusingly applied to a variety of other fishes.
The Common Perch is well known and popular as both a food and a sport fish. They have two dorsal fins, the first spiny (for protection) and the second soft-rayed.

Figure 2.3.30: Perch (Perca fluviatilis) (illustration by Philippa Mitchell).

Perch are carnivores and inhabit quiet ponds, lakes, streams, and rivers. They are well known for their habit of lurking motionless in shady parts of slow flowing waters, but nevertheless they are fierce predators. They spawn in spring, the female at that time laying strings of eggs in the shallows among water plants, branches, and the like. The Common, or European, Perch is greenish with dark, vertical bars on the sides and reddish or orange colouring in the lower fins. It grows to a maximum weight of about 3 kg, rarely more.

174

Pike (*Esox lucius*)

The Pike is a voracious freshwater fish, of the family *Esocidae*, and it is caught both commercially and for sport. It can be recognized by its elongate body, small scales, long head, shovel like snout, and large mouth armed with strong teeth. The dorsal and anal fins are far back on the tail. It has pale, bean-shaped spots on the body and lacks scales on the lower parts of the gill covers. It is a fairly common and prized game fish with a maximum size and weight of about 1.4 metres and 21 kg.

Figure 2.3.31: Pike (Esox lucius) (illustration by Philippa Mitchell).

Solitary hunters, Pike lie motionless in the water or lurk in a clump of weeds. As the prey comes within reach, they make a sudden rapid lunge and seize it. They usually eat small fishes, insects, and aquatic invertebrates, but larger forms also take frogs, waterfowl and small mammals. They spawn in weedy shallows from late winter through spring. The Pike's fierce looking set of needle-sharp teeth in the upper jaw point backwards to prevent prey from escaping.

Trout (*Salmo spp.*)

Trout are closely related to Salmon, both members of the family *Salmonidae*, which are usually restricted to freshwater, though a few types migrate to the sea between spawnings. They are important sport fishes and are often raised in hatcheries for later transfer to ponds, lakes and waterways. Two species are common in British waters: the Brown Trout and the Rainbow Trout. The Brown Trout (*Salmo trutta*) is a common European trout that has been widely introduced into suitable waters around the world.

Figure 2.3.32: Brown Trout (Salmo trutta) (illustration by Philippa Mitchell).

Rainbow Trout (*Oncorhynchus mykiss*), noted for their spectacular leaps and hard fighting when hooked, are brightly coloured fish of lakes and swift streams. They are covered with small black spots and have a reddish band along either side.

Trout usually live in cool freshwater, often among submerged objects or in riffles and deep pools. They are native to the Northern Hemisphere but have been widely introduced to other areas. Their diet consists of insects, small fishes and their eggs, and crustaceans. Trout spawn between autumn and spring and bury their eggs in a gravel nest scooped out by the female on a streambed. The eggs take two to three months to hatch, and the newly hatched trout, or fry, become known as fingerlings when they leave the nest and begin feeding on plankton.

Salmon (*Salmo salar*)

The adult Atlantic Salmon averages about 4.5 kg in weight and is a powerful fish which has the ability to leap waterfalls or barriers in the river as high as 3 m or more. One fascinating aspect of the behaviour of salmon (and some trout species) is their homing instinct: their ability to return to the stream of their birth after migrating thousands of kilometres in the ocean over 1 - 3 years. Salmon are silvery-sided fishes while in the ocean, but during the breeding season (October to March) a change in coloration occurs that varies from one species to another, but the males generally develop hooked jaws. Atlantic salmon, though fished commercially in certain areas, are valued chiefly as sport fish.

Figure 2.3.33:   *Salmon (Salmo salar) (illustration by Philippa Mitchell).*

Female Salmon lay their eggs in small hollows called 'redds' which they make in gravel beds. The eggs depend on having a continuous supply of fresh, oxygenated water. As soon as the eggs hatch and the yolk sac is absorbed, the salmon fry migrate to sea, returning 1-3 years later to the same place to spawn themselves.

2.3.5   Cold-blooded Creatures of British Waterways

Rivers and canals support a vast array of invertebrates, ranging from the large crayfish to microscopic single-celled zooplankton such as the microscopic amoeba.   Between these extremes are tiny mites, snails, mussels, leeches, worms and, most interesting of all, thousands of insects of all shapes and sizes.

2.3.5.1 Amphibians

The Common or Grass Frog (*Rana temporaria*) is famed for its leaping ability, powered by its long, muscular back legs, and is easiest to spot in spring when the adults emerge from their winter retreats.   The shade and markings of the Common Frog's skin vary enormously but the basic colour ranges from a pale greenish-grey, through bright yellow to a dark olive-coloured brown. The skin can be marked with spots, speckles or marbling in black, brown or red. The only regular markings are the dark cross-bars on the limbs, and streaks behind and in front of the eyes.

Figure 2.3.34:   Common Frog (Rana temporaria) (illustration by Philippa Mitchell).

One of the most distinctive features of the frog is its large jewel-like eyes, each of which is protected by a thick immovable upper and lower lid and a thin movable transparent inner eyelid, known as the nictitating membrane. The frog makes good use of its wide mouth and long tongue to snap up whole invertebrates. Slugs and worms are a favourite diet, but it will also catch flies and insects.

Frogs hibernate in winter so they are not usually seen until February or March when they emerge from their winter retreat and begin to congregate (travelling up to half a mile) at breeding sites (such as ponds with water flowing in and out of them or canals). The males attract females by their croaking chorus and the female lays over 2000 eggs as the male releases his sperm to fertilise them. Each egg is 2-3 mm in diameter and enclosed in an envelope of jelly. The mass of eggs, which swell up once in contact with water, is known as 'frog spawn' and can easily be found in ponds, ditches, canals or other slow moving water bodies in spring time. Only a few eggs survive to grow into adult frogs, most being eaten by predators such as Herons, Gulls, Ducks, Snakes, Hedgehogs, Shrews, Badgers, Rats, Weasels, Stoats, Otters, Mink and Foxes.

Those which survive develop into a tadpole in 10-21 days, gaining nourishment from the egg yolk, until the mouth forms when it can eat algae. It breathes by means of 3 pairs of external gills, and normally the hind leg stumps appear after about 5 weeks, and the young adult frog (12-15 mm long) stage is reached after about 12 weeks (in May/June). By October/November they are about 20 mm long, double their size by the following autumn, and reach sexual maturity in the third year.

2.3.5.2 Insects

A remarkable variety of insects have become adapted to life in the water or on its surface, some eating aquatic plants while others are predators on these vegetarians. The vegetarians are usually present in greater numbers than the predatory insects. However, it is often difficult to tell them apart since, for example, the larva of one species might be a predator, while the adult is a vegetarian and *vice versa.* The struggle for life in water involves different insects in four main habitats within the canal or river: the surface, just below the surface, the open water and the bed. Each habitat has its own community of predators and vegetarians, each adapted to the particular problems of its chosen niche.

Dragonflies and Damselflies are probably the best known and most easily observed insects of rivers. A very common life cycle for many river insects involves an aquatic larva stage and a free-flying terrestrial adult stage. Apart from the young of Dragonflies and Damselflies, juvenile Mayflies, Stoneflies and some bugs are also called 'nymphs'. This term is reserved for larvae which metamorphose into adults without going through a pupal stage. Thus, these insects have larvae which, when mature, crawl out of the water to shed their skins and become instant airborne adults. The Mayflies, which belong to this group, are probably best known to fishermen because of their importance as a source of fish food. Mayflies are also unique in the insect world in having two, not one, adult stages. Despite this, Mayflies live for only a day.

The other insect group to arouse interest is that of the Caddisflies, which rank as the most resourceful of aquatic house builders. Some of the larvae build protective mobile homes of tiny stones, while others crawl around inside tubes of plant stems and leaf debris, disguised as sticks.

Surface Life. The surface of the water collects floating debris, such as pollen grains, dead insects and leaves, that provides food for a variety of insects. This plant material attracts large congregations of the most primitive of insects, **Springtails**. There are two British species which have adapted to life on the water, the most common of the two being the tiny (1.5 mm) *Podura aquatica*. These may be seen with the naked eye as blue-black clusters of creatures which leap about on the surface of stagnant waters when disturbed. Along with the bodies of dead insects, these springtails are preyed upon by a whole host of bugs and beetles. These include the **Watercrickets** and **Pond Skaters**, both of which belong to the bug order *Hemiptera*, despite their common names. As with all bugs, these surface dwellers have piercing mouthparts with which they suck the juices of their prey. A common surface predator is the **Whirligig Beetle** which feeds upon small insects that fall on to the water surface. Unlike the predatory bugs, the Whirligig Beetle can dive for food beneath the water surface as well.

The insect order Odonata, the Dragonflies, is represented on British waterways by two suborders, the Zygoptera, or Damselflies, and the Anisoptera, the Dragonflies themselves. In summer the territorial nature of the Dragonflies can be seen as they patrol their own patch of water like whirring miniature helicopters. The beauty of the terrestrial adult contrasts markedly with the drab and ugly aquatic larvae, yet both stages are carnivorous. Damselflies share much in common with the Dragonflies, but they are much smaller and more delicate, their flights being silent, gentle flits from reed to reed. Dragonflies have stout bodies and powerful flight, their hind wings are broader at the base than their forewings and, when at rest the wings are always held out flat on either side (Figure 2.3.55 a). Damselflies, on the other hand, have more slender bodies and weak, fluttering flight (Figure 2.3.35 b). Their fore and hind wings are similar in shape and, when at rest, are held over the back, either together or slightly parted. Their eyes are more widely separated than those of Dragonflies. There are about 15 species of Damselfly in Britain today, and almost half these species have blue and black bodies, with variable markings. So this does not make for easy identification of Damselflies. The Damselfly larvae are also more slender than those of Dragonflies as shown in Figure 2.3.35 c.+

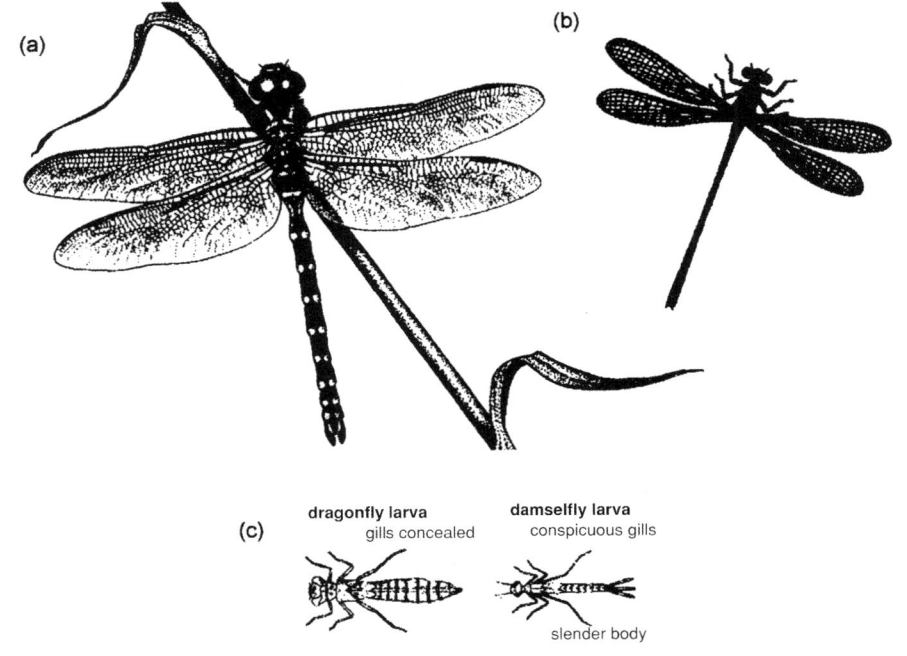

Figure 2.3.35: (a) Aeshna juncea, one of the commonest of the larger dragonflies with a wingspan of about 95 mm; (b) Ischnura elegans, the Common ischnura damselfly (about 30 mm long); and (c) dragonfly and damselfly larvae compared.

Under the film. Living just below the surface film of still water are the vegetarian larvae of some species of Biting Midges and Non Biting Midges. These feed on algae and decaying plant material, respectively. Living plants also provide food for some aquatic beetle larvae and at least one group of moth caterpillars called **China Mark Moths**. The larvae of reed beetles, long and narrow beetles with brilliant metallic sheens, feed on submerged plants and obtain their oxygen supplies by tapping into the air spaces of their food plant. The caterpillars of China Mark Moths live inside protective cases made from fragments of the floating leaves of water plants beneath which they feed.

Life is hazardous close to the surface, as many of the larger insect predators regularly rise to the surface to replenish their air supply, and may take a quick meal at the same time. Species such as the **Water Boatman** and the **Great Diving Beetle** would find easy pickings among the herbivorous larvae that they see on the leaves of surface plants.

181

Open water. Many of the insect predators are found swimming in areas of open water. Among the more prominent are the Water Beetles; these include some of the largest aquatic insects. Among these are the fearsome *Dytiscus* species, commonest and largest of which is the **Great Diving Beetle** *(Dytiscus marginalis)* with a length of 3-5 cm. It attacks other aquatic creatures, including small fish and tadpoles as well as virtually any other insect it encounters. Equally ferocious are the **Greater Water Boatmen** of which we have four species in Britain. These large bugs, some 15 mm long, often take on insects, and even fishes, bigger than themselves. They subdue their prey by injecting them with a poison.

Life on the bed. Above a certain speed and volume, water carries fine particles away, leaving no foothold for rooted plans. Typical of headstreams, such conditions occur throughout many of Britain's northern and western river systems. Their stony substratum harbours an abundant fauna as seen in Figure 2.3.36.

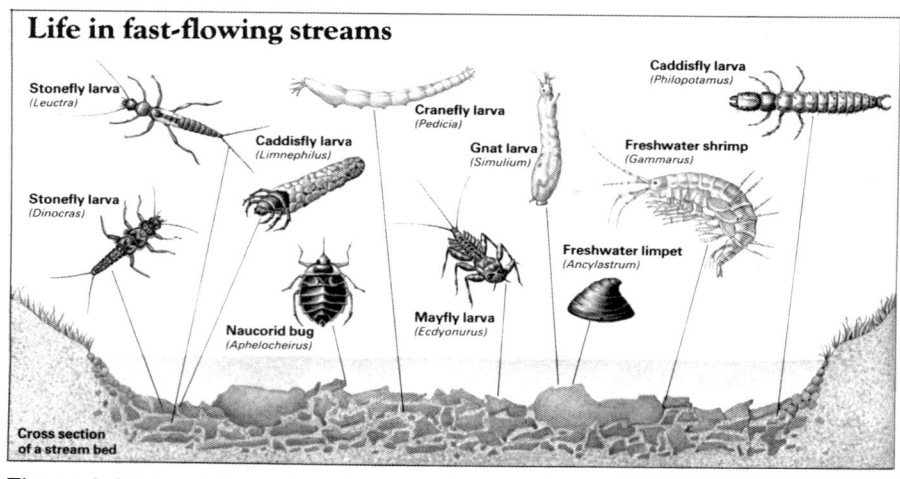

Figure 2.3.36: Life in fast flowing streams (source: The Reader's Digest, The Living Countryside – Along the Riverbank © 1985).

However, these animals face an unending struggle to find enough to eat. Some are specialised to cling on to an exposed surface, while others obtain their food by filtering the water. Insects predominate and the larvae of Stoneflies, Mayflies and Caddisflies are, almost without exception, aquatic. This is also true of two families of the True Flies, the Non-biting Midges (Chironomids) and the Buffalo Gnats (Simuliids). In other groups the common stream dwellers are made up of: a few crustaceans, notably *Gammarus* (the freshwater shrimp) and sometimes crayfishes; a few snails, of which *Ancyclastrum*, the freshwater limpet, is well adapted to life in a fast flowing current; of arachnids, many species of water mite; the flatworms; some worms; and of the fish the trout, the bullhead and the stone loach.

In lowland river reaches, by far the most prolific place to live for many vegetarians and predators alike, is on the bed. Here are found a whole range of water plants and a rich supply of organic silt and debris washed down from the upper reaches, which form the basis for the food chain. This is where the larval, or nymphal, stages of most aquatic insects live and feed. All face the problem of how to obtain oxygen without continually moving up to the surface to replenish stores. Most overcome this problem by possessing gills which allow oxygen from the water to diffuse into the insect. However, not all species live in oxygen-rich water; some larvae, especially those of flies, live in muddy deoxygenated places in stagnant ponds and ditches. The larvae of some species of Non-biting Midges overcome this problem by extracting oxygen from their surroundings and then storing it by means of haemoglobin in their bodies. The so called Rat-tailed Maggots, larvae of some hoverflies, have snorkel-like siphons which can extend up to 15 cm to reach the water surface and air.

Although some species of **Mayfly** and **Stonefly** larva (Figure 2.3.36) are carnivorous, most are vegetarian and eat fragments of plants. The Mayfly larva may live anything from a few months to three years, depending upon the species, before reaching adulthood. **Stonefly** larvae, also known as 'creepers', especially to fishermen, live for one to three years before becoming adult. Larvae of these two insect groups are often abundant in streams and rivers and provide a rich source of food for other insects, fish and even birds such as the dipper. Every stretch of standing or running water holds at least one species of Caddisfly whose larvae usually conceal themselves in protective cases of sticks, gravel, leaves or even snail shells.

The most abundant of bed and plant dwelling insect predators are the larvae of Water Beetles. Just as the adult beetles rule the open waters, so the larval stages are the 'tigers' of the pond bed. Even species such as the Great Silver Water Beetle whose adult is a vegetarian, have predatory larvae with sharp curving jaws with which they feed on Water Snails. In contrast to the energetic Water Boatmen or Pond Skaters, many bugs use the strategy of waiting for a meal to come to them. The **Water Scorpion** (Nepa cinerea) can grow to a length of 30 mm and has a long spiny 'tail' through which it obtains oxygen by pushing it above the water surface. These bugs sit among water plants and rely upon their mottled brown camouflage to blend into the background. Any suitable sized insect, fish or other small creature that comes within striking distance of the Water Scorpion's menacing forelegs is grabbed and sucked dry.

A similar, but longer and more slender bug which uses the same strategy, is the **Water Stick Insect** *(Ranatra linearis)*. Unlike the Water Scorpion, this bug is not totally reliant upon stealth, as it can swim well and is capable of flight. About 6.5 cm in length, the Water Stick Insect has long thin legs. The forelegs are used for grasping their prey, which consists of much the same species preyed on by the Water Scorpion. Rivalling the Great Diving Beetles as the tigers of the watery jungle are the nymphs of the Dragonflies and their smaller relations the Damselflies. These are both stalkers which rely upon stealth and patience to grab suitable prey in their extendible jaws or 'mask'. Once caught in the pincer like grip the prey is pulled back under the larva's head and eaten. The adult and larval dragonflies not only exploit different food sources, just as their land-dwelling counterparts do, but they also live in different environments. This is an important strategy allowing insects to diversify and colonize a wide range of habitats. Few insects show this better than the dragonflies, the contrast between the ugly functional larva and the sleek sparkling adult is almost unparalleled in the insect world.

2.3.5.3 Molluscs

Freshwater **Mussels** are molluscs with many features in common with their close relatives, the Marine Oysters and Mussels. They are all bivalves, their bodies being enclosed in two flap-like shells known as valves. Of the five larger species of Freshwater Mussel you are most likely to find, the **Swan Mussel** (*Anodonta cygnea*) is the largest, growing up to 22 cm in length and commonly occurring in canals, lakes, ponds and reservoirs over most of the British Isles. Mussels live by drawing water through their shells. The water passes over gills where oxygen and food is removed, and so there is no need to move to catch food, though mussels can move very slowly when necessary (at a top speed of about one mile per year !). The **Pearl Mussel** (*Margaritifera margaritifera*) sometimes produces valuable pearls inside its shell. Although in Roman times pearl fisheries were quite common, this Mussel is now only locally fished commercially. It produces the pearl from nacre (mother of pearl) which lines the shell and is secreted to surround a foreign body such as a grain of sand which has entered the shell. As it prefers fast flowing soft water, it is found mainly deep in the swift rivers of south-west and northern England, Wales and Scotland, where it burrows into the sand which accumulates in the lee of large boulders.

To conclude this section, we have seen only a flavour of the variety of life which Britain's rivers and inland waterways can support. There is much much more to see than it has been possible to describe here. The references section at the end of Part 2 will list guides and further texts which will help you to find out more about the less common species which I have not attempted to describe here.

2.4   River Management

"River management is the art of resolving conflicting demands upon a natural resource and at the same time attempting to define and conserve the essential features of that resource".

(Wood, 1981)

Substantial demands are made of rivers both to support abstractions and to accept industrial and domestic effluent, while at the same time there is a growing demand for use of our rivers as a recreational resource. In Britain, the high population density in the south and east of the country means that there is a high level of water consumption in that part of the country (see the map in Figure 2.4.1 (a)). It is the south and east which also has the lowest mean annual rainfall in the UK (see the map in Figure 2.4.1 (b)). This uneven spread of population, and the east-west rainfall gradient, combine to make some English rural rivers and many British urban rivers very badly over-subscribed.

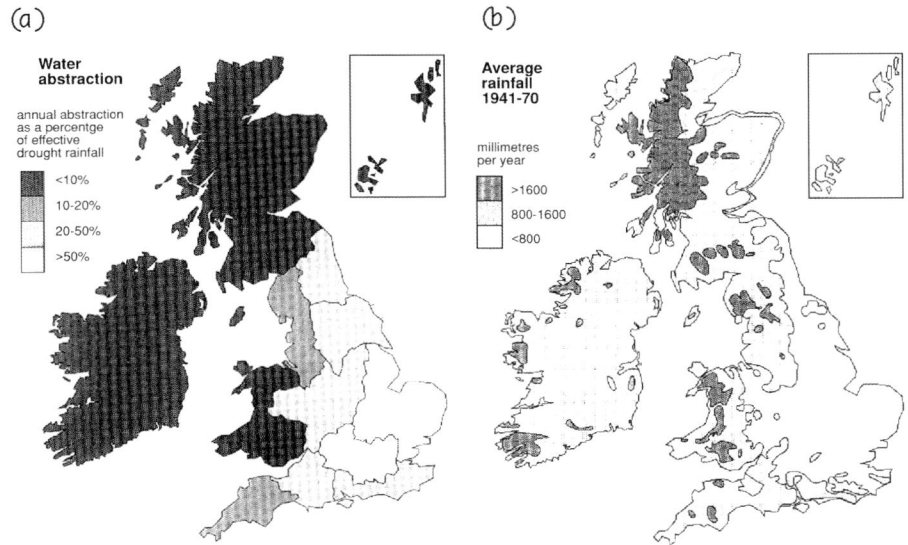

Figure 2.4.1: Maps to show: (a) water abstraction, and (b) average rainfall in the UK.

However, even in remote rural areas, conflicting demands are evident. For example, leisure activities such as angling have a need to conserve a variety of physical river characteristics, while the demands of the agricultural community might be to improve land drainage by lowering the water table. There are few British rivers and almost no English rivers where the river regime has not been affected by such demands.

As a result there are now several common ground rules employed in the Water Industry to help define a river's essential characteristics, and to test whether or not new demands will be acceptable. These essential characteristics range from the hydraulic capacity of the channel, to the frequency and magnitude of low flows, and the quality of the river water itself. These ground rules are by no means written in stone and may not be easily available to the public, but they have been developed through a long history of river engineering and water supply practice which has developed alongside river conservation measures.

It was the Industrial Revolution, with the resulting growth in demand for water supply and for sewage disposal, which brought about legislation to deal with river water quality and resource management. In the 19th century, epidemics of water borne disease led the new towns and cities to look for remote, wholesome and more reliable water supplies via a series of private Acts of Parliament. They also looked to provide more adequate means of sewage disposal, for by that time many rivers were in an appalling condition. The Thames, for example, was in a particularly bad state, the stench being so bad that sheets drenched in disinfectant had to be hung over the windows of Parliament !

In 1865, a Rivers Commission was appointed to look into ways of preventing the pollution of rivers. This resulted in the Rivers Pollution Prevention Acts of 1876 and 1893. However, these Acts disregarded one of the Commission's conclusions which was that effective river management could only be conducted over entire river basins unhampered by the artificial boundaries of local governments. It must be remembered that river management is not just concerned with the river channel and its banks, but must be concerned with the whole drainage basin since the river channel is inextricably linked to the rest of the catchment (as we saw in Section 1.2).

In 1902, the Royal Commission on Salmon Fisheries and the Royal Commission on Sewage both encouraged the formation of local river boards, but that was only achieved in England and Wales in 1930, with the establishment of Catchment Boards to exercise pollution control and drainage functions. In 1948, the River Boards Act created river basin bodies responsible for land drainage, pollution prevention and fisheries. In 1963, the Water Resources Act achieved a measure of amalgamation of the River Boards, renaming them River Authorities.

Although this was a major step forward, and still today is the cornerstone of resource management legislation, the River Authorities themselves have now been replaced by the Environment Agency (EA) in England and Wales, by the Scottish Environment Protection Agency (SEPA) in Scotland and in Northern Ireland the Department of the Environment for Northern Ireland. The management organisations that have been created have evolved policies to resolve the conflicting demands made on rivers by people living in or near their catchments.

2.4.1   Water Quantity

2.4.1.1 Water Availability and Use in The British Isles

The imbalance of available water between areas of the UK, and from one year to the next, is evident in Figure 2.4.1. Annual average rainfall varies from less than 500 mm in the lowlands of eastern England, to over 3000 mm in the uplands of western Britain and Ireland (Figure 2.4.1 (b)). This pattern results from both the southwesterly prevailing winds and the mountainous terrain of the north and west. This same topography, along with other factors, has resulted in the population density in Britain being highest in the south east, and decreasing the further north and west you go. So, the demand for water is greatest precisely in the areas where the rainfall is lowest (Figure 2.4.1). In the north and west of the British Isles, the annual demand is less than half the **effective drought rainfall,** the effective rainfall (annual rainfall less evaporation) during a one-in-fifty-years drought. However, in East Anglia, demand reaches two-thirds of the effective drought rainfall and in the Thames region demand exceeds it, the deficit in dry years being made up by re-use of river water, drawdown of water reservoirs, and imports from other regions.

2.4.1.2 Management of Surface Water

Much of our water in the south and south east of Britain is supplied from groundwater **aquifers**. However, surface water provides the major supplies in most of the British Isles. Small communities can be supplied directly from a spring or stream, but reservoirs allow seasonal and inter-annual variations in flow and rainfall to be evened out more reliably. Towns can be supplied by pipeline or aqueduct directly from a reservoir, or by a river in which the flow is maintained at a steady level by the input of surplus water. This water might come from a reservoir upstream on the same river system, one in an adjacent drainage basin, or from an aquifer. On the other hand, reservoir water can be used to recharge aquifers where rainfall is insufficient to balance extraction (as occasionally occurs in South East England).

Reservoirs are usually constructed in the deep valleys of upland areas. Lowland reservoirs have a greater surface area and evaporation rate for a given volume of stored water. A reservoir can also be created at sea level behind an **estuarial barrage. Desalination** of sea water is a last resort for most countries due to the high costs of energy involved.

2.4.1.3 Water Supplies in the Future

Reservoirs play a key role in managing the amount of water in Britain's rivers today. However, most are now owned privately. Reservoir managers are constantly playing a balancing game. On the one hand they need to have sufficient water stored in the reservoir to be able to supply direct to customers or to release it slowly to maintain river levels during times of drought, and in many cases, they also want the level of water in the reservoir to be high enough to preserve its amenity value, particularly over the summer, when activities such as sailing and windsurfing are likely to take place. On the other hand, some reservoirs also need to make sure there is sufficient capacity to be able to store flood water during times of heavy rainfall to prevent the river bursting its banks.

The British Isles are not short of water. The UK utilizes only 25% of its groundwater and less than 10% of its surface water. Estimates for Ireland are 2.5% and 2% respectively. However, the regional imbalance of available water (Figure 2.4.1 b) means that future supply strategies must be carefully planned, particularly for the drier, more populated areas of eastern Ireland and southeastern England. Demand for water in England and Wales is growing only slowly, by about 4% over the decade 1980-1990.

A steady increase in piped mains supply, mostly for domestic purposes, was balanced by a decrease in industrial use. This decrease, due to the decline of heavy industry, was unforeseen by the water supply authorities. Reservoirs were built to satisfy anticipated industrial growth, so that most northern and western regions had a large surplus of supply capacity by the year 2000. Predicted increases in demand over the next thirty years leave only the southeast short of water. There is a vigorous debate about whether to meet this shortfall by constructing more reservoirs, by pumping surplus water from the northwest, or by stemming the present 25% leakage of mains water from broken pipes. Some surplus of supply capacity over average demand is maintained to allow for occasional years of drought. A new factor in this assessment is the risk of climate change induced by global warming. The current predictions are that the beneficial effect of wetter winters in a warmer British Isles climate, would be offset by greater summer evaporation and more climatic variability.

From the white water canoeist's point of view, for example, classic upland river reaches such as the upper Tryweryn in North Wales, are totally dependent on reservoir releases to provide suitable paddling conditions. Thus, negotiation and agreements between canoeing representatives and the reservoir managers are vital in maintaining this resource.

2.4.2   Water Quality and Pollution

All of our lives depend upon a healthy water system. When rivers become polluted, by accident, negligence or a deliberate act, the results can be catastrophic. Drinking water and irrigation supplies can be put at risk or the entire wildlife population of a river can be destroyed. Despite growing public awareness, thousands of pollution incidents still occur every year. These are caused by farm waste, pesticides and fertilizers in rural areas, oil and chemical leaks, spillages or discharges from road accidents, industrial estates, car parks and garages. All can pollute rivers and groundwater; and, homeowners too, have added to the problem through wrongly connected pipes or careless oil and waste disposal.

2.4.2.1 History of River Pollution in Britain

In Britain, one of the main uses of rivers is for the disposal of domestic and industrial waste. This dates back only to the closing years of the 19th century when the water closet was widely introduced as a means of safely and conveniently removing human sewage from developing towns and cities. The growth of large urban areas was not in itself the cause of river pollution, nor was the impoundment of remote upland streams to produce cheap supplies of water. Rather, it was the widespread introduction of water-borne sewage disposal, together with the growth in industrial effluent, which produced water pollution some generations after the Industrial Revolution was underway. Therefore, the extensive use of British rivers for effluent disposal is less than 120 years old, and post-dates the Industrial Revolution and the development of major urban areas by several generations.

Indeed, both the River Trent at Nottingham, and the River Tame in Birmingham, were separately used in the middle years of the 19th century as local sources of water supply. Today, the River Tame downstream of Birmingham contains about 90% effluent during low flow. In the summer of 1976 even the River Severn near Gloucester, with a catchment area of 10000 square kilometres, was almost entirely dependent for its flow upon a combination of releases from reservoir storage and effluent discharges. The natural discharge of the River Severn was virtually nil at Gloucester because of the effects of abstraction. The management of river water quality is thus extremely important, both at times of normal low flow in urban rivers, in rivers used for public water supply, and in rural rivers in times of drought.

In Britain, the first significant pollution prevention legislation was passed in 1876. This prohibited four forms of pollution; from mine water; from sewage; from trade effluent and from solids disposal. The 1876 Act was not successful, and attempts at controlling rather than prohibiting polluting discharges followed. In 1912, the Eighth Report of the Royal Commission on Sewage Disposal recommended two criteria for an acceptable standard of a sewage effluent, provided that there was an adequate dilution available from the receiving watercourse. That dilution was taken to be a minimum of eight times the quantity of the effluent under low-flow conditions. The criteria for the effluent discharge itself, put forward by the Royal Commission, were a maximum demand of 20 parts per million of dissolved oxygen (BOD) and a maximum of 30 parts per million of suspended solids. This would result in river water downstream of the discharge which would have a BOD of less than 4 mg l^{-1}. Since 1912, these Royal Commission limits of '20/30' have been widely applied and almost to the present day have been used as a standard for sewage effluents.

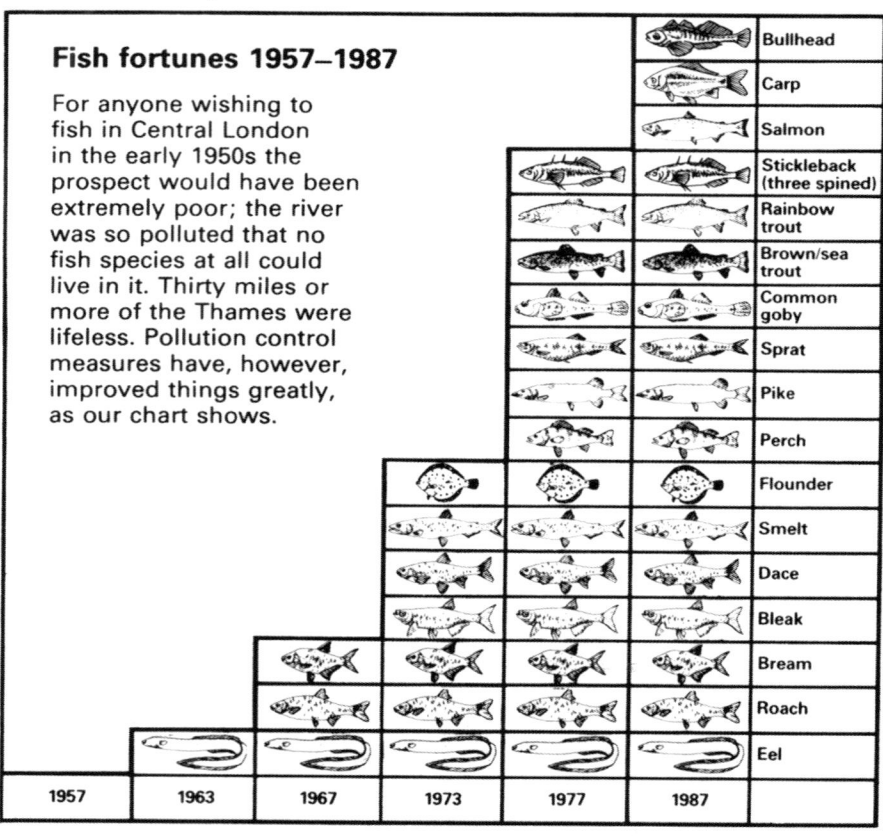

Figure 2.4.2: The effect of pollution control measures on fish diversity in the River Thames, 1957-87 (source: The Reader's Digest, The Living Countryside – Along the Riverbank © 1985).

In 1951, the Rivers (Prevention of Pollution) Act replaced the earlier 1876 legislation. Prohibition was replaced by a system of discharge consents with new discharges being required to comply with minimum standards. In 1961, this system was extended to cover existing discharges. In 1974, the Control of Pollution Act (COPA) received the Royal Assent. Amongst other powers,

190

COPA allowed any person or group to take proceedings against a polluter, including of course the Water Authorities, themselves responsible for the operation of the sewage works which are the chief source of pollution load.

The record of the British Water Industry in improving water quality over the past half century has been very good indeed. For example, between 1958 and 1975 in England and Wales there was a rise from 86.1% to 91.4% of total river length which could be classed as of good quality (DOE, 1978). This apparent slight rise of only 5% represents a very significant national investment in pollution control and some dramatic changes in particular areas. For example, the tidal Thames, which in the middle of the 18th century, had a good run of salmon, had become seriously polluted by 1800. Even in 1950, the lower Thames was so heavily polluted that for several months of the year no dissolved oxygen could be detected. To all extent and purpose the tidal Thames was a dead river with no fish life, an unpleasant and characteristic smell, and a poor appearance. However, the effects of the improvement and diversion of sewage effluent and stricter trade effluent control can be seen by the improvements in fish diversity in the River Thames (1957-87) shown in Figure 2.4.2. The offensive odour has disappeared and amenity and appearance are vastly improved.

Similar dramatic improvement has been seen in other major rivers, for example the Clyde, the Tees, the Trent and the Pennine Rivers of Yorkshire and Lancashire. Some of the changes in river water quality in the Severn and the Trent between 1962 and 1978 include more than halving of BOD levels and the general improvement of river water from one class to the next highest class. This is testimony both to the investments made in effluent treatment, and to the hard work of the pollution control authorities.

2.4.2.2 Control Of River Pollution Today

Operational since April 1 1996, the Environment Agency (EA) was formed from the National Rivers Authority (NRA), Her Majesty's Inspectorate of Pollution (HMIP), Waste Regulation Authorities (WRAs) and units from the Department of the Environment. It is a non-departmental public body sponsored by the Department of the Environment, Transport and the Regions, Ministry of Agriculture, Fisheries and Food (MAFF) and the Welsh Office. Its main functions include: pollution prevention and control; waste minimisation; management of water resources; flood defence; improvement of salmon and freshwater fisheries; conservation; navigation and the use of inland and coastal waters for recreation.

All water pollution is an offence under the Water Resouces Act (1991) and polluters can be prosecuted.

Run-off from farmland, roads and urban areas, plus discharges from sewers are the two main sources of freshwater pollution. Specifically, these may be:

- Farm slurry, improperly spread or stored,

- Agricultural pesticides and fertilizers, carelessly used, stored or applied,

- Accidents, often preventable with good planning,

- Wrong connections, causing household sewage or industrial waste to enter surface water drains, producing lasting damage to river life and endangering public health,

- Oil, chemicals and detergents, rinsed or disposed of into surface water drains - as good as tipping them straight into a river,

- Milk, fruit juice, alcohol, cream, yoghurt and any other organic drink or foodstuff entering a surface water drain. These can be up to a thousand times more destructive than raw sewage or chemical waste and, even in small amounts, can wipe out whole river populations through oxygen starvation.

It is most important that all of us understand the pathways to river pollution: sewers, drains and groundwater.

Waste water from homes and factories discharges to foul sewers. It flows to a treatment plant where the solid matter is removed and the remaining water is treated to reduce the level of dissolved organic chemicals. The treated water is then discharged into a river or groundwater with the Agency's consent. Water entering surface water drains, in contrast, is not treated and is carried eventually to rivers, streams or soakaways. If a wrong connection occurs in the pipework of any domestic or commercial property, whole rivers can become severely contaminated. However, most pollution from these drains results from heavy rainfall flushing urban roads, parks, factory or farm yards (where there may be decomposing food, pet droppings etc.) into drains. This is especially so in late summer after a long dry spell leading to a build up of pollutants which then are available to be washed into rivers.

Groundwater feeds wells, boreholes and rivers, and provides nearly 30% of all public water supplies. Spillages from a factory or tanker, for example, can seriously pollute these supplies. Dumping of waste and leaks from storage tanks (even small leaks), can, over time, carry pollutants to our groundwater. Figure 2.4.3 shows how the chemical quality of rivers and canals, 1988-96 (source Environment Agency, SEPA, Environment and Heritage Service) has improved in recent years. There has been an overall net upgrading in the chemical water quality of almost 26 per cent of the length of rivers and canals in England and Wales between 1990 and 1996.

192

Chemical water quality of rivers and canals: 1988 – 1996

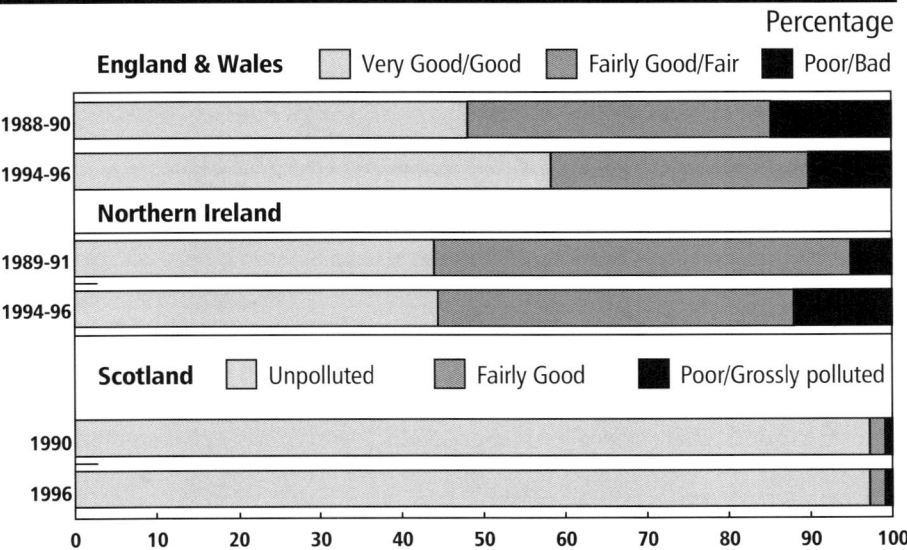

1994-96 Figures (1995 for Scotland)			Percentage
Country	V Good/ Good	Fairly Good/ Fair	Poor/ Bad	Total river lengths surveyed (km)
England & Wales	59	32	10	40,800
Northern Ireland	44	43	12	2,360
Country	Unpolluted	Fairly Good	Poor/Grossly polluted	Total river lengths surveyed (km)
Scotland	97	2	1	50,260

Inland waters are used for supplying drinking water, for industrial and agricultural abstraction and may also be used for the disposal of treated domestic sewage, industrial wastes and farm effluents. Increasingly, inland waters are being used for a variety of leisure activities.

There was an overall net upgrading in the chemical quality of almost 26 per cent of the total length of rivers and canals in England and Wales between 1990 and 1996.

Source: *Environment Agency, SEPA, Environment and Heritage Service*

Figure 2.4.3: The chemical quality of rivers and canals, 1988-96 (source Environment Agency, SEPA, Environment and Heritage Service).

Figure 2.4.4 shows the biological water quality of rivers and canals, 1990-96 (source: Environment Agency, SEPA, Environment and Heritage Service) and shows that rivers in Scotland tend to be of the highest biological quality, but that most of the UK rivers are of good or moderate quality. It also shows that there was a net upgrading in the biological quality of nearly 12 per cent of the total length of the rivers and canals in England and Wales between 1990 and 1995.

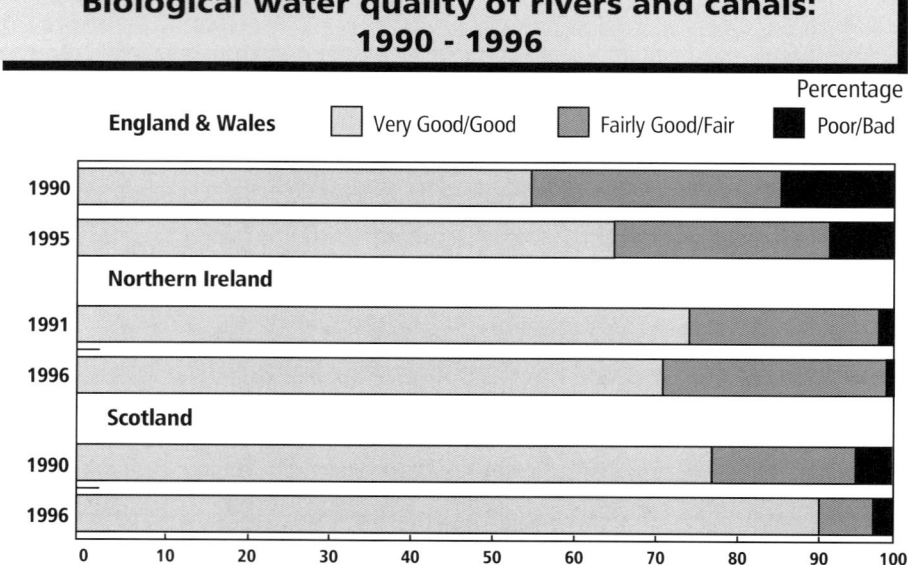

1995 Figures (1996 for N Ireland)			Percentage
Country	V Good/ Good	Fairly Good/ Fair	Poor/ Bad	Total river lengths surveyed (km)
England & Wales	66	27	7	37,560
Northern Ireland	72	28	1	2,330
Scotland	90	8	2	16,710

Biological grading is based on the monitoring of small animals (invertebrates) which live in, or on the bed of, rivers and canals.

Most UK rivers are of good or moderate biological quality. Those in Scotland tend to be of the highest quality. There was an overall net upgrading in the biological quality of nearly 26 per cent of the total length of rivers ands canals in England and Wales between 1990 and 1995.

Source: *Environment Agency, SEPA, Environment and Heritage Service*

Figure 2.4.4: Biological water quality of rivers and canals, 1990-96 (source: Environment Agency, SEPA, Environment and Heritage Service).

2.4.3   Specific Water Quality Issues for Recreationalists

Every day a vast amount of sewage, industrial effluent and agricultural waste is discharged to our rivers and inland waterways. Many of these same waterways, or lakes fed by them, are used for recreational activities such as swimming, canoeing, rowing, sailing and windsurfing. Although in most cases the waste has been treated, the major objectives of the treatment processes are to decrease the level of suspended solids and to reduce the biochemical oxygen demand (BOD) of the effluent. However, the House of Commons Environment Committee (1990) noted that the levels of bacteria and viruses in effluent from treated sewage can be appreciable.

Watercourses receiving such effluents are likely to contain harmful micro-organisms or **pathogens**. On ingestion, or contact with a susceptible individual, these pathogens may cause infection and illness. Oils and detergents present in the water may also cause skin irritation, and naturally occurring toxins released from algae can cause symptoms ranging from skin irritation to an unusual form of pneumonia.

The lower dilution and dispersal of effluents in freshwater, as opposed to marine, receiving environments, coupled with the fact that bacteria and viruses have longer survival times in freshwater, produce a higher potential risk to human and animal health. Data sources on the recreational use of water and associated infections are given in Table 2.4.1.

Table 2.4.1: Recreational use of water and infections (source: Fewtrell, 1991).

Disease	Organism	Data source
Gastrointestinal infections	*Campylobacter*	Galbraith *et al.* (1987)
	Cryptosporidium	Gallagher *et al.* (1989)
	Salmonella typhi	Galbraith *et al.* (1987)
	Salmonella paratyphi	Galbraith *et al.* (1987)
	Shigella sonnei	Rosenberg *et al.* (1976)
	Viruses	Baron *et al.* (1982)
Infectious hepatitis	Enterovirus 72	Bryan *et al.* (1974); Philipp *et al.* (1989)
Skin infections	*Trichobilharzia ocellata*	Harvey and Price (1981); Eastcott (1988)
Leptospirosis	*Leptospira icterohaemorr-hagiae*	Galbraith *et al.* (1987)
Cyanobacterial poisoning	*Microcystis aeruginosa*	Turner *et al.* (1990)
Viral infections	Various	Denis *et al.* (1974); Hawley *et al.* (1973

Infectious hepatitis. The incubation period for hepatitis-A is at least three to four weeks and may be as long as several months, which obviously leads to difficulties in tracing the source of infection. However, in the US in 1969, there was an outbreak of hepatitis-A which has been attributed to consumption of polluted lake water during recreation (Bryan *et al.*, 1974). In the UK a case of hepatitis-A associated with swimming in Bristol City Docks prompted a study to determine the presence of hepatitis-A antibodies in regular dock users (Philipp *et al.*,1989). This is dealt with in more detail below.

Gastrointestinal infections are caused by a variety of agents, probably the best known being the *Salmonella typhi* and *S. paratyphi,* both of which can be contracted through sewage-polluted waters. There are also a number of viral agents which cause gastroenteritis.

Skin infection. In the UK there have been two well documented outbreaks of 'swimmers' itch' in freshwater lakes (Harvey and Price ,1981; Eastcott, 1988). Swimmers' itch (*Cercarial dermatitis*) is caused by *Trichobilharzia ocellata* (a parasite of ducks) and occurs when mobile *cercariae* attempt to invade the skin of humans, resulting in a prickling sensation on leaving the water, followed by a rash. *T. ocellata* has a complex life cycle requiring aquatic snails as intermediate hosts; management is therefore effected by reducing the snail population.

Leptospirosis. Leptospirosis (or Weil's disease) is a potentially fatal disease caused by infection with pathogenic *Leptospira* organisms. Animals and humans become infected either directly, through contact with infected urine (mainly rats and cattle), or indirectly, via contaminated freshwater or wet soil. Virulent leptospires gain entry to the body through cuts and abrasions of the skin and through mucosal surfaces of the mouth, nose and conjunctiva. The degree of severity of the disease may vary from hepatorenal failure and meningitis, associated with classic Weil's syndrome (due to infection with L. *icterohaemorrhagie),* to a milder flu-like illness with severe headache, more often found in infections associated with *L. hardjo,* a cattle-associated *Leptospira.*

Compared with many other pathogens, leptospires have a comparatively low resistance to adverse physical and chemical conditions. They are rarely found in water of pH below 6 - 8. Their survival in polluted water and salt water is poor. However, in the right circumstances, such as clean freshwater at roughly neutral pH, leptospires are viable for up to six months.

Leptospirosis was predominantly associated with sewer workers, but recent years have seen a shift in epidemiological trends, which are probably due to the introduction of preventative measures, such as the proper covering of cuts and abrasions. Now farmers and recreational water users are increasingly the main risk groups. Table 2.4.2 compares the 15-year period between 1933 and 1948 with a five-year period between 1978 and 1983, highlighting the changing incidences of the disease.

It can be seen from the table that the annual incidence of leptospirosis is small, especially when compared with the estimated 1 - 4 million people over the age of 16 who take part in outdoor swimming activities. However, the number of people using water for recreational purposes is increasing, as is the rat problem. It is possible, therefore, that there will be a greater incidence of leptospirosis in the future, especially as doctors become more aware of the changing epidemiology of the disease and make more accurate diagnoses. In an effort to counter this expected increase, sporting bodies such as the British Canoe Union and the Royal Yachting Association are issuing leaflets to their members highlighting the risks of leptospirosis and measures which can be taken to avoid infection.

Table 2.4.2: Human leptospirosis in the British Isles (number of cases) (source: Fewtrell, 1991).

Type of contact	1933-48	1978-83
Farmer	45	170
Abattoir/meat worker	21	8
Veterinarian	0	4
Coal miner	139	2
Sewer/water worker	95	5
Fish worker/farmer	216	3
Armed forces personnel	97	3
Rat bite or contact	11	27
Dog contact	2	11
Bathing and water sports	48	49

Source: Adapted from Waitkins (1990).

Cyanobacterial poisoning. An increasing problem in fresh recreational water is the presence of toxic algal blooms. This is not a new problem: the first documented incident in the UK was at Llangorse Lake in Wales in the twelfth century. The causative agents of these algal blooms are blue-green algae, or cyanobacteria. These have been suspected of having human and animal toxicity since the mid-nineteenth century. It is only recently, however, that algae have started to present major health and amenity problems.

The toxins produced by cyanobacteria include hepatotoxins (such as the microcystitis) and neurotoxins. Ingestion of microcystins by animals can cause circulatory shock coupled with rapid and fatal liver damage. The neurotoxin group includes a neuromuscular blocking agent, which in animals can cause death within 30 minutes due to muscle paralysis leading to respiratory collapse. In 1989, ingestion of water containing toxic algal scum led to the death of several dogs and lambs at Rutland Water in Leicestershire. Warning notices were promptly erected around the reservoir, banning the recreational use of the water in order to protect public health. Fortunately, to date, no human deaths have been attributed to blue-green algae, although recently the first UK cases of suspected cyanobacterial poisoning were reported following contact with freshwater containing *Microcystis aeruginosa* (Turner *et al.*, 1990). Two army recruits were admitted to hospital with a rare form of pneumonia four to five days after participating in a canoeing exercise on Rudyard Lake in Staffordshire. The men were shown to have developed lung deposits similar to those seen in animals inoculated with algal toxins. Subsequently, a further eight recruits who had been canoeing had symptoms which might have been associated with cyanobacterial poisoning, including sore throats, headaches, abdominal pains, dry coughs, vomiting and blistered mouths.

Viral infections. There are potentially a large number of pathogenic viruses present in polluted water. It has been suggested that only a few of these pathogens are required to cause infection. In fact, the minimum infective dose may be as low as one viral particle. Although waterborne outbreaks of infections caused by these viruses are difficult to recognize, there have been reports of gastroenteritis due to Norwalk virus (Baron *et al.*, 1982) and minor outbreaks of disease from freshwater swimming, due to Coxsackievirus A and B (Hawley *et al.*, 1973; Denis *et al.*, 1974).

The UK press has speculated on the possibilities of catching AIDS from recreational exposure to water. A recent publication examined the survival of human immunodeficiency virus (HIV), the causative agent of AIDS, in tap water, sewage and seawater (Slade *et al.*, 1989). It was found that times required for a tenfold reduction in HIV concentration were 1 - 8 days in tap water, 1 - 6 days in seawater and 2 - 9 days in sewage. Whilst it was concluded that HIV was very unlikely to pose a threat to disinfected water supplies, no comment was passed on infection via recreational water use. Fortunately, however, these results, coupled with the findings of an epidemiological study (Pike, 1987) which found no indication that water or sewage is involved in HIV transmission, suggest that there is no risk of contracting AIDS from the recreational use of water.

Two epidemiological studies have been conducted at Bristol Docks, the first in response to a number of people reporting gastrointestinal illness following a snorkel event held in the docks in 1981. A similar event was closely monitored the following year. It was found that 27 per cent of the swimmers who participated in the event experienced gastrointestinal symptoms within 48 hours of entering the water. The incidence of the symptoms experienced by the participants was found to be significantly higher than those experienced by control groups. Limited clinical follow up of participants reporting symptoms was attempted, but only two samples were obtained and no causative organisms were identified (Philipp *et al.*, 1985).

The second study followed a fatality from Weil's disease (leptospirosis) and a case of hepatitis-A associated with water immersion in the docks. The study examined a number of regular dock users (windsurfers and waterskiers) for antibodies to leptospirosis and hepatitis-A. One person demonstrated evidence of a past leptospiral infection and several people had evidence of previous hepatitis-A, but there was no causal association with the docks water (Philipp *et al.,* 1989). Despite the findings, warning notices were posted around the docks listing sensible precautions. Whether a snorkel event in Bristol Docks can be deemed typical of a normal recreationalist's use of fresh water is dubious.

Other more recent studies are perhaps more relevant. Fewtrell *et al.* (1992) reported that there was little quantitative information on the relation between water quality and disease attack rates after recreational activities in fresh water. They conducted a prospective cohort study to measure the health effects of white water and slalom canoeing in two channels with different degrees of microbial contamination. Site A, fed by a lowland river, showed high enterovirus concentrations (arithmetic mean 198 pfu per 10 litre) and moderate faecal coliform concentrations (geometric mean 285/dl); at site B, from an upland impoundment, all samples were free of enteroviruses and the geometric mean faecal coliform concentration was 22/dl. Between 5 and 7 days after exposure, canoeists using site A had significantly higher incidences of gastrointestinal and upper respiratory symptoms than canoeists using site B, or non-exposed controls (spectators). Like seawater bathers, fresh water canoeists can be made ill by sewage contamination. They concluded that the hazard of fresh water may be best measured by counting of viruses rather than bacteria.

Fewtrell *et al.* (1994) reported on four studies which were carried out at separate locations to investigate the relationship between health effects and low contact water sports. Intensive microbiological sampling was conducted in parallel to the health studies at each site. The two sports examined were marathon canoeing and rowing. The extremes of water quality were at the estuarine sites on the River Torridge, where pollution levels varied from a geometric mean faecal coliform value of 62/100 ml at the Appledore/Instow site to 4613/100 ml at the Bideford site. A comparison of 'exposed' and 'unexposed' groups, 5-7 days after exposure, showed that the health effects of low contact water sports are minimal, within the water quality ranges which were studied.

2.4.3.1 Standards and Legislation

In the UK, the principal legislation covering recreational waters is the EC Bathing Water Directive (76/160/EEC). This legislation sets down microbiological and physico-chemical standards for recreational water. It is aimed at protecting public health and the environment, at reducing pollution in bathing water and at encouraging long-term improvements in amenity. The directive requires that designated sites should be sampled fortnightly, throughout the bathing season, for total coliforms and faecal coliforms (Table 2.4.3). However, it must be remembered that these standards are based on limited epidemiological studies, and compliance with the directive does not indicate a total lack of risk. Rather, compliance indicated that the risk is present, but is considered to be low but acceptable. The UK now has over 400 designated marine bathing places, but few freshwater sites. The lack of designation of freshwater sites is surprising in view of the increasing use of many inland recreational facilities, and research has indicated that bacteria and viruses have longer survival times in fresh, rather than salt, waters (Chamberlin and Mitchell, 1978). Indeed, some pathogens such as *Leptospira spp* only survive in fresh water. Sporting organizations such as the International Canoe Federation (ICF) have formulated their own water quality guidelines. The ICF recommend that faecal coliform and faecal streptococci levels do not exceed 1000 per 100 ml and 250 per 100 ml respectively. In addition, water should not contain chemicals or algae in concentrations that could endanger human health. However, since there are no official standards applying to the recreational use of inland waters, and with occasional exceptions (such as regular water quality sampling which takes place on the River Trent at the Holme Pierrepont National Water Sports Centre white whater course), there is little microbiological monitoring of surface waters as a check on recreational use.

Table 2.4.3: Microbiological standards of EC bathing water directive (source: Fewtrell, 1991).

Parameter	Guide	Imperative	Minimum sampling frequency
Total coliforms 100 ml^{-1}	500	10 000	Fortnightly
Faecal coliforms 100 ml^{-1}	100	2 000	Fortnightly
Faecal streptococci 100 ml^{-1}	100	-	Discretionary
Salmonellae litre^{-1}	-	0	Discretionary
Enteroviruses (pfu[a] 10 l^{-1})	-	0	Discretionary

[a]plaque-forming units

2.4.3.2 Management Policy

There have been a number of management strategies proposed. One example is that suggested by Jones and Godfree (1989). This system scores the recreational site on a number of factors, including National Water Council classification, the proportion of river volume which is sewage or trade effluent, the proximity of the location to sources of pollution and bacteriological quality. A location scoring between 0 and 10 is considered to be suitable for primary contact sports (such as swimming, where there is a real likelihood that water will be swallowed and there will be water contact with the nose, ears and eyes). Locations scoring 0 - 16 can be used for secondary contact sports (such as angling and pleasure cruising, where there is a reasonable expectation that any water contact will be limited and accidental). Sites scoring 16-20 are considered to be unsuitable for recreational use. Although this is a useful and workable system, it relies on a knowledge of the micro-biological quality of the water, which is often absent.

Reports in the literature have indicated that there is a range of health risks associated with the recreational use of freshwater. Studies have been conducted to try to link water quality with rates of illness, and to obtain a measure of the degree of risk, with a view to formulating standards. Unfortunately, due to methodological flaws we are still in the position of having little scientifically valid data. Until freshwater sites are monitored, it will be difficult to make informed management decisions about the suitability of use. Unlike the bathing water directive, where monitoring is confined to the summer months, it is vital that freshwater sites are monitored throughout the year because the use of wet suits extends the season of recreational use. There is also a need for research into health effects of chemical pollution since, currently, very little is known on this subject.

The question of whether freshwater recreation should be a cause for concern is full of uncertainty at the present time. In the light of gaps in current knowledge and legislation, people are entitled to become concerned. Compared to the risks of drowning, the dangers from infection from the recreational use of freshwater are probably small. It is, however, an area about which the public are entitled to credible scientific information and moves are being made in the right direction. Sewage treatment systems, such as chemical disinfection and membrane filtration, are now being introduced (CES, 1988) and, although costly, their introduction would markedly reduce the microbiological loadings of our rivers. Membrane filtration is claimed to be capable of virtually complete removal of bacteria and viruses. In the final analysis, the decision on whether or not to use a facility must be left to the individual, but it should be an informed decision based on microbiological and chemical monitoring and the application of sensible standards.

2.4.4 Management of Wildlife and Nature Conservation on Rivers and Inland Waterways

2.4.4.1 Background

The government has recently issued a challenge on increasing the opportunities for sustainable development and biodiversity. **Sustainable Development** is about ensuring quality of life for now and generations to come. **Biodiversity** represents the richness and variety of plants, birds, animals and insects that exist throughout the world. Biodiversity is now recognised as having a central role in climate control (e.g. producing oxygen and developing soil), as an indicator of the health of our environment, and as the source of all our food, medicines and welfare.

Biodiversity is being lost at an alarming rate. In the UK 100 species have been lost this century. Thus, the UK's biodiversity policies are about ensuring a future for these species and the habitats on which they depend. The UK Government's Biodiversity Action Plan (BAP) is to prepare species and habitat action plans with monitoring arrangements. Achieving these plans presents a considerable challenge. Work to achieve recovery of species and the enhancement and restoration of habitats is well precedented, but the scale of the task, some 400 species and 38 habitat action plans running simultaneously, will stretch the resources of all organisations involved, both within and outside Government.

Local Agenda 21 (LA 21) is a national initiative examined at a local level. It aims to take the principles of sustainability and create a framework in which they can be developed in local action plans. It attempts to overcome the response that says "too difficult" and promotes the culture that says "can do". Each local authority has a Local Agenda 21 Officer, and many conservation groups (e.g. Groundwork Trust) are paving the way in LA21 assessments and action plans.

As agricultural, industrial and urban development have proceeded apace over the last century or so, the natural environment, and its wildlife, has come under increasing pressure. This is particularly true of the aquatic environment, where agricultural drainage and industrial pollution have contributed greatly to a steep decline in the extent of wetland habitats. In addition to this, we have seen a gradual increase in the use of rivers and waterways over the last 30 years, as seen by research findings of the Inland Waterways Association (discussed in section 2.1.2 earlier).

The danger of loss of significant habitat types has led to the introduction, since 1949, of a wide range of legislative measures to protect wildlife and wildlife habitats in Britain. These include protection of particular habitats and rare species, as well as imposition of duties on public bodies to further the conservation of flora and fauna. A wide range of statutory and non-statutory designations is applied to particular sites, as detailed later in this section, but perhaps the most important mechanism within the system is the notification of Sites of Special Scientific Interest (SSSIs).

In addition to these SSSIs, certain species are listed as requiring special protection and official permission may be required before disturbing or damaging these animals or plants. Both the habitat and species protection measures are relevant to those interested in rivers and navigable waterways. A number of waterway sites are notified as SSSIs and many harbour flora and fauna are designated to be of nature conservation importance. The approach to management of navigable waterways is important in influencing nature conservation interests. Operations such as dredging can obviously have a major impact, while the passage of boats may enhance or damage wildlife conservation interests, depending on its intensity and local circumstances.

Biological succession is the process whereby a wetland will naturally evolve through marsh and scrub to become dry land, unless factors exist to arrest the process at a particular point. Many of the factors, such as regular flooding, that achieved this in past times, have been eliminated by modern management of the water environment (as outlined in Section 2.4.1), so where an aquatic habitat is of conservation importance, specific management measures may be necessary to maintain the interest. Well planned dredging and appropriate levels of boat traffic may make a significant positive contribution to this management process.

Recreational use of waterways and the protection of wildlife conservation interests are therefore inextricably linked. On the basis that discussions to balance the sometimes conflicting requirements of these interests will be - more fruitful the better the participants are informed, this section summarises nature conservation protection measures of relevance to those interested in navigable waterways.

The rationale for the purpose of conserving important river wildlife habitats was spelt out in general terms as long ago as 1947 in Command 7122 (Ministry of Town and Country Planning, 1947). This White Paper recommended the establishment of a series of National Nature Reserves which would:

> "preserve and maintain, as part of the nation's natural heritage, places which can be regarded as reservoirs for the main types of community and kinds of wild plants and animals represented in this country, both common and rare, typical and unusual, as well as places which contain physical features of special or outstanding interest".

This definition clearly spans a wide range of values and caters for those who simply enjoy spending a day in unspoilt countryside as well as for the more serious students of natural history.

2.4.4.2 Notification of Sites of Special Interest

Identification and notification of sites meriting protection as SSSIs is the responsibility in England of English Nature (EN); in Wales the responsible body is the Countryside Council for Wales (CCW) and in Scotland it is Scottish Natural Heritage (SNH). Sites were originally designated under the National Parks & Access to the Countryside Act (1949), but this has now been superseded by section 28 of the Wildlife & Countryside Act 1981 (as amended), and this section relates to the current procedure.

Sites are identified on the basis of application of specific criteria within geographical areas known as areas of search, which correspond mainly with counties. Detailed selection criteria are laid out (NCC, 1989); these include naturalness, typicality, diversity, rarity, size, fragility and geographical position (a detailed description of these is given in Appendix I of Newbold *et al.*, 1983). Aquatic sites are generally designated principally on the basis of the plant community, although certain animals such as newts or dragonflies may also be involved in the assessment.

Once a site has been identified as qualifying for SSSI status, EN, CCW or SNH will 'notify' this to: all owners or occupiers; the local planning authority; the relevant Secretary of State; relevant water and sewerage companies, internal drainage boards and the Environment Agency; owners of minerals on the land; other affected public bodies (Ministry of Agriculture, Fisheries & Food (MAFF), Forestry Authority, etc). The notification will include: a letter explaining that the area is of special interest and explaining the requirement to consult EN, CCW or SNH about listed operations; a map showing location and boundaries of the site; a statement of the site's special interest; a list of operations which appear to EN to be likely to damage the special interest of the site. These are known as 'Potentially Damaging Operations' or PDOs.

There is then a consultation period of at least three months, during which time interested parties may make representations or objections. EN, CCW or SNH officers will respond to representations and try to negotiate an agreement. If disputes cannot be resolved, the final decision rests with the Councils of EN, CCW or SNH. Voluntary bodies such as the Inland Waterways Association (IWA) may be given the opportunity to put forward their views, but they have no statutory role, and the views of the owner of the waterway will clearly have to be taken fully into account also. Within nine months of initial notification, EN, CCW or SNH must confirm or withdraw the notification. They may modify it at this stage to take account of consultation, but may not increase the area or add to the list of PDOs.

During the consultation period, the site enjoys full protection as an SSSI in relation to PDOs. Where sites cease to fulfil the relevant criteria, EN, CCW or SNH may denotify them and they are then removed from the provisions described above. SSSIs may also be notified to protect sites of geological interest and these may also be relevant in relation to waterway restoration and management.

2.4.4.3 Management and Protection of SSSIs

The principal mechanism for protection of SSSI is through the list of 'Potentially Damaging Operations' (PDO's) of which there are 28 activities, mainly relating to agriculture and land management / construction. However, those outlined below may relate in some way to recreational small boat users:

Those related to changes to river course and features:

- Drainage including the installation of mole, tile, tunnel or other artificial;
- Modification of the structure of water courses (e.g. rivers, streams, springs, ditches, drains, oxbows, backwater channels and mill leats / races), including their banks and beds, as by re-alignment, damming, regrading, dredging, shoal removal, excavation and the repair of locks, weirs, sluices, fish traps, fish ladders, fords, croys, fishing platforms and new stock watering points;
- Infilling of ditches, drains, ponds, pools, marshes, oxbows, backwater channels or mill leats/races;
- Construction, removal or destruction of roads, tracks, footpaths, walls, fences, hardstandings, banks (including bank protection work), ditches or other earthworks;
- Modification of natural or man made features including clearance of boulders, large stones, loose rock or scree and battering, buttressing or grading rock faces, river banks, cuttings and rock outcrops;

Those related to damage during recreational activity include:

- Killing or removal of any wild animal, excluding pest control and existing game and coarse fishing;
- Destruction, displacement, removal or cutting of any plant or plant remains, including tree, shrub, waterweed, dead or decaying wood, moss, lichen, fungus or turf other than mowing of permanent grass and traditional hedge management;
- Use of vehicles, vessels or craft likely to damage riparian and geomorphological and riparian features or disturb species of interest;
- Recreational or other activities likely to damage riparian and geomorphological and riparian features or disturb species of interest.

Provided river and inland waterway users adhere to the Guidelines for Low Impact River Users in Appendix I, all of the above potentially damaging effects can easily be avoided.

Relevant PDOs for a particular site are selected from a standard list. These operations are not necessarily prohibited but, because they may damage the scientific interest of the site, permission must be sought from EN, CCW or SNH before carrying out such operations, unless the operation is covered by a Planning Consent, a Management Agreement or is a case of emergency.

If the owner/occupier wishes to carry out a PDO they must first seek consent from EN, CCW or SNH, who will consider the proposal and may give consent or try to negotiate suitably modified proposals. If consent is refused, the owner/occupier must not carry out or permit the operation for four months after the application for consent. To do so is an offence, punishable by a fine of up to £1000. If no agreement is reached within this period, which can be extended by mutual agreement, the PDO may be carried out unless EN, CCW or SNH obtains a Nature Conservation Order (NCO) from the Secretary of State. Where a NCO is in force, any person wishing to carry out a PDO must give 3 months notice, during which time consultation with EN, CCW or SNH will take place. This period may be extended to 12 months if EN, CCW or SNH offer to negotiate a Management Agreement (see below). If after this time no agreement can be reached, EN, CCW or SNH may apply for a compulsory purchase order to secure protection of the site.

Thus, a PDO must not be carried out in an SSSI unless:

- EN, CCW or SNH has given written consent;
- The consultation period has expired since the date of application for consent;
- The PDO is carried out under a Management Agreement between the owner/occupier and EN, CCW or SNH;
- The PDO has planning consent under the Town & Country Planning Acts;
- The PDO is an emergency operation and details are supplied immediately to EN, CCW or SNH.

EN, CCW or SNH will usually be willing to consent, via the landowners, to existing levels of recreational use and may accept an increase in certain circumstances. However, any proposals for changes in recreational use will need to be discussed with EN, CCW or SNH (unless covered by a Management Agreement).

On navigable waterways, many potentially damaging operations form part of routine maintenance and operational management programmes and may indeed be essential to maintain the scientific interest of the site. To avoid the need for repeated consultation and written consent from EN, CCW or SNH, routine and planned programmes may be covered by a Management Agreement, negotiated between the waterway owner/occupier and EN, CCW or SNH staff. Such agreements are EN, CCW or SNH 's preferred way forward and offer benefits for both parties. A Management Agreement can be reached at any time during the notification process or thereafter and will typically include the following items:

- Definition of aims and objectives for the SSSI;
- Management Action Plan - identifying management tasks to be undertaken, appropriate methods, seasonal timing of operations, locations etc.;
- Programme for monitoring the effects of the Action Plan.

Where extra costs are incurred as a result of constraints imposed by EN, CCW or SNH to protect nature conservation requirements, these bodies may make a financial contribution.

In 1981 the Wildlife and Countryside Act modified the 1975 Land Drainage Act to give the Water Authorities (as were in operation then) the requirement to 'further' conservation of flora and fauna. The 1989 and 1991 Water Resource Act gave responsibilities to 'promote' conservation. Also, the 1981 Wildlife and Countryside Act and late additions to it put various species on schedules and required them and their habitats to be protected.

2.4.4.4 Relevance to Rivers and Inland Waterways

Sites designated as SSSI may include the channels of navigable or derelict waterways, as well as reservoirs/feeders and bankside sites. On British Waterways property alone, out of a total of more than 50 SSSIs, there are over 20 that include the waterway channel, including some on busy Cruising Waterways such as the Leeds and Liverpool Canal, the Chesterfield Canal and the Kennet and Avon. SSSIs also exist on the Broads and on other waterways. Reasons for notification may include terrestrial vegetation, ornithological interests and geological exposures within the canal corridor or associated with reservoirs, as well as aquatic flora and fauna.

2.4.4.5 Inland Waterway Restoration

While canals were clearly built primarily for navigation, the purpose and uses to which they are put today may, in many cases be very different. For instance, their use by commercial traffic has declined and, as we have seen earlier, recreational use has increased. Aquatic habitats have become rarer, putting more value on any existing wetland (natural or not). When considering restoration of disused waterways, it is the Restoration Committee of the Inland Waterways Association (IWA) which promotes the restoration of canals and undertakes the planning and political lobbying necessary to achieve this. It is the Waterway Recovery Group which undertakes the actual physical work of waterway restoration. The rate of growth of informal use of waterways and boating use of BW waterways is greater than the rate of restoration of waterways (IWAAC, 1996) which in Great Britain averages 13.5 km (8.4 miles) per year, a growth rate of 0.25% per year. The effect of the introduction of propeller driven motor boats is also a major factor to be taken into account, as most canals in UK were built for use by craft powered by sails or haulage from the bank. On river navigations in particular, historical navigation practices may be a far cry from the expectations of the modern motor cruiser owner. Even if restoration plans do not include navigational use by motor vessels, careful planning is required to ensure that nature conservation interests are taken fully into account.

All these factors, and many more, need to be taken into account in planning the future of our waterways and this will usually best be achieved by consultation between all interested parties at the earliest possible stage. EN, CCW and SNH must consult owners and occupiers, but have no obligation to consult other bodies such as canal societies or the IWA. Such consultation is most likely to be achieved if a good relationship has been developed in advance between all interested parties.

2.4.4.6 Other Habitat Designations and Species Protection

A variety of other nature conservation designations may be applied to sites of interest and these are summarised briefly below. All sites to be designated as being of national or international importance under any legislation must first be designated as SSSI.

- **National Nature Reserves**

    National Nature Reserves (NNRs) are designated under section 35 of the Wildlife & Countryside Act (1981), where SSSI are regarded as being of national importance. They may be owned or leased by EN, CCW or SNH or managed in accordance with Nature Reserve Agreements. NNRs are managed primarily for nature conservation.

- **SPA/Ramsar sites**

    Sites of international importance for birds may be designated as Special Protection Areas (SPAs) under the EC Directive on the Conservation of Wild Birds (the Birds Directive) or, for waterfowl, as Ramsar sites under the Ramsar Convention. The UK is required to follow policies to conserve these sites to protect the relevant bird species.

- **Local Nature Reserves**

    Local Nature Reserves (LNRs) can be designated under section 21 of the National Parks & Access to the Countryside Act (1949). LNRs are designated by local authorities who must own the site or reach a suitable agreement with the owner. EN, CCW or SNH must be consulted. As well as protecting wildlife features, LNRs have a particular role to play in education and providing access to wildlife areas for local people. Some LNRs may also qualify as SSSIs.

- ### *Local Development Plans*

  Local Planning Authorities (LPAs) have responsibilities under the Countryside Act (1968) to conserve natural beauty and amenity. Under the Planning & Compensation Act (1991), LPAs are required to include nature conservation policies in Structure, Local and Unitary Development Plans and one section of the Habitats Regulations extends this to include landscape features of importance to wildlife. Some authorities have produced separate wildlife strategies for their areas. In many cases, areas identified as being of local nature conservation importance, often with the assistance of the local wildlife trust, are also included in local development plan policies. These sites are generally known as 'second tier' sites and go under a variety of names in different areas.

  The implementation of development plan policies operates largely through the planning consent system. Development within SSSIs can be granted planning permission, as mentioned above, but the LPA must first consult EN, CCW or SNH and give 14 days for their response. The area around an SSSI may be defined by EN, CCW or SNH as a consultation area (up to a maximum of 2 km from the site), and the LPA will also need to consult EN, CCW or SNH about specified developments within this area or about any other development likely to affect the SSSI. In cases where a development requires a formal Environmental Assessment, EN, CCW or SNH are statutory consultees.

- ### *Special Areas of Conservation*

  The EC Directive on the Conservation of Natural Habitats and of Wild Fauna and Flora (the Habitats Directive) is currently being implemented in the UK under the Conservation Regulations (the Habitats Regulations) and involved designation of Special Areas of Conservation (SAC) for both habitat and species. These will enjoy similar protection to SSSIs but this is strengthened in relation to developments falling under the Permitted Development Rights of planning control law.

Nature conservation is also protected via the route of protection of designated species. The Wildlife & Countryside Act, other specific Acts (e.g. the Badgers Acts) and the EC Habitats Directive, detail protection measures for a variety of indigenous animals and plants, including the great crested newt, bats, otters, badgers and a large number of birds. In addition, introduction into the wild of certain species (including some fish) is prohibited.

These measures apply throughout England and Wales, and Scotland, not just within SSSIs, and any waterway restoration plans must take account of any relevant restrictions for species protection.

2.4.4.7 Duties Of Other Public Bodies

- ### *Environment Agency (in England and Wales)*

  In 1996, under a new Environment Act, the duties of the former National Rivers Authority (NRA) were taken over by the Environment Agency (EA). Under the Water Resources Act (1991), EA has duties to 'promote' conservation of flora and fauna, which built on earlier powers given to the Water Authorities in 1981 which were to 'further' conservation of flora and fauna. In relation to pollution control responsibilities, EA has to take conservation into account. Increasingly, this is being carried out through Local Environment Agency Plans (LEAPs), previously Catchment Management Plans, covering policies for all aspects of management of natural waters within a river basin. These include assessment of catchment resources, uses and activities; consulting customers on issues; and establishing long-term visions for each catchment.

  In Scotland the equivalent body is the Scottish Environment Protection Agency (SEPA) and in Northern Ireland, the Department of the Environment.

- ### *British Waterways*

  The British Waterways Act (1995) gives BW the same duties to further conservation as are required of the EA.

Part 2: Bibliography

Archer, D. (1992) *'Land of the Singing waters: Rivers and Great Floods of Northumbria'*, Spreddon Press, Northumbria.

Barnes, R. S. K. and Mann, K. H. (1980) *'Fundamentals of Aquatic Ecosystems'*, Blackwell Scientific, Oxford.

Baron, R. C., Murphy, F. D., Greenberg, H. B., Davis, C. E., Bergman, D. J., Gary, G. W., Hughes, J. M. and Schonberger, L. B. (1982) *'Norwalk gastrointestinal illness: an outbreak associated with swimming in a recreational lake and secondary person-to-person transmission'*, American Journal of Epidemiology 115 (2), 163-172.

Boon, P. J., Calow, P. and Petts, G. E. (Eds.) (1992) *'River Conservation and Management',* John Wiley and Sons, Chichester.

Briggs, D. J. (1977) *'Sediments'*, Butterworths, London.

British Canoe Union (1989) 'Canoeing Handbook', British Canoe Union, Nottingham.

British Waterways (1991) 'The Kennet & Avon Canal: A Plan for the Environment, Tourism and Leisure', British Waterways, Devizes, November 1991.

British Waterways (1995) *'Informal visitors to waterway towing paths'*, British Waterways, Watford, 1995.

British Waterways (1996) *'Visits to Inland Waterways 1994: An analysis of inland waterway data from the UK Day Visits Survey'*, Market Research Unit, British Waterways, Watford, Research Paper No. 79, April 1996.

British Waterways Board and Nature Conservancy Council (1986) *'Management of Canal SSSIs: guidance on the management of Sites of Special Scientific Interest and other provisions of the Wildlife and Countryside Act 1981'*, BWB/NCC, London.

Brown, A.G. and Quine, T. A. (1999) *'Fluvial Processes and Environmental Change'*, John Wiley and Sons Ltd., London.

Bryan, J. A., Lehmann, J. D., Setiady, 1. F. and Hatch, M. H. (1974) *'An outbreak of hepatitis-A associated with lake water',* American Journal of Epidemiology 99 (2), 145-154.

Burton, A. (1982) *'The Changing River: An Account of some British Rivers and their History',* Victor Gollancz, London.

Carling, P. A. (1987) *'Bed stability in gravel streams with reference to stream regulation and ecology',* in K. Richards (Ed.), River Channels, Environments and Process. Blackwell, Oxford, Institute of British Geographers Special Publication 17, 272-294.

Carling, P. A. and McCahon, C. P. (1987) *'Natural siltation of Brown Trout (Salmo trutta L.) spawning gravels during low flow conditions'*, in Craig, J. F. and Kemper, J. B. (Eds.), Regulated Streams, Advances in Ecology, Plenum Press, New York, 229-244.

Chamberlin, C. E. and Mitchell, R. (1978*) 'A decay model for enteric bacteria in natural waters',* In R. Mitchell (Ed.), Water Pollution Microbiology, John Wiley, New York.

Clowes, A. and Comfort, P. (1982*) 'Process and Landform: An Outline of Contemporary Geomorphology'*, Oliver and Boyd, Edinburgh.

Cock O.J. (1974) 'A Short History of Canoeing in Britain', Chameleon Press, London.

Countryside Recreation Network (1996) *'UK Day Visits Survey 1994'*, CRN, Cardiff, June 1996.

Chorley, R. J. (Ed.) (1969) *'Introduction to Fluvial Processes'*, Methuen, London, 218 pp.

Croft, P. (1975) 'The wildlife of a canal', Shropshire Conservation Trust Bulletin 3, 5-8.

Croft, P. S. (1986*) 'A key to the major groups of British Freshwater Invertebrates',* Field Studies 6, 531-579. An AIDGAP Publication of the Field Studies Council, Offprint No. 181.

Cullingford, R. A., Davidson, D. A. and Lewin, J. (1980) 'Timescales in Geomorphology', Chichester, Wiley.

Deitrich, K. (1974*) 'Investigation into the pollution of water by two-stroke outboard motors'*, Gesundheits Ingenieur 85, 342-347.

Denis, F. A., Blanchovin, E., DeLignieres, A. and Flamen, P. (1974) *'Coxsacki A_{16} infection from lake water'*, Journal of the American Medical Association 228*,* 1370-1371.

Derbyshire, E. (Ed.) (1976) *'Geomorphology and Climate'*, Wiley, Chichester,

DOE (1978) 'River Pollution Survey of England and Wales, updated 1975', HMSO, London.

Doherty, A. and McDonald, M. (1992) *'River Basin Management'*, Aspects of Applied Geography, Hodder & Stoughton, London.

Eastcott, H. R. (1988*) 'Swimmer's itch: a surfacing problem'*, Communicable Disease Report, Public Health Laboratory Services, London.

Environment Agency (1998) *'Freshwater Fisheries and Wildlife Conservation: a good practice guide'*, EA, Bristol.

Fewtrell, L. (1991) *'Freshwater recreation: a cause for concern?'*, Applied Geography 11, 215-226.

Fewtrell, L., Godfree, A. F., Jones, F., Kay, D., Salmon, R. L. and Wyer, M. D. (1992) *'Health Effects of white-water canoeing'*, Lancet 339, 1587-1589.

Fewtrell, L., Kay, D., Salmon, R.L., Wyer, M.D., Newman, G. And Bowering, G. (1994) *'The Health-Effects Of Low Contact Water Activities In Fresh And Estuarine Waters'* Journal Of The Institution Of Water And Environmental Management 8 (1), 97-101.

Furniss, P. and Lane, A. (1992) *'Practical Conservation: Water and Wetlands'*, Open University / Nature Conservancy Council, Hodder & Stoughton, London.

Gallagher, M. M., Herdon, J. L., Nims, L. J., Sterling, C. R., Grabowski, D. J. and Hull, H. H. (1989) *'Cryptosporidiosis and surface waters'*, American Journal of Public Health 79, 39-42.

Galbraith, N. S., Barrett, N. J. and Stanwell-Smith, R. (1987*) 'Water and disease after Croydon: a review of water-borne and water-associated disease in the UK 1937-86'*, Journal of the Institution of Water and Environmental Management 1, 7-21.

Gardiner, J. L. (Ed.) (1991) *'River Projects and Conservation: A Manual for Holistic Appraisal'*, John Wiley and Sons, Chichester.

Gardiner, V. and Dackombe, R. (1981) 'Geomorphological Field Manual', London, George Allen & Unwin.

Gordon, N. D., McMahon, T. A. and Finlayson, B. L. (1992*) 'Stream Hydrology: an introduction for ecologists'*, John Wiley & Sons, London.

Goudie, A. (1981) 'Geomorphological Techniques', George Allen & Unwin, London.

Gregory, K. J. and Walling, D. E. (1973) *'Drainage basin form and process'*, Edward Arnold, London, 456 pp.

Gregory, K. J. (Editor) (1977) *'River Channel Changes'*, Wiley, New York, 448pp.

Hanwell, J. D. and Newson, M. D. (1973) 'Techniques in Physical Geography', Macmillan.

Harvey, R. W. S. and Price, T. H. (1981*) 'Observations on infections associated with South Wales natural waters'*, Journal of Applied Bacteriology 51, 369-374.

Haslam, S. M. (1978*) 'River Plants: The Macrophytic Vegetation of Watercourses'*, Cambridge University Press, Cambridge.

Haslam, S. M. (1994) *'River Pollution: an ecological perspective'*, Wiley, London.

Haslam, S. M. and Wolseley, P. A. (1981*) 'River Vegetation: Its Identification, Assessment and Management'*, Cambridge University Press, Cambridge.

Hawley, H. B., Morin, D. T., Geraghty, M. E., Tomkow, J. and Phillips, C. A. (1973) *'Coxsackievirus B epidemic at a boys' summer camp: isolation of virus from swimming water'*, Journal of the American Medical Association 226, 33-36.

Helawell, J. M. (1986) *'Biological Indicators of Freshwater Pollution and Environmental Management'*, Elsevier, London.

Hey, R.D., Bathurst, J. C. and Thorne, C. R. (Eds.) (1982*) 'Gravel-Bed Rivers: Fluvial Processes, Engineering and Management',* Wiley, New York, 875 pp.

Hilton, J. and Phillips, G. L. (1982) *'The effects of boat activity on turbidity in a shallow Broadland river',* Journal of Applied Ecology 19, 143-150.

Hopkins, T. and Brassley, P. (1982) *'Wildlife of Rivers and Canals',* Moorland Publishing, Ashbourne.

House of Commons Environment Committee (1990) *'Pollution of Beaches',* HMSO, Fourth report of the Environment Committee, London.

House of Commons Environment Committee (1995*) 'The Environmental Impact of Leisure Activities, Volume I',* HMSO, Fourth report of the Environment Committee, London.

Inland Waterways Amenity Advisory Council (1996a) *'Britain's Inland Waterways: An Undervalued Asset',* Consultative Report, IWAAC, London, March 1996.

Inland Waterways Amenity Advisory Council (1996b) *'Waterway Restoration Projects of Great Britain and Northern Ireland',* Supplementary Paper 6 to IWWAC, 1996a.

Inland Waterways Association (1995) *'SSSIs, Wildlife Conservation and Inland Waterways',* Inland Waterway Association Restoration Committee, London.

Inland Waterways Association (1997) *'Technical Restoration Handbook: Use and Benefits of Waterways for Recreation',* IWA, London.

Jackivicz, T. P. and Kuzminski, L. (1973a) *'The effects of the interaction of outboard motors with the aquatic environment: a review',* Environmental Research 6, 436-454.

Jackivicz and Kuzminski (1973b) *'A review of outboard motor effects on the aquatic environment',* Journal of the Water Pollution Control Federation 45, 1759-1770.

Jaackson, R (1988) *'River recreation boating impacts',* J. Waterway, Port, Coastal, and Ocean Engin., 114, 363-367.

Jones, F. and Godfree, A. F. (1989) *'Recreational and amenity use of surface waters: the public health implications',* Water Science and Technology 21 (3), 137-142.

Knighton, D. (1998) *'Fluvial forms and Processes',* Edward Arnold, London.

Lagler, K. F., Hazzard, A. S., Hazen, W. E. and Tomkins, W. A. (1950) *'Outboard motors in relation to fish behaviour, fish production and angling success',* Trans. N. Am. Wildl. Conf., 15, 280-303.

Lane, A. and Tait, J. (1992) *'Practical Conservation: Woodlands'*, Open University / Nature Conservancy Council, Hodder & Stoughton, London.

Langmuir, E. (1995) *'Mountaincraft and Leadership: a handbook or mountaineers and hillwalking leaders in the British Isles'*, 3rd Edition, MLTB / Scottish Sports Council, Manchester/Edinburgh.

Lee, J. V., Dawson, S. R., Ward,S., Surman, S. B. and neal, K. R. (1997) *'Bacteriophages are a better indicator of illness rates than bacteria amongst users of a white water course fed by a lowland river'*, Wat. Sci. Tech. 35 (11-12), 165-170.

Leopold, L. B., Wolman, M. G. and Miller, J. P. (1964) *'Fluvial Processes in Geomorphology'*, Freman, San Francisco, 522pp.

Lewin, J. (1980) *'British Rivers'*, George Allen & Unwin.

Lewis, G. and Williams, G. (Eds) (1984) *'Rivers and Wildlife Handbook'*, Royal Society for the Protection of Birds / Royal Society for Nature Conservation, Sandy, UK.

Liddle, M. J. (1997) *'Recreation Ecology: the Ecological Impact of Outdoor Recreation and Ecotourism'*, Chapman and Hall, London.

Liddle, M. J. and Scorgie, H. R. A. (1980) *'The effects of recreation on Freshwater Plants and Animals: A Review'*, Biological Conservation 17, 183-206.

Maitland, P. S. (1977) *'Coded Checklist of Animals Occurring in Freshwater in the British Isles'*, Natural Environment Research Council, Swindon.

Maitland, P. S., Newson, M. D. and Best, G. A. (1990) *'The impact of afforestation and forestry practice on freshwater habitats'*, Focus on Nature Conservation Report 23, Nature Conservancy Council, Peterborough, 80pp.

Maitland, P. S. and Turner, A. K. (Eds.) (1985*) 'Angling and Wildlife in Fresh Waters'*, Proceedings of a symposium organised by the Scottish Freshwater Group and the British Ecological Society, Grange-over-Sands, Institute of Terrestrial Ecology, ITE Symposium No. 19, 83pp.

M & S Research Marketing Consultancy Ltd. (1991) *'The British Waterways System: Perception and Use of the Inland Waterways'*, Business Planning Unit, Research Report No. 45, British Waterways, Watford, July 1991.

McCormack, F. (1994) *'Water Based Recreation: Managing Water Resources for Leisure'*, ELM, Huntingdon.

Milner, N. (1984) *'Fish'*, In Lewis, G. and Williams, G. (Eds.) *Rivers and Wildlife Handbook, RSPB,* Sandy, Chapter 4.

Morris, R. (1989) *'Microbiological quality of an inland surface water used for recreational purposes'*, In D. Wheeler, M. L. Richardson and J. Bridges, (Eds.) *Watershed 1989: the future for water quality in Europe,* Pergamon, Oxford, 353-356.

Moss, B. (1977) *'Conservation problems in the Norfolk Broads and rivers of East Anglia, England – phytoplankton, boats and the causes of turbidity'*, Biological Conservation 12, 95-115.

Moss, B. (1983) *'The Norfolk Broadland: experiments in the restoration of a complex wetland'*, Biology Review 58, 521-561.

Moss, B. (1988) *'Ecology of Freshwaters'*, 2nd edition, Blackwell Scientific, Oxford.

Murphy, K. J. and Eaton, J. W. (1983) *'Effects of pleasure-boat traffic on macrophyte growth in canals'*, Journal of Applied Ecology 20, 713-729.

Nature Conservancy Council (1983) *'The Conservation of Rivers'*, Leaflet by Interpretative Branch, Nature Conservancy Council, Peterborough.

Nature Conservancy Council (1989) *'Criteria for selection of biological SSSIs'*, NCC, London.

Newbold, C., Purseglove, J. and Holmes, N. (1983) *'Nature Conservation and River Engineering'*, Nature Conservancy Council, London.

Newson, M. D.(1994) *'Hydrology and the River Environment'*, Clarendon Press, Oxford.

Newson M. D. and Lewin, J. (1990) *'Climate change, river flow extremes and fluvial erosion - scenarios for England and Wales'*, Progress in Physical Geography 15 (1), 1-17.

Patmore, J. A. (1983) *'Recreation and Resources'*, Blackwell, Oxford.

Pearce, H. G. and Eaton, J. W. (1983) *'Effects of recreational boating on freshwater ecosystems – an annotated bibliography'*, Waterway Ecology and the Design of Recreational Craft, Appendix B. Inland Waterways Amenity Advisory Council, London.

Pearson, R. G. and Jones, N. V. (1975) *'The effects of dredging operations on the benthic community of a chalk stream'*, Biological Conservation, 18, 273-278.

Pearson, R. G. and Jones, N. V. (1978) *'The effects of weed-cutting on the macro-invertebrate fauna of a canalised section of the river Hull, a northern English chalk stream'*, Journal of Environmental Management, 7, 91-97.

Petts, G. E. (1984) *'Impounded Rivers: Perspectives for Ecological Management'*, John Wiley & Sons, Chichester.

Petts, G. E. and Foster, I. D. L. (1985) *'Rivers and Landscape'*, Edward Arnold, London, 274 pp.

Philipp, R., Waitkins, S., Caul, O., Roome, A., McMahon, S. and Enticott, R. (1989) *'Leptospiral and Hepatitis A antibodies amongst windsurfers and waterskiers in Bristol city docks'*, Public Health 103, 123-129.

Pigram, J. (1985) *'Outdoor Recreation and Resource Management'*, Biddles, Kings Lynn.

Pike, E. B. (1987) *'Aids: implications for the water industry'*, Medmenham: Water Research Centre, Report PRU 1529-M.

Rees, J. R. and Tivy, J. (1977) *'Recreational impact on lochshore vegetation'*, J. Scott. Ass. Geogr. Teach. 6, 93-108.

Richards, K. S. (Editor) (1987) *'River Channels: Environment and Processes',* Blackwell, New York, 391 pp.

Richards, K. S. (1982) *'Rivers: Form and Process in alluvial channels',* Methuen, London, 361 pp.

Richards, S. (1990) 'Living with the Physical Environment', Unwin Hynman, London.

Rosenberg, M. L., Hazlett, K. K., Schaeffer, J., Wells, J. G. and Pruneda, R. C. (1976) *'Shigellosis from swimming',* Journal of the American Medical Association 236, 1849-1852.

Scorgie, H. R. A. (1978) *'Effects of aquatic herbicides on freshwater ecosystems',* Internal Report to the Nature Conservancy Council.

Sidaway, R. (1991) *'A Review of Marian Developments in Southern England',* RSPB/WWF UK, Sandy.

Sidaway, R. (1994) *'Recreation and the natural heritage: a research review',* Scottish Natural Heritage Review, No. 25, Scottish Natural Heritage/Scottish Sports Council, Edinburgh.

Slade, J. S., Pike, E. B., Elgin, R. P., Colbourne, J. S. and Kurtz, J. B. (1989) *'The survival of human immunodeficiency virus in water, sewage and sea water',* Water Science and Technology 21 (3), 55-59.

Solbe, J. F. de L. G. (Ed.) (1986) *'Effects of Land Use on Fresh Waters: Agriculture, Forestry, Mineral Exploitation, Urbanisation',* Ellis Horwood, Chichester.

Stoner, J.H. and Gee, A.S. (1985) *'Effects of forestry on water quality and fish in Welsh rivers and lakes',* Journal of the Institution of Water Engineers & Scientists, 39, 27-45.

Stott, T. A. (1997a) *'A Comparison of Stream Bank Erosion Processes on Forested and Moorland Streams in the Balquhidder Catchments, central Scotland',* Earth Surface Processes & Landforms, 22 (4), 383-400.

Stott, T. A. (1997b) *'Forestry effects on bedload yields in mountain streams',* Journal of Applied Geography, 17, 55-78.

Stott, T. A. (1999) 'Stream bank and forest ditch erosion: preliminary responses to timber harvesting in mid-Wales', In Brown, A.G. and Quine, T.A. (Eds.), *'Fluvial Processes and Environmental Change',* John Wiley and Sons Ltd., London, 47-70.

Stott, T. A. and Marks, S. (1998) *'Bank erosion and suspended sediment dynamics: responses to timber harvesting in mid Wales UK',* Proceedings of the International Symposium on Comprehensive Watershed Management (ISWM-'98), 7-10 September 1998, Beijing, China, 213-220.

Stott, T. A. (in press) *'Bedload transport in rivers: trapping and tracing',* Geography Review.

Sukopp, H. (1971) *'Effects of man, especially recreational activities, on littoral macrophytes'*, Hidrobiologia Bucuresti 12, 331-340.

Tait, J., Lane, A. and Carr, S. (1992) *'Practical Conservation: Site Assessment and Management Planning'*, Open University / Nature Conservancy Council, Hodder & Stoughton, London.

Tanner,M. F. (1973) *'Water resources and recreation'*, Study 3, Sports Council, London.

Thomas, M. (1995) *'Weather for Hillwalkers and Climbers'*, Alan Sutton Publishing Ltd., Gloucestershire.

Thornes, J. B. (1990) *'Vegetation and Erosion, Processes and Environments'*, John Wiley & Sons, Chichester.

Townsend, C.R. (1980) *'The Ecology of Streams and Rivers'*, Studies in Biology 122, Arnold.

Turner, P. C., Gammie, A. J., Hollinrake, K. and Codd, G. A. (1990) *'Pneumonia associated with contact with Cyanobacteria'*, British Medical Journal 300, 1400-1401.

Varey, M. (1998) *'An Investigation into what Recreational Canoeists do for Recreational Canoeing'*, Unpublished Undergraduate Dissertation, Liverpool John Moores University, 60pp.

Schneider, E. Von and Wölfel, H (1978) *'Suggested modes of protection for wild animals in connection with construction of shipping canals and canalised inland waterways'*, Zeitschrift für Jadwissenschaft, 24, 72-88.

Waitkins, S. (1990) *'Leptospirosis: a water-related health hazard'*, In Polluted Water and Recreation, Central Council of Physical Recreation, London, 18-23.

Ward, D. (1990) *'Recreation on Inland Lowland Waterbodies: does it affect birds ?*' RSPB Conservation Review, 62-68, Royal Society for the Protection of Birds, Sandy.

Water Space Amenity Commission (1980) *'Conservation and Land Drainage Guidelines'*, London.

Welsh Water Authority (1980) *'A Strategic Plan for Water-Space Recreation and Amenity'*, Directorate of Resource Planning, Welsh Water Authority.

Williams, D. (1991) *'The Hydrology of White Water Rivers'* in Storry, T. (Ed.) *British White Water,* Constable, London.

Wood, T. R. (1981) *'River Management'*, In Lewin, J. (Ed) *British Rivers,* George Allen & Unwin, London, Chapter 6.

Woodcock, N. H. (1994) *'Geology and Environment in Britain and Ireland'*, University College London Press, London.

Appendix I: Guidelines For Low Impact River Users

This code has been produced by the British Canoe Union and is designed to ensure that canoeists do not come into conflict with each other or with other users of rivers and inland waterways who may live or earn their living on or around them. So please observe it at all times.

Earning a Welcome - to enjoy their sport canoeists need to be welcome

- **Be friendly and polite to local residents**
- **Drive slowly with care and consideration**
- **Park sensibly without causing any obstruction**
- **Be as quiet as possible**
- **Unload kit tidily and take all litter home**
- **Get changed out of public view**
- **Get permission before going onto private property**
- **Avoid wildlife disturbance and environmental damage**
- **Be considerate to other water users**
- **Avoid being an intrusion on local life**
- **Support local businesses if you can**
- **Say "Thank You" for help you receive**
- **Leave no trace of your visit**
- **Follow the country code (see below)**

Enjoy the countryside and respect its life and work
Guard against all risk of fire
Fasten all gates
Keep your dogs under close control
Keep to public paths across farmland
Use gates and stiles to cross fences, hedges & walls
Leave livestock, crops and machinery alone
Take your litter home
Help to keep all water clean
Protect wildlife, plants and trees
Take special care on country roads
Make no unnecessary noise

These are some good ways for canoeists to earn a welcome in the countryside.

Appendix II: Roles and Responsibilities in the Freshwater Environment

Bodies responsible for policy and regulation include:

- Department of the Environment, Transport and the Regions;
- Ministry of Agriculture, Fisheries and Food (MAFF);
- Environment Agency (EA);
- Office of Water Services (OFWAT);
- Forestry Authority;
- Countryside Council for Wales (CCW) / Scottish Natural Heritage (SNH);
- Joint Nature Conservation Committee

The Environment Agency (EA), formed from the National Rivers Authority (NRA), Her Majesty's Inspectorate of Pollution (HMIP), Waste Regulation Authorities (WRSs) and units form the Department of the Environment,Transport and the Regions, on 1 April 1996 is responsible for the management of the main rivers of England and Wales. Among the main functions of the EA are:

- addressing climate change;
- improving air quality;
- managing our water resources;
- enhancing biodiversity;
- managing our freshwater fisheries;
- delivering integrated river basin management;
- conserving the land;
- managing waste;
- regulating major industries.

The EA monitors and controls the conservation and redistribution of surface water and groundwater supplies. It provides flood warning and flood protection for people and property from rivers and the sea. It maintains and develops salmon, trout, freshwater and eel fisheries and has statutory duties to help in the conservation of special environmental sites, and to promote conservation of natural beauty and wildlife that depends on the aquatic environment. The EA is also responsible for inland navigation control on some rivers including boat registrations and it manages sites ranging from the Thames Barrier to facilities for angling, sailing and walking as part of its duty to develop recreation. The equivalent body in Wales is the Countryside Council for Wales (CCW) and in Scotland it is Scottish Natural Heritage (SNH).

EA implements EC directives such as the Habitat and Birds Directive and the UK Biodiversity Action Plan. Environmental protection and enhancement at a local level is achieved through the production of Local Environment Agency Plans (LEAPs)

Bodies responsible for the management of water:

- Water companies

- British Waterways

- Internal Drainage Boards

- Broads Authority

- Landowning bodies (National Trust, Forest Enterprise, sand and gravel companies)

- Private land managers and their representative bodies (e.g. Country Landowners Association, National Farmers Union)

Other bodies with an interest in rivers and canals:

- Industry (individual companies and their associations, e.g. CBI)

- Local Authorities / Local Government Associations

- National Park Authorities

- Voluntary Conservation Organisations (RSPB, Wildlife Trusts, CPRE, WWF, WWT, FoE, Plantlife,etc)

- Angling and fishing associations and their representative bodies

- Inland Waterways Association

- Inland Waterways Amenity Advisory Council

- Royal Commission on Environmental Pollution

- Countryside Commission

- Sports Council (BCU, RYA, ARA etc)

Research and technical bodies (e.g. Universities, Research Councils, Institute of Hydrology, Institute of Terrestrial Ecology, Institute of Freshwater Ecology, Aquatic Weed Research Organisation etc.)

Appendix III: Useful Addresses and Web Sites

Agricultural Development and Advisory Service (ADAS)
Nobel House, 17 Smith Square

Amateur Rowing Association (ARA)
The Priory, 6 Lower Mall, Hammersmith, London W6 9DJ
WWW: http://www.regatta.rowing.org.uk/ARA.html

Association for Science Education (ASE)
College Lane, Hatfield, Herts. AL10 9AA
Magazine, journal, outlet for School Natural Science Society publications.
WWW: http://www.ase.org.uk/

Association of Thames Yacht Clubs (ATYC)
ATYC Honorary Secretary, Crek House, Hamm Court, Weybridge, Surrey, KT13 8YB.

British Association of Nature Conservationists (BANC)
Lings House, Billing Lings, Northampton N3 8BE
E-mail: the.editor@indyfox.ndirect.co.uk
WWW: http://www.greenchannel.com/banc/

Biodiversity Information Unit
The Natural History Museum, Cromwell Road, London SW7 5BD
E-mail: BIU@nhm.ac.uk   WWW: http://www.nhm.ac.uk/biu/homepage.html

British Canoe Union (BCU)
Adbolton Lane, West Bridgford, Nottingham, NG2 5AS
Governing Body for the Sport of Canoeing. 22 000 members
E-mail: Info@bcu.org.uk   WWW: http://www.bcu.org.uk

BBC Education Information
Villiers House, Ealing Broadway, London W5 2PA
WWW: http://www.bbc.co.uk/education/home/

British Ecological Society (BES)
Burlington House, Piccadilly, London WIV OLQ
WWW: http://www.demon.co.uk/bes/

British Museum (Natural History)
Cromwell Road, South Kensington, London SW7 5BD
Charts, posters, books and exhibitions.
WWW: http://www.british-museum.ac.uk/

British Petroleum plc (BP)
Education Liaison Officer, Britannic House, 1 Finsbury Circus, London EC2M 7BA
Posters, films and videos.
WWW: http:bpamoco.com/_nav/edu/index.htm

British Sub Aqua Club (BSAC)
Telfords Quay, Ellesmere Port, South Wirral, Cheshire, L65 4SY.
WWW: http://www.bsac.com/

British Trust for Conservation Volunteers (BTCV)

36, St. Mary's Street, Wallingford, Oxon. OX10 OEU.
Involves volunteers in practical conservation work in both rural and urban environments. Useful packs on pond construction & water habitat maintenance.
WWW: http://www.greenchannel.com/btcv/

British Trust for Ornithology (BTO)
The National Centre for Ornithology, The Nunnery, Thetford, Norfolk IP24 2PU
WWW: http://birdcare.com/birdon/birdaction/bto.html

British Waterfowl Association (BWA)
c/o New Gill, Bishopsdale, Leyburn, N. Yorks. DL8 3TQ.
WWW: http://www.btnternet.com/~palmiped/page3.html

British Waterways (BW)
 Willow Grange, Church Road, Watford, Hertfordshire, WD1 3QA.
Responsible for managing 2,000 miles of inland waterways/canals in Britain.
WWW: http://www.britishwaterways.co.uk

Centre for Alternative Technology (CAT)
Machynlleth, Powys, Wales SY20 9AZ
WWW: http://cat.org.uk/

Civic Trust
17 Carlton House Terrace, London SW14 5AW.
WWW: http://www.civictrust.org.uk/

Council for Environmental Education (CEE)
94,London Street, Reading, Berks. RG1 4SJ.
Coordinating body for environmental education, resource centre, newsheetlproject packs
WWW: http://www.cee.org.uk/

Council for National Parks
246 Lavender Hill, London SW11 1LJ

Council for the Protection of Rural England (CPRE)
25 Buckingham Palace Road, London, SW1W OPP.
WWW: http://www.greenchannel.com/cpre/index.htm

Countryside Agency (CA)
John Dower House, Crescent Place, Cheltenham, Gloucestershire, GL50 3RA.
New statutory body working to conserve and enhance the countryside, to promote social equity and economic opportunity for the people who live there, and to help everyone, wherever they live, to enjoy this national asset
WWW: http://www.countryside.gov.uk/

Countryside Council for Wales (CCW)
Government's statutory adviser on sustaining natural beauty, wildlife and the opportunity for outdoor enjoyment in Wales and its inshore waters. The national wildlife conservation authority.
WWW: http://www.ccw.gov.uk/

County Wildlife Trust/County Trusts for Nature Conservation
- see Royal Society for Nature Conservation.

Department of the Environment for Northern Ireland
Clarence Court, 10-18 Adelaide Street, Belfast BT2 8GB

Department of the Environment, Transport and the Regions (DETR)
Eland House, Bressenden Place, London, SW1E 5DU
WWW: http://www.detr.gov.uk/

Directorate of Environmental Policy and Analysis
Romney House, 43 Marsham Street

English Nature (EN)
Northminster House, Peterborough, PE1 IUA.
Government organisation concerned with the promotion of nature conservation in Britain. Many publications, including those on ponds and wetlands. Runs a grant scheme for conservation areas in school grounds).
WWW: http://www.english-nature.org.uk/start.htm

Environment Agency (EA)
Rio House, Waterside Drive, Aztec West, Almondsbury, Bristol , BS12 4UD
WWW: http://www.environment-agency.gov.uk

Field Studies Council (FSC)
Central Services, Montford Bridge, Shrewsbury, Shropshire, SY4 1HW.
Field centres, teachers' courses, etc.

Friends of the Earth, England & Wales (FoE)
26-28 Underwood Street, London NI 7JQ
Study packs, posters, resource sheets.
WWW: http://www.foe.co.uk/

Friends of the Earth - Scotland
Bonnington Mill, 72 Newhaven Mill, Edinburgh EH6 5QG
E-mail: foescotland@gn.apc.org   WWW: http://www.foe-scotland.org.uk

Forestry Commission
231 Corstorphine Road, Edinburgh EH12 7AT
WWW: http://www.forestry.gov.uk/

Foundation for Environmental Education in Europe (FEEE)
European Secretariat, Tidy Britain Group, Elizabeth House,
The Pier, Wigan, WN3 4EX
E-mail main@feee.org   WWW: http://www.feee.org/

Geographical Association (GA)
343 Fulwood Road, Sheffield, S. Yorks. S10 3BP
The national subject teaching organisation for all geographers. 11,500 members and 60 local branches in England, Wales and Northern Ireland. Nationally, hundreds of teachers contribute to the objectives of the Association through section committees, working groups and working parties. The

224

Association is working to provide curriculum support for teachers and safeguard and extend geography's contribution to education at all levels.
WWW: http://www.geography.org.uk/

Global Environment Directorate
2 Marsham Street, London SW1P 3EB

Greenpeace UK
Canonbury Villas, London, N1 2PN

Groundwork Trusts
c/o Groundwork Foundation, Bennetts Court, Bennetts Hill, Birmingham, B2 5ST
*Promote environmental improvement through encouragement of partnerships with **private,** public and voluntary sectors. Can you give addresses of local Groundwork Trust*
WWW: http://www.groundwork.org.uk/

Inland Waterways Association (IWA)
P. O. Box 114, Rickmansworth, WD3 1ZY.
The Inland Waterways Association was founded in 1946 to campaign for the retention, restoration, conservation and appropriate development of the inland waterways. It has over 18 000 members throughout the country.
E-mail: iwa@waterway.demon.co.uk   WWW: http://waterway.demon.co.uk

Institute for Earth Education
P.O. Box 14, Mortimer, Reading, Berks. RG7 3YA
The world's alternative to agency- and industry-sponsored supplemental environmental education.
WWW: http://www.slnet.com/cip/iee/

Joint Nature Conservancy Council (JNCC)
Monkstone House, City Road, Peterborough PE1 1JY
E-mail: feedback@jncc.gov.uk   WWW: http://www.jncc.gov.uk

Marine Conservation Society
9 Gloucester Road, Ross-on-Wye, Herefordshire HR9 5BU
The Marine Conservation Society is the leading environmental charity in the UK dedicated solely to protecting the marine environment
WWW: http://www.mcsuk.mcmail.com/

National Association for Humane and Environmental Education (NAHEE)
c/o P. Neal, Wolverhampton Polytechnic, Walsall Campus, Gorway, Walsall WS1 3BD

The National Trust
36 Queen Anne's Gate, London SW1H 9AS
E-mail: enquiries@ntrust.org.uk   WWW: http://www.nationaltrust.org.uk

Natural Resources Institute (NRI)
Central Avenue, Chatham Maritime, Kent ME4 4TB
WWW: http://www.nri.org

Natural Environment Research Council (NERC)

Headquarters, Polaris House, North Star Avenue, Swindon SN2 1EU
WWW: http://www.nerc.ac.uk
CEH - Centre for Ecology and Hydrology, WWW: http://www.ceh-nerc.ac.uk
IFE - Institute of Freshwater Ecology,   WWW: http://www.ife.ac.uk
IH - Institute of Hydrology,   WWW: http://www.nwl.ac.uk/ih/
ITE - Institute of Terrestrial Ecology,   WWW: http://www.nmw.ac.uk/ite/

Royal Society for Nature Conservation (RSNC), The Wildlife Trust Partnership
22 The Green, Witham Park, Waterside South, Lincoln LN5 7JR
Produces wide range of materials, mostly under auspices of WATCH (junior club)
Umbrella Organisation for all County Wildlife TrustsICounty Trusts for Nature Conservation.

Royal Society for the Prevention of Cruelty to Animals (RSPCA)
The Causeway, Horsham, W. Sussex RH12 1HG
(junior membership, information packs and kits, booklets, posters).
WWW: http://www.rspca.org.uk/

The Royal Society for the Protection of Birds (RSPB)
UK Headquarters, The Lodge, Sandy, Bedfordshire SG19 2DL
Teachers' packslstudy notes, newsletter, posters plus wide range of materials for junior wing - the Young Ornithologists' Club
WWW: http://www.rspb.org.uk

Royal Yachting Association (RYA)
RYA House, Romsey Road, Eastleigh, Hampshire SO50 9YA.
UK Governing Body for the sports of sailing, powerboating and windsurfing. Administers sailing and boating training standards in 1200 establishments, 500 000 members.
E-mail: admin@rya.org.uk   WWW: http://www.rya.org.uk

Scottish Natural Heritage (SNH)
12 Hope Terrace, Edinburgh EH9 2AS
WWW: http://www.snh.gov.uk

Scottish Wildlife Trust (SWT)
Cramond House, Kirk Cramond, Cramond Glebe Road, Edinburgh EH4 6NS

Shell Education Service, Shell UK Ltd.
Shell-Mex House, Strand, London WC2R ODX
(films, posters, wallcharts).

Thames Water Authority (TWA)
Nugent House, Vastern Road, Reading, Berks. RG1 8DB
(posters, wallcharts, leaflets).

The Environment Council
80 York Way, London NI 9AG *(leaflets).*
The Environment Council is an independent charity dedicated to enhancing and protecting Britain's environment through building awareness, dialogue and effective solutions.
WWW: http://www.greenchannel.com/tec/

Tidy Britain Group
The Pier, Wigan, Greater Manchester WN3 4EX *(project packs, notes.)*

Tree Council
Room 101, Agriculture House, Knightsbridge, London SWLX 7NJ
Advises on planting trees in urban and rural areas, school grounds, etc.

WATCH - see RSNC above - national club for young people. School membership available.

Water Space Amenity Commission (WSAC)
1 Queen Anne's Gate, London SWLH 9BT
Leaflets on recreational use.

Water Authorities (see local telephone directory for addresses)
Produce materials and support charity "Water Aid" (1 Queen Anne's Gate, London SWLH 9BT)

The Wildfowl and Wetlands Trust (WWT) *(+ seven Centres nationwide*
Slimbridge, Gloucestershire GL2 7BX
Packs, leaflets, visits.
WWW: http://freespace.virgin.net/j.tubb/wwtmain.htm

Wildlife and Countryside Directorate
2 Marsham Street, London SW1P 3EB
 Countryside Division, Tollgate House, Houlton Street, Bristol BS2 9DJ
European Wildlife Division, Tollgate House, Houlton street, Bristol BS2 9DJ
Global Wildlife Division, Tollgate House, Houlton Street, Bristol BS2 9DJ
E-mail: global.wildlife@gtnet.gov.uk,
WWW: http://www.wildlife-countryside.detr.gov.uk/gwd/

The Woodland Trust
Autumn Park, Dysart Road, Grantham, Lincolnshire NG31 6LL

World Wide Fund for Nature (WWF UK)
Panda House, Weyside Park, Godalming, Surrey GU7 1XR
resources throughout the curriculum, books, posters, project packs, tapes, etc.
E-mail: wwf-uk@wwf-uk.org   WWW: http://www.wwf-uk.org

WWF Scotland
8 The Square, Aberfeldy, Perthshire, PH15 2DD
WWW: http://www.wwf-uk.org/action/scotland.htm

Appendix IV: Accompanying Web Site with Useful Links

This book is accompanied by a Web Site at:

http://www.staff.livjm.ac.uk/ecststot

From this site there are useful links to a range of water recreation and related sites as well as to many of the organisations listed in Appendix III.

Glossary

A

abiotic factors: those aspects of the physical and chemical environment around us that affect the distribution of organisms e.g. light, water availability, temperature etc.

abrasion: the wearing away of rock on the bed of a river or of bedload in a river channel, rather like sandpapering action.

abstraction of water: the removal of water from a river for public or private use.

actual evapotranspiration: the actual evapotranspiration is that which takes place even though the amount of water which is available exceeds it. This term can usually be applied in the British context.

algal bloom: excessive growth of algae in a water body, usually in spring or autumn, which may be a sign of, or associated with eutrophication.

amphibious: can live on land or in water, e.g. frogs.

aquifer: a layer of rock which holds water and allows water to percolate through it.

attrition: as bedload in a river is moved downstream, boulders collide with other material and the impact may break the rock into smaller pieces. In time these angular rocks become increasingly rounded in appearance.

B

bankfull stage or discharge: is the point when the level of water has reached the top of the channel banks and any further increase in discharge will result in flooding of the surrounding land.

bars: depositional features formed on the bed of a river. They can take the form of small islands in mid-channel, or they can be attached to banks and are most frequently found on the inside of meanders.

baseflow: that part of a storm hydrograph which is very slow to respond to a storm, but by continually releasing water from the lower ground, it maintains the river's flow during periods of low precipitation.

base level: this is the lowest point to which erosion by running water can take place. In the case of rivers, the ultimate base level is sea level. Exceptions are when the river flows into an inland sea or there happens to be a temporary, local base level, such as where a river flows into a lake, where a tributary joins the main river or where there is a resistant band of rock crossing a valley.

bedload: the coarse sediment on the bed of a river which may be transported at times of high discharge.

biodegradable: term applied to materials, such as contained in litter, which will eventually be broken down by micro-organisms, e.g. an apple core.

biotic factors: the animals and plants themselves who compete with each other for space, food, light etc.

bluff line: The edge of a flood plain most distant from the river channel is often marked by a prominent break in slope known as a bluff line.

bottomset beds: the lowest layers of sediment in a delta. The finest materials are carried furthest and form the bottomset beds which are composed of fine clays.

Boulder clay or **till:** the mass of rocks and finely ground rock flour left behind when ice melts after a glaciation.

Bronze Age: the stage of prehistoric cultural development when BRONZE, an alloy of copper and tin, first came into regular use in the manufacture of tools, weapons, and other objects. It marks the transition between the NEOLITHIC PERIOD (a phase of the Stone Age), when stone tools and weapons were predominant, and the succeeding IRON AGE, when the large-scale use of various kinds of metals was introduced. The Bronze Age occurred at different times in different parts of the world, but was between about 2 500 and 750 B.C. in Britain.

C

capacity (to transport load): is the total load actually transported by a river.

capillary action: the process by which water moves upwards through a soil profile.

carnivores: animals which live by eating other animals.

cavitation: a form of hydraulic action caused by bubbles of air collapsing. The resultant shock waves hit and slowly weaken the river banks. This is the slowest, least effective erosion process.

chlorophyll: green pigment in plants which helps them to absorb sunlight which is essential in the process of photosynthesis.

cilia: specialised cells with tiny strands of cytoplasm which act like beating 'hairs' on the lining of the nose or surface of a flatworm.

climatic optimum: a warm period between 6 000 and 3 000 B.C when global mean sea level rose.

colonisation: the spread of plants and animals into new habitats.

competence of a river: refers to the maximum size of material the river is capable of transporting.

condensation: the process by which a substance changes from the vapour to the liquid state. Clouds, for example, are formed by the condensation of water vapour in the atmosphere.

condensation level: term which describes a level in the atmosphere at which moisture vapour condenses into droplets which make clouds. Sometimes also referred to as the 'dew point'.

cotyledon: storage organ in plant seeds.

critical erosion velocity: is the approximate velocity of flow in a river needed to pick up and transport, in suspension, particles of various sizes from clay to boulders.

culverts: drainage pipes or tunnels which take storm water under roads or buildings.

D

data logger: a scientific piece of equipment into which sensors feed data. The readings are taken at pre-set time intervals. Data are normally retrieved by downloading into a computer.

delta: depositional feature formed at t he moutn of a river where it enters a lake or the sea. It is caused by the river losing energy and depositing its load.

desalination: the removal of salts from sea water to produce fresh potable water.

detritivores: scavengers, animals that feed on detritus (dead and decaying plant and animal material).

discharge: the amount of water flowing in the channel at a particular point or cross-section. The standard units of measurement are cubic metres per second (cumecs).

drainage basin: the area of land on the Earth's surface which drains all the rain water that falls on it, apart from that removed by evaporation, into a river or stream which eventually carries the water to the sea.

dynamic equilibrium: the idea that a river is capable of existing in a state of balance with the rate of erosion being equal to the rate of deposition.

E

effective drought rainfall: the effective rainfall (annual rainfall less evaporation) during a one-in-fifty-years drought.

effluent: term applied to liquid waste discharged into watercourses, e.g. silage effluent.

embryo (plant seed): the early stages in the growth of a plant seed.

entrenched meanders: have a symmetrical cross-section and result from either a very rapid incision by the river or the valley sides being resistant to erosion (e.g. the River wear near Durham).

estuarial barrage: dam built across an estuary to create a lake or reservoir.

eutrophication; the build up of nutrients in a water body to the point where it starts to cause problems associated with algal growth for example.

evaporation: the process by which a substance changes from the liquid to the vapour state. Evaporation of surface water by the heat of the sun, from oceans, lakes, rivers etc., is the cause of the water vapour in the atmosphere.

evapotranspiration: term used by hydrologists to account for both evaporation and transpiration combined together since, in practice, in a vegetated drainage basin it can be difficult to measure each separately.

F

falling or receding limb: is the segment of a storm hydrograph where discharge is decreasing and the level of the river or stream is falling.

farm effluent: waste farm materials which are usually associated with the keeping of animals, that enters rivers and watercourses and may cause pollution, e.g. from silage or cow sheds.

field capacity: once excess moisture has drained away, the remaining moisture that soil holds is said to be its field capacity.

flash lock: a movable weir, or barrage, across a river or drainage cut which made it possible to dam and then release suddenly a mass of water, thus allowing a shallow-draft barge to float over a minor obstruction.

flood plain: a plain, bordering a river, which has been formed from deposits of sediment carried down by the river. When a river rises and overflows its banks, the water spreads over the floodplain depositing a layer of sediment.

flocculation: the coagulation of clay particles, sometimes caused by the meeting of fresh and salt water in an estuary, which produces an electric charge causing particles flocculate.

food chain: a way in which living organisms are connected, and dependant on each other, through feeding relationships.

food pyramid: a way of showing the relative numbers of organisms at each trophic level in a food chain.

food web: a means of showing the complex feeding relationships between organisms in an ecosystem.

fossils: ancient remains of organisms encased in layers of rock.

G

grade (of a river): the concept of grade supports the idea that a river is capable of existing in a state of balance, or **dynamic equilibrium**, with the rate of erosion being equal to the rate of deposition.

groundwater (storage): water which exists in the pores and crevices of the Earth's crustal rocks, having entered them mainly as rainwater percolating from the surface.

H

habitat: the natural environment of a plant or animal.

headstream: another tern for the upper course of a river also called upland river.

headward erosion (or spring sapping): a process characteristic at the source of a river where throughflow reaches the surface and the river erodes back towards its watershed as it undercuts the overlying rock, soil or vegetation.

helicoidal flow: a corkscrew flow pattern which occurs at meander bends in rivers.

herbivores: animals which entirely feed on plant material.

honeypot: the term 'honeypot' is used to describe popular tourist sites or attractions.

hydraulic action: the sheer force of the water as the turbulent current hits river banks, e.g. on the outside of a meander bend.

hydraulic radius: the ratio between the area of the cross-section of a river channel and the length of its wetted perimeter.

hydrological cycle: the water cycle. The natural cycling of water evaporated from the oceans via clouds and rain, onto the land surface and eventually back to the sea.

hydrograph: a hydrograph is a means of showing the discharge of a river at a given point over a short period of time.

hydrosphere: all water on the Earth. It includes all water on the Earth's surface - in the oceans and ice sheets, as well as water in the atmosphere.

I

impermeable: rocks that do not allow water, e.g. rain water, to soak into them. Granite is an example of this kind of rock.

incised meanders: when isostatic uplift of the land, or fall in sea level, continues for a lengthy period, the river may cut downwards to form incised meanders.

Industrial Revolution: describes the historical transformation of traditional into modern societies by industrialisation of the economy. There was a dramatic increase in per capita production that was made possible by the mechanisation of manufacturing and other processes that were carried out in factories

infiltration: the passage of rain water through the ground surface into the soil.

infiltration capacity: the maximum rate at which rain water can pass through the ground surface into the soil.

ingrown meanders: occur when the uplift of the land, or incision by the river, is less rapid than when entrenched meanders form, allowing the river to have time to shift laterally and to produce an asymmetrical cross valley shape (e.g. the River Wye at Chepstow).

interception: the trapping for rainfall by objects (such as tree canopy, vegetation surfaces or roof tops) before it reaches the ground.

interlocking spurs: form in a V-shaped valley down which a river with a winding course is flowing. They are the portions of the valley walls which project from both sides to the concave bends of the river and so obscure the view upstream.

invertebrates: animals without a backbone, e.g. insects.

ions: when chemicals dissolve they break up into ions, e.g. salt or sodium chloride (NaCl) splits into Na^+, Cl^- .

Iron Age: marks the period of the development of technology, when the working of iron came into general use, replacing bronze as the basic material for implements and weapons. It is the last stage of the archaeological sequence known as the three-age system (Stone Age, Bronze Age, and Iron Age) and began around 750 B.C in Britain and ended around the time of the Roman invasion in the first century A.D.

isostatic uplift: following deglaciation, when the weight of ice which built up during an ice age is removed, the land which was depressed into the Earth's mantle by the weight of ice, rises again. This is still believed to be happening today in several parts of the earth's crust.

K

knickpoint: where the isostatic uplift of land is rapid, a river does not have sufficient time to erode vertically to the new sea level, and so it may descend as waterfalls over recently emerged sea cliffs. In time, the river cuts downwards and backwards and the waterfall, or knickpoint, retreats upstream and marks the maximum extent of the newly graded profile

L

lag time: the time between the peak rainfall and the peak discharge in a river.

laminar flow: is a horizontal movement of water rarely experienced in rivers, but when it does occur, water in the channel would travel over sediment on the river bed without disturbing it. Most flow in rivers is turbulent.

larva: (plural = larvae) stage in an insect's life cycle.

lateral erosion: sideways erosion by a river as opposed to vertical erosions (downcutting).

levee: the natural bank of a river formed during flooding by the deposition of sediment. Sometimes artificial levees are built to prevent flooding of the land next to a river.

load: term applied to the material, usually sediment or dissolved materials, transported by a river.

lock staircases: a series of locks in a canal which is necessary when canals go up or down hills.

long profile: the section view of a river from its source to mouth showing the average gradient. Such profiles are typically concave.

M

macrophytes: water loving plants.

meander: a curve in the course of a river which continually swings from side to side in wide loops, as it progresses across flat country.

micro-organisms: organisms which are too small to be see with the naked eye.

moorland gripping is land improvement practice undertaken by upland farmers. It involves the digging of open drains to remove excess water from the soil, thus drying out the land and improving production.

O

organic matter: dead parts of plants or animals which enter watercourses, e.g. dead leaves.

overland flow: the flow of water over the ground surface. It usually takes place when the soil is saturated with water, or when it is frozen or baked hard by the sun.

ox-bow lake or cut-off: a lake formed when a meandering river, having bent in almost a complete circle, cuts across the narrow neck of land between the two stretches, and leaves a backwater or lake.

P

pathogens: tiny organisms which cause illness.

percolation: the movement of soil water into the bedrock below.

permeable: rocks which allow water to soak into them, eg. sandstone.

photosynthesis: the chemical process by which green plants make their food (sugars).

plankton: microscopic plants and animals which float in water, often giving it a green or brown appearance.

plunge pool: deep pool which forms below a waterfall due to the force of the water falling under gravity.

point bar: sediment deposited on the convex slope on the inside of a meander bend may take the form of a curving point bar. Its particles are usually graded in size with the largest material being found highest up the slope.

pollard: the cutting back of a tree to encourage new growth.

pollution: can be regarded as the introduction by human activities, directly or indirectly, of substances or energy into the environment which results in harmful effects that may endanger human health or harm living things and their ecosystems.

porous: term given to rock which has numerous pores in which water can reside, e.g. chalk.

porosity (of soil): the amount of air space within a soil (which could potentially be filled by water).

portage: term given to a point in a river journey when the small boat user will have to leave the river and carry his/her boat around an obstacle such as a dangerous weir or rapids.

potential evapotranspiration: the amount of evapotranspiration that would occur if there was sufficient moisture available, e.g. in deserts there is a high potential evapotranspiration.

potholes: where there are hollows in the bedrock of a river bed, particularly if the rock is limestone, pebbles are likely to become trapped. As the current produces turbulent eddies the pebbles will be swirled around in the hollows and enlarge them to form potholes.

precipitation

term given to all forms of moisture which fall from the sky by natural processes eg. rain (most common in Britain), snow, sleet, hail, drizzle, mizzle, fog

primary forest: the original forest cover which grew after the last ice age ended.

R

regime: the regime of a river describes the annual variation in discharge.

rejuvenation: when sea level falls in relation to the land (or the land rises in relation to the sea), this movement causes land to emerge from the sea, increasing the gradient of the river and therefore increasing the rate of fluvial erosion.

residence time (of water): the length of time and particular unit or molecule of water spends in a particular location, e.g. the ground, a lake.

riffles: areas of shallower water in a river channel where rapids may develop. They usually separate deeper pools and alternate down a river's course.

rising limb: the part of a storm hydrograph which shows the increasing stream or river discharge.

river terraces: a platform of land formed beside a river flowing across a plain, when for some reason the river has commenced vertical down cutting again, possibly because of rejuvenation.

rivulet: a small river.

roughness coefficient: roughness of a river channel is difficult to measure, but Manning, a river engineer, calculated a roughness coefficient by which he interrelated three factors affecting the velocity of a river: hydraulic radius, channel slope and boundary roughness.

runoff: term used to describe the general flow of water from the land to the sea

S

saltation: is the process whereby small pebbles, sand and gravel are temporarily lifted up by the current and bounced or 'jumped' along the bed in a hopping motion.

salts are precipitated: when salts dissolved in water turn back to solids, usually being deposited on something solid.

secondary interception: where rainfall is intercepted at a higher level, such as by a tree canopy, then drips through as throughfall and may be intercepted a second time (secondary interception) by understory vegetation.

settling velocity: the velocity at which particles of a given size become too heavy to be transported in the flow of a river and so will fall out of suspension and be deposited.

sinuosity: term used to describe how meandered a river is. It can be calculaed as the actual river length divided by the straight line distance.

solution or corrasion: the dissolving of rocks by river water, a significant form of erosion.

solution load: the dissolved materials carried as part of a river's load.

soil moisture deficiency: when evapotranspiration exceeds precipitation and any surplus soil moisture is used.

soil moisture recharge: the replacement of soil moisture after rain.

stage board: a board fixed securely in a river or stream which is graduated (usually in m and cm) and shows the river level or stage.

stemflow: the movement of rainfall down the outside of stems of plants or trunks of trees.

substrate: term used to describe he nature of the bed or a river – it refers to the type of rock, whether it is rough or smooth, which in turn will affect the living creatures that can exist.

succession: term used to describe the gradual process of colonisation of an area of bare rock or soil by plants.

suspended sediment or load: the fine particles of sand, silt or mud carried by a river which sometimes make it appear brown or grey.

sustainable: means ensuring that the needs of the present are met without compromising the ability of future generations to meet their own needs. Sustainability is about improving the quality of peoples' lives whilst maintaining the capacity of the Earth to provide for future generations.

T

thalweg: the point in a river with the fastest flow. This usually swings to the outside on meander bends.

throughfall: the process whereby rainfall intercepted by vegetation, and trees in particular, drips from leaves and branches once the interception capacity of the canopy has been exceeded.

throughflow: the movement of water through a layer of soil – usually in the downhill direction.

traction: when the largest cobbles and boulders roll or slide along the bed of a river. Some of these may be moved only during times of extreme flood.

transpiration: is a biological process by which water is lost from a plant through the minute pores (stomata) in its leaves.

turbulent flow: is the dominant type of flow in rivers and consists of a series of erratic eddies, both vertical and horizontal, generally in a downstream direction.

turbidity: term used to describe the clarity of river water. It would be impossible to see the bottoms of a river with high turbidity (it would appear brown and dirty), whereas a river with low turbidity would appear clear.

V

velocity: speed. Can be measured in a river either by using a special instrument called a current or flow meter, or by floating an object over a known distance and timing it. Speed is equal to distance travelled divided by time taken. Usually measured in metres per second (m s^{-1}).

vertical erosion: the downcutting by a river which ultimately produces river valleys.

W

water table: the upper level of the zone of saturation within a soil or rock. Below the water table all pore spaces within the soil or rock are filled with water.

watershed: the elevated boundary line separating the headstreams of different river systems or drainage basins. It often, but not always, follows the ridge of a line of hills.

wetted perimeter: when viewing a river channel cross section, the wetted perimeter is the length of the bed and banks which is in contact with the water in the channel.

Z

zone of saturation: term given to an area of soil or rock which is completely saturated with water and can absorb no more.

P

pathogens, 51, 62, 196
Pearl mussel, 184
Perch, 175
percolation, 16, 106
permeable, 14, 25, 30
pesticides, 56
photosynthesis, 33, 42
phytoplankton, 100
Pike, 176
plankton, 44
platyhelminthes, 37
plunge pool, 122
point bar, 127
point sources of pollution, 52
pollard, 136
pollution, 51, 53, 193-5
Pond Skaters, 180
pools, 124
Poplar, Black, 135
porosity (of soil), 105
porous, 30
portage, 21
potential evapotranspiration, 104
potholes, 120
precipitation, 102, 104
primary forest, 4

R

Ragged Robin, 82, 155
rapids, 123
Reed, Common, 81, 147-8
regime (of a river), 112
rejuvenation, 129
reptiles, 39
residence time (of water), 30
riffles, 125
rising limb, 108
river terraces, 29, 131-2
rivulet, 14
roughness coefficient, 116
rowing, 93-5

Royal Yachting Association, 232
runoff, 12
Rutland Water, 199

S

Salmon, 178-9
saltation, 118
Sand Martin, 83, 165-6
secondary interception, 105
seed bearing plants, 36
SEPA, 54, 187
settling velocity, 120
Severn, River, 50, 64, 71-4, 111, 190
sewage, 99, 193
sinuosity, 125-7
skin infection, 196
soil moisture deficiency, 106
soil moisture recharge, 106
solution load, 118
solution or corrasion, 120
speed, 18, 68
Sprigtails, 180
stage board, 21
stemflow, 105
Stonefly, 183
substrate, 32
succession, 43
surface life, 180
suspended sediment or load, 32, 118
sustainability, 11
sustainable, 11, 49, 203
Swan Mussel, 184
Swan, Mute 82, 164-5

T

Tame, River, 190
Tay, River, 79, 102
Teal, 166-7
tectonic, 128

Tees, Barrage, 76, 89
Thames swans, 164-5
Thames terraces, 132
Thames, River, 191
Thornton Force Waterfall, 78
throughfall, 105
throughflow, 16, 105
traction, 118
transpiration, 104
Trent, River, 190-1
tributaries, 14
Trout, Brown, 177-8
Tryweryn, Afon, 50, 77, 89
turbidity, 33
turbulent flow, 113

U

Urbanisation, 25, 109

V

valley-in-valley feature, 130
vegetation, 121
velocity, 42, 115
vertebrates, 38
vertical erosion, 122
viral infections, 199
v-shaped valley, 122
Vyrnwy, River, 50

W

Washburn, River, 50
water balance, 106
Water Boatman, 181
Water Crowfoot species, 148-9
water cycle, 13
Water Lily, White, 81, 149
Water Plantain, Common, 142
water quality, 188

water quantity, 187
Water Scorpion, 184
Water Shrew, 167-8
Water Stick Insect, 184
water table, 106
Water Vole, 168-9
Watercricket, 181
waterfall, 27, 122
watershed, 14
Weil's disease (see leptospirosis)
wetted perimeter, 114
Whirligig Beetle, 181
Willow, 136-7
Wye, River, 64, 90, 111

Y

Yellow Flag Iris, 150

Z

Zone of saturation, 106